THE
BIBLE
HAS THE
ANSWER

**Practical Biblical Discussions of
100 Frequent Questions**

HENRY M. MORRIS

ISBN: 0-8010-5905-4

"This special edition, part of Project CLAIM, a ministry of
Christ for Greater Manila was produced with the special permission
of Baker Book House, Grand Rapids, Michigan 49506."

Published by:

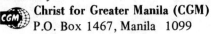 **Christ for Greater Manila (CGM)**
P.O. Box 1467, Manila 1099

jointly with

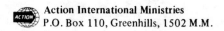 Action International Ministries
P.O. Box 110, Greenhills, 1502 M.M.

This book is gratefully dedicated
to my mother
MRS. IDA HUNTER MORRIS

CONTENTS

ACKNOWLEDGMENTS

I would like to thank Dr. Tim LaHaye for reviewing the manuscript and for writing a very generous Introduction to the book. I also appreciate the interest of the editors and staff of the *News Messenger,* of Montgomery County, Virginia, in publishing the original articles from which the book was taken, and in giving permission now to republish them in book form. I am grateful also to my beloved wife, Mary Louise, for her encouragement at all times and, specifically, for her help in reviewing the proofs and typing the indexes. The publisher, Mr. Charles H. Craig, and the typesetter, Mr. Earl Powell, have, as always, been most helpful and effective in their part of the work.

Finally, I want to dedicate this book to my mother, Mrs. Ida Hunter Morris. She typed the manuscript for this book as she has for most of my previous books, and her faithful help and prayers have played an important part in any ministry they may have had.

HENRY M. MORRIS

FOREWORD

Solid and satisfying answers, whether to the problems of the world or to the needs of the individual life, seem hard to come by these days. It is easy enough to raise questions, but few people can offer more than opinions and speculations in response to these problems.

But the Bible does have the answer, either explicitly or implicitly, to every possible problem! "Thy Word is a lamp unto my feet, and a light unto my path" (Ps. 119:105). It is not that the Bible and Biblical Christianity have been tried and found inadequate. Rather they have been found offensive to man's baser nature and therefore not tried. For that individual, or that nation, who genuinely desires the truth and who is willing to obey the truth when he finds it, the Holy Scriptures will be found wonderfully "profitable for doctrine, for reproof, for correction, for instruction in righteousness, that the man of God may be perfect, throughly furnished unto all good works" (II Tim. 3:16, 17).

During the past several years the writer has had the privilege, even though not at the time engaged in what is normally considered a full-time Christian ministry, of speaking to hundreds of groups around the country—churches, colleges, men's organizations, youth clubs, scientific meetings, service organizations, seminars, and others, in 35 states, as well as Canada and Mexico, representing many different denominational and non-denominational constituencies. These sessions normally dealt with what may be called "scientific Biblical creationism" and practical Christian evidences, as well as Biblical studies in general. Most of these meetings were followed by question-and-answer sessions with the audience.

It was noteworthy that, regardless of the type or location of the audience, the same general questions were raised again and again. These evidently are problems that concern many people. Accordingly, the writer has attempted in this book to deal briefly but incisively with 100 of the more common and important of these questions.

The answers have already been helpful to many, as published originally in the *News Messenger*, the bi-weekly newspaper for Montgomery County, Virginia, where the writer lived from 1957 through 1970. The response of many of the wonderful people in this community to these articles has been most gratifying. It is, of course, now fervently hoped that their publication in this form will make them useful on a much wider scale.

The writer hopes that the book may be especially helpful to people who are seriously considering the claims of Christ and His gospel, but who still have real questions and reservations that need to be settled before they can yield their minds and hearts to Him. The way of salvation is therefore a recurring theme through many of the answers given in the book.

The reader who elects to read straight through the book may find there is a certain amount of repetition. This is because each "answer" has been made essentially self-contained. Thus, readers who are looking only for answers to specific questions, or readers who simply like to browse, will find the structure of the book appropriate for this use. At the same time there is a basic and orderly development of Biblical doctrine in the actual sequence of chapters and sections.

Naturally there are numerous Bible quotations and references throughout the book, since it is the Bible (and not the writer of this book) that has the answer! For the most part (and for good reason, as discussed in Question I-5) the standard King James translation has been used. However, these quotations have occasionally been modified when the original languages actually warrant such changes and when they are helpful in giving the essential thrust of the meaning. Similarly on many occasions, only a part of a verse is quoted, rather than a full passage, but care has been taken that the use of a verse in such fashion is not inconsistent with its context. Wherever a Biblical reference is given, the reader is by all means encouraged, if he will, to look it up in his Bible and read it in its whole setting.

The writer would be most happy to hear from those who find the book helpful in their own lives, especially from any who may be led to accept Jesus Christ as personal Lord and Saviour through reading it. For such people, and for this purpose, the book is written.

HENRY M. MORRIS
San Diego, California
February, 1971

INTRODUCTION

Dr. Henry M. Morris offers a unique combination of scientific scholarship and practical, spirit-filled Christianity. These characteristics abound not only in his personal life but also in his writings. He has already made masterful contributions to Christian evidences in seven other books, which have been widely received. Although he writes as a scientist and educator, he possesses the rare ability to make his writings easily understood by laymen.

The Bible Has the Answer may well prove to be one of his finest books. It is highly practical in that it covers the most commonly asked questions confronting people today. The answers are interesting, Biblical, and very logically presented. Unlike many authors, he does not avoid the difficult questions, but presents a Biblical answer for the most complex problem. For example, "Was Jonah really swallowed by a whale? What about Joshua's long day? Is there life on other planets? Is evolution a scientific fact? Where did Cain get his wife?" His subject matter covers a broad area, from proof for the divine authorship of the Word of God to a thorough discussion of the Bible and science, and on to very practical matters concerning everyday living.

This book will do much to correct the false idea that "no men of science believe the Bible." Being a scientist himself, he is in a position to know many other scholars and scientists who believe the Bible *is* the Word of God. It is refreshing to read his statement, "The fact is, true science has always confirmed the Bible! It is not science, but scientism (that is, the extension of scientific theories to a supposedly complete philosophy of life and meaning) that has attacked the Bible." Probably no man in America is better equipped to call this fact to the attention of our skeptical generation.

After reading this excellent manuscript, I could not help but conclude that it deserves a place among the key books every Christian should have. Next to the Bible, one needs a concordance, a Bible dictionary and Bible atlas, a commentary, and this book of Bible answers. It will prove a handy reference book for years to come for Sunday School and Bible School teachers, pastors, scientists, and any Christian who has doubts or questions about his faith or some Bible teaching. I hope it will be read by college and high school young people who have to face the atheistic humanism of our educational system. This book will do much to stabilize the faith of its readers and help them to "be ready always to give an answer to every man that asketh you a reason of the hope that is in you with meekness and fear. . . ." (I Peter 3:15).

TIM F. LaHAYE
Pastor, Scott Memorial Baptist Church and
President, Christian Heritage College
San Diego, California

Chapter I

THE WORD OF GOD

1. *Question: "How do we know the Bible is true?"*

Answer: There have been hundreds of books written on the subject of the evidences of the divine inspiration of the Bible, and these evidences are many and varied. Most people today, unfortunately, have not read any of these books. In fact, few have even read the Bible itself! Thus, many people tend to go along with the popular delusion that the Bible is full of mistakes and is no longer relevant to our modern world.

Nevertheless the Bible writers claimed repeatedly that they were transmitting the very Word of God, infallible and authoritative in the highest degree. This is an amazing thing for any writer to say, and if the forty or so men who wrote the Scriptures were wrong in these claims, then they must have been either lying or insane or both. But, on the other hand, if the greatest and most influential book of the ages, containing the most beautiful literature and the most perfect moral code ever devised, was written by deceiving fanatics, then it is hopeless to look elsewhere for meaning and purpose in this world!

If one will seriously investigate these Biblical evidences, he will find that their claims of divine inspiration (over 3,000 times the various writers stated in one way or another that they were transmitting God's Word to man) were amply justified. The remarkable evidence of fulfilled prophecy is one case in point. Hundreds of Bible prophecies have been fulfilled, specifically and meticulously, often long after the prophetic writer had passed away.

Just as one example, Daniel the prophet predicted in about 538 B.C.[1] (Dan. 9:24-27) that Christ would come as Israel's promised Saviour and Prince 483 years after the Persian emperor would give the Jews authority to rebuild Jerusalem, which was then in ruins. This was clearly and definitely fulfilled,[2] hundreds of years later.

---

[1] Even those "liberal" scholars who reject the traditional authorship of the book of Daniel accept its composition at no later than about 300 B.C.
[2] See Article III - 2.

1

Another group of prophecies (for example, Ezek. 37:22; Isa. 11:11; Luke 21:24, and many others) predict the restoration of the Jews to the land of Israel as a true nation in the latter days. For almost 1,500 years this seemed utterly impossible, and yet we have now seen it fulfilled in our own generation!

There are extensive prophecies dealing with individual nations and cities and with the course of history in general, all of which have been literally fulfilled. More than 300 prophecies were fulfilled by Christ Himself at His first coming. Other prophecies deal with the spread of Christianity, as well as various false religions, and many other subjects.

There is no other book, ancient or modern, like this. The vague, and usually erroneous, prophecies of people like Jeane Dixon, Nostradamus, Edgar Cayce, and others like them are not in the same category at all, and neither are other religious books such as the Koran, the Confucian Analects, and similar religious writings. Only the Bible manifests this remarkable prophetic evidence, and it does so on such a tremendous scale as to render completely absurd any explanation other than divine revelation.

The historical accuracy of the Scriptures is likewise in a class by itself, far superior to the written records of Egypt, Assyria, and other early nations. Archaeological confirmations of the Biblical record have been almost innumerable in the past century. Dr. Nelson Glueck, probably the greatest living authority on Israeli archaeology, has said: "No archaeological discovery has ever controverted a Biblical reference. Scores of archaeological findings have been made which confirm in clear outline or in exact detail historical statements in the Bible. And, by the same token, proper evaluation of Biblical descriptions has often led to amazing discoveries."[3]

Another striking evidence of divine inspiration is found in the fact that many of the principles of modern science were recorded as facts of nature in the Bible long before scientists confirmed them experimentally. A sampling of these would include the roundness of the earth (Isa. 40:22), the almost infinite extent of the sidereal universe (Isa. 55:9), the law of conservation of mass and energy (II Peter 3:7), the hydrologic cycle (Eccl. 1:7), the vast number of stars (Jer. 33:22), the equivalence of matter and energy (Heb. 1:3), the law of increasing entropy (Ps. 102:25-27), the paramount importance of blood in life processes (Lev. 17:11), the atmospheric cir-

[3] *Rivers in the Desert* (New York: Farrar, Strauss and Cudahy, 1959), p. 31.

2

culation (Eccl. 1:6), the gravitational field (Job 26:7), and many others. These are not stated in the technical jargon of modern science, of course, but in terms of the basic world of man's everyday experience; nevertheless, they are completely in accord with the most modern scientific facts.

It is significant also that no real mistake has ever been demonstrated in the Bible, in science,[4] or history, or any other subject. Many have been claimed, of course, but conservative Bible scholars have always been able to work out reasonable solutions of all such problems.

The remarkable structure of the Bible should also be stressed. Although it is a collection of 66 books, written by 40 or more different men over a period of 2,000 years, it is clearly one Book, with perfect unity and consistency throughout. The individual writers, at the time of writing, had no idea that their message was eventually to be incorporated into such a Book, but each nevertheless fits perfectly into place and serves its own unique purpose as a component of the whole. Anyone who diligently studies the Bible will continually find remarkable structural and mathematical patterns woven throughout its fabric, of intricacy and symmetry incapable of explanation by chance or collusion. And the one consistent theme of the Bible, developing in grandeur from Genesis to Revelation, is God's great work in the creation and redemption of all things, through His only Son, the Lord Jesus Christ.

The Bible is unique also in terms of its effects on individual men and on the history of nations. It is the all-time best seller, appealing both to hearts and minds, beloved by at least some in every race or nation or tribe to which it has gone, rich or poor, scholar or simple, king or commoner, men of literally every background and walk of life. No other book has ever held such universal appeal nor produced such lasting effects.

Those nations that have honored the Scriptures in their national life, God has honored and blessed. This has been true in particular of the British Empire and the United States, from which have gone out most of the world's stock of Bibles and most missionaries and preachers of the Word in modern times. Tragically, England's rapid decline in recent years has followed her descent into the morass of apostasy and unbelief in the past several decades, and our nation is now quickly traversing the same route.

[4] Certain alleged scientific errors in the Bible, especially associated with the early chapters of Genesis, are discussed in Chapters VII and VIII.

One final evidence that the Bible is true is found in the testimony of those who have believed it. Multitudes of people, past and present, have found from personal experience that its promises are true, its counsel is sound, its commands and restrictions are wise, and its wonderful message of salvation meets every need for time and eternity.

2. Question: "In what sense and to what extent is the Bible the inspired Word of God?"

Answer: The men who wrote the Bible claimed that their writings were supernaturally inspired by God. The Bible, especially the Old Testament, abounds with statements such as "Thus saith the Lord: . . ."; "The Word of the Lord came unto me, saying . . .," and similar assertions.

In the prophetic books, for example (Isaiah, Jeremiah, et al.), statements of this sort occur more than 1,300 times! In the historical books (Samuel, Kings, Chronicles, etc.) there are over 400 such statements. In the Mosaic writings (Genesis, Exodus, Leviticus, Numbers, Deuteronomy) there are almost 700. Almost half of the entire book of Exodus consists of statements and instructions given as direct quotations from the voice of God Himself! Altogether there are more than 2,600 such direct claims of inspiration found in the Old Testament.

The Jewish people at the time of Christ were in full agreement on the divine inspiration of the Old Testament Scriptures, and this was basic in all their thinking. They accepted exactly the same books that we have now in the Old Testament, and no others, as inspired and authoritative.

The writers of the New Testament make this fact very clear, quoting directly from the Old Testament more than 320 times and making hundreds of additional allusions to it. There are more than 60 quotations from the book of Genesis alone. Always these quotations are assumed to be of absolute divine authority, settling every question with which they deal.

It is of particular importance that the Lord Jesus Christ likewise shared this high evaluation of the Scriptures. He said, in fact, that "the Scriptures cannot be broken" (John 10:35). He quoted from many parts of the Bible, including especially many that have been ridiculed by modern skeptics. Thus, He accepted as true the account of man's creation, quoting from both Genesis 1 and Genesis 2, in Matthew 19:4. He referred to the great Flood, accepting it as worldwide (Matt. 24:37-39). He cited the destruction of Sodom (Luke 17:26-32) and the miracles of Elijah (Luke 4:25-27).

He believed in the Mosaic authorship of the Pentateuch (John 5: 46, 47; Luke 20:37, 38) and also that Isaiah wrote both parts of the book of Isaiah (Matt. 4:14-16; 12:17), seemingly unimpressed by the fact that twentieth-century critics would later deny these claims. He accepted the writings of Daniel as true prophecies (Matt. 24:15).

With respect to the nature of inspiration, we are told that "God in divers manners spake in time past unto the fathers by the prophets" (Heb. 1:1). Sometimes (as when He gave the ten commandments), God used the method of direct dictation to His prophet. Often He spoke through visions or dreams. More commonly, He used the prophet's own background, training, experience, and research as the vehicle through which to have His Word recorded. It is not the method, but the result, of inspiration which is important. Though God may have used various methods and may often have used the particular scribe's own style and abilities, He nevertheless so guided the whole process that the final result was perfectly and infallibly the Word of God. As Peter says, "Holy men of God spake as they were moved by the Holy Ghost" (II Peter 1:21).

It is certain, furthermore, that Christ and the apostles believed that inspiration extended to the very words of Scripture. Paul, for example, in Galatians 3:16, proves his argument merely by showing that the passage he is quoting has a certain word in the singular rather than in the plural ("seed" instead of "seeds"). Similarly, the Lord Jesus in Matthew 22:32 draws a tremendous conclusion about the resurrection from a single word in an Old Testament passage ("am" instead of "was"). Scores of similar examples could be cited. The Lord Jesus in fact said "Till heaven and earth pass, not one jot or one tittle [that is, the very punctuation marks!] shall in no wise pass from the law, till all be fulfilled" (Matt. 5:18). Those modern-day preachers and professors of religion who seem to take delight in finding supposed mistakes in the Bible thus in effect are calling God a liar!

As far as the New Testament Scriptures are concerned, Christ promised that His apostles would be guided by the Holy Spirit when the time came for them to write their respective books (John 14:26; 16:13, 14). They also make frequent claims of their own divine guidance. Paul, for example, said, "I certify you, brethren, that the gospel which was preached of me is not after man. For I neither

5

received it of man, neither was I taught it, but by the revelation of Jesus Christ" (Gal. 1:11, 12).

The final portion of God's Word to be inscripturated was to be the wonderful book of the Revelation, sent by Christ Himself (Rev. 1:1) through the last of the apostles, John. When this was completed, the Lord said: "I testify unto every man that heareth the words of the prophecy of this book, if any man shall add unto these things [that is, as do the modern cultists and false prophets who profess to receive new revelations and words from God], God shall add unto him the plagues that are written in this book" (Rev. 22:18).

Even more ominously, He then said: "If any man shall take away from the words of the book of this prophecy [that is, as do the liberal and modernistic preachers and seminary teachers of the present day, not to mention the multitudes of intellectual unbelievers everywhere], God shall take away his part out of the book of life, and from the holy city, and from the things which are written in this book" (Rev. 22:19). These are solemn words and ought certainly to be heeded.

The true doctrine of Biblical inspiration is summarized in the classic passage of the Apostle Paul, II Timothy 3:16: "All scripture is given by inspiration of God." That is, not just a part, but all, of Scripture is inspired. Similarly, not just the thoughts, but the "scriptures"—that is the "writings," the actual words written down, are inspired. Finally, the Scriptures were not derived from men who were inspired, but rather were "given by inspiration of God" (that is, literally, "God-breathed"). As such, the Bible, the Holy Scriptures, is both the necessary and sufficient guide for all faith and life.

3. Question: "Is the Bible authoritative when it deals with facts of history and science, or only in matters of religion?"

Answer: A widely held opinion today suggests that the Bible is indeed a great book of faith and religious insights, but that it is encased in a framework of fallible human writings, which often contain errors. Thus many say that the Bible may have valid meaning and authority when it serves as a vehicle of "existential encounter" with God, but its historical narratives and descriptions of natural phenomena are not to be taken very seriously.

This temporizing approach to the Bible has been advocated by liberal and "neo-orthodox" theologians and preachers for the past two generations or more and now largely dominates the Sunday School literature, as well as the seminaries, of most of the large de-

6

nominations. Likewise, public school curricula and textbooks, though usually careful to avoid open advocacy of atheism, completely reject the authority of the Bible in matters of historical fact, while "damning it with faint praise" as a book of religion—which, ergo, has no place in a public school!

But, as Jesus said, "If I have told you earthly things, and ye believe not, how shall ye believe, if I tell you of heavenly things?" (John 3:12). That is, if we cannot rely on God's Word when it records matters of science and history (which, presumably, we can verify through our own observations and experience), then how can we possibly trust it when it deals with matters of salvation, heaven, the spiritual world, and eternal life, which are entirely beyond the reach of scientific observation and experimentation?

This is the underlying reason why most young people have rejected not only the scientific authority of the Bible but also its religious and moral authority, and along with that the authority of the church, the school, the home, and everything. Each person has become, in effect, his own god, with his own self-determined standards of truth and morality.

Nevertheless, each person is still keenly aware of his own personal inadequacy and his desperate need for some frame of reference and authority. So he desperately casts about for some bedrock of infallibility to which he can give his life. He may try to find this in "Science" or "Communism" or "Humanism" or whatnot. But he soon finds that scientists are biased, fallible, selfish, sinful human beings just like everyone else, and so are communists and humanists. Neither the scientific method nor Marxist philosophy has been given to man by divine revelation, and all man-made systems are bound to be inadequate and self-contradictory.

As a matter of fact, everything in this world (physical systems, biological organisms, sociological units, and even individual souls) is in what the Bible calls "the bondage of corruption" (Rom. 8:21). This principle has been formalized scientifically as the Law of Increasing Entropy (that is, "in-turning," or self-destructing) but, more fundamentally, is the historical result of the Curse placed on man's entire dominion because of his sin. The world and its individual souls are in desperate need of redemption, and none of man's own philosophical or scientific inventions can ever accomplish it.

The only real solution is a return to that faith in the absolute integrity of the Word of God which characterized the apostles and, indeed, most of our American forefathers. "Science" has never disproved any statement of the Bible—rather, most scientists have simply repudiated it because of their own unwillingness to submit to God's authority as Creator and coming Judge.

It should be obvious that the Bible cannot be divided up into two sets of verses—those which are considered basic to faith and those which are expendable. There are certainly no objective criteria available for any selective discrimination of this sort The Bible itself makes no such distinctions—it presents itself as a unified whole, every portion of it completely trustworthy and infallibly inspired, absolutely authoritative in faith and practice.

As far as man's judgment is concerned, his opinions are notoriously subjective and changeable. One man, for example, may decide that the Virgin Birth of Christ is a biological impossibility and irrelevant to the spiritual value of the example and teachings of Christ. Another may decide (quite properly) that miracles are surely possible with God, and that the Virgin Birth is an inescapable corollary of both the deity and the sinless humanity of Jesus Christ. What one judges to be of no relevance religiously, another believes to be absolutely essential to his faith.

Similarly, someone may say that the first chapter of Genesis does not try to tell us about the actual events of creation, but only that God is Creator. But another may reply that the very first verse of Genesis gives us *that* information, and the rest of the chapter becomes a mere appendage of irrelevant and misleading information if such is the case. Furthermore, he says, the later Biblical writers, and even Jesus Christ Himself, accepted Genesis as true and factual history, and, if they were wrong about this foundational revelation, how can we trust them about anything else?

If the Word of God is thus to be reduced to a miscellaneous aggregation of existential insights and relativistic irrelevancies, we should be honest enough to discard it altogether! How much better, however, to return in repentant faith to the God of our fathers, believing in the absolute integrity and perspicuity of His written Word. Not one statement has ever been disproved by any real facts of science or history, and God will surely honor and bless the faith and witness of anyone who fully believes and obeys His Word.

4. Question: "How can a person know how to interpret the Bible?"

Answer: *The proper way to interpret the Bible is not to interpret it at all!* It was written to be understood and obeyed and should therefore be read like any other book of information and instruction. If God is truly the Author of the Bible, as Christians have always believed, then it is certainly reasonable to assume that He could say what He means!

The Bible was written as God's revelation (not as a mystery-book, in some secret code), to all men, of all times and places. It therefore is meant to be understood by all people. He used ordinary men, from many backgrounds (soldiers, shepherds, fishermen, doctors, tax collectors—as well as kings and priests) to write different books of the Bible. Just so, it is significant that people of all backgrounds—rich and poor, educated and uneducated, old and young, of every race and nationality—have read and loved, believed, and understood the Bible—more so than for any other book ever written.

This does not mean, of course, that the Bible does not use figures of speech and poetic language on occasions. There are parables and allegories, visions and symbols, all through the Bible. This is likewise true of other books, but this does not keep us from understanding these books—assuming they were intended to be understood. Authors use such figures as devices of emphasis and illustration, not of confusion.

Whenever a Biblical writer uses figurative or poetic language, he makes this evident in the context, and the truth intended to be conveyed by the figure is likewise evident in the context. When symbols are used, they also are defined and explained, either in the immediate context or in related passages in other parts of the Bible. The best rule to follow is to take the Bible literally unless the context clearly requires a symbolic meaning; if the latter is true, then the meaning is to be found in the Scriptures themselves—not from modern science, or from one's own imagination, or from specially gifted "interpreters," or from any other source.

Now the above discussion is not intended to suggest that a thorough understanding of the Bible can be obtained by a quick and superficial scanning of its pages. As the unique and infallible Word of God, it is inexhaustible—an endless mine of rich truth and perfect counsel which no one can ever completely explore. Although the basic message of any passage can be comprehended by anyone who will study and believe it, that same passage will continue to yield new treasures of blessing and guidance over and over again.

It is true, of course, that many people do seem to find the Bible hard to understand. There are probably three main reasons for this. Or, to put it another way, there are three prerequisites to a good understanding of the Bible. These are: (1) faith, (2) obedience, and (3) study.

One must first of all approach the Bible as the very Word of God, if he would really understand it. It is not his prerogative to pass judgment on its validity and veracity. The Bible is to judge him, not he the Bible! "Without faith it is impossible to please him; for he that cometh to God must believe that he is, and that he is a rewarder of them that diligently seek him" (Heb. 11:6). There is an abundance of evidence for the divine inspiration of the Bible, more than enough to satisfy anyone of open heart and willing mind, if he is interested enough to investigate it. But before he can really understand and receive the message of the Bible, he must be at least willing to believe it. Otherwise, though he read it through a thousand times, it will remain a closed book to him. "The natural man receiveth not the things of the Spirit of God, for they are foolishness unto him; neither can he know them, because they are spiritually discerned" (I Cor. 2:14).

Secondly, one must obey those parts of the Bible which he does understand, before he can expect to gain further understanding. "Be ye doers of the word, and not hearers only, deceiving your own selves" (James 1:22). The first and most important command to obey, of course, is to turn in repentance and faith to the Lord Jesus Christ, receiving Him as one's Saviour and Lord. "Search the scriptures," He said, "for in them ye think ye have eternal life; and they are they which testify of me. And ye will not come to me, that ye might have life" (John 5:39, 40).

Finally, one must begin to study the whole Bible, and continue daily, year after year, all his life. "Study to show thyself approved unto God, a workman that needeth not to be ashamed, rightly dividing the word of truth" (II Tim. 2:15). The more he studies (and, of course, believes and obeys) the more he will understand, and the more precious and certain the Bible will continue to grow. "All scripture is given by inspiration of God, and is profitable for doctrine, for reproof, for correction, for instruction in righteousness: that the man of God may be perfect, throughly furnished unto all good works" (II Tim. 3:16, 17). The Bible is a marvelous unity in all its diversity, perfectly divine in all its common humanity. Every part throws light on every other part, so that all must be understood in some measure if any would be understood in full measure. Thus there is no end to study for complete understanding; yet every moment of sincere Bible study will bring some understanding, and is time profitably invested, with eternal dividends.

5. *Question: "With many modern translations of the Bible now available, should we abandon the King James Version?"*

Answer: One indication that the Bible is still very much alive, even in these days when so many strident voices are denying its authority in the modern world, is the continuing demand for new translations, not only in modern English but also in other languages. Parts or all of the Bible are now available in more than 1,200 different languages (twice as many as in 1920), and this number is increasing steadily. The Wycliffe Bible Translators, for example, now have a staff of missionary linguists working in almost 500 different tribes, reducing their previously unwritten languages to written form in order to be able to give them the Bible in their own languages.

As far as the English language is concerned, at least 25 important translations and paraphrases have received wide usage in the twentieth century, all in so-called "modern" English, instead of the supposedly archaic sixteenth-century English of the King James Authorized Version. The need for so many *different* modern-speech versions, however is not at all evident (except possibly the need for new profits for the promoters!). Yet still more translations in English are being produced nearly every year.

A modern-speech version does have certain advantages, of course. The Scriptures as originally given were in the common language of the people and were certainly intended by God to be understood and used by ordinary people, not just by priests and scholars. It is equally important today that all men should have access to the Bible in a language that is meaningful to *them*. There is no doubt that one or another of the modern translations has been of help to many a person who, for some reason, was not reached by the King James Version.

Nevertheless, there is good reason for continuing to regard the latter as our basic English version, with the others used whenever appropriate for supplementary reading and study. In the first place, no modern translation has yet met the test of universal acceptability, as has the King James for more than 350 years. On the contrary, the very number of new translations is confusing, each with its own advocates and its own peculiar claims and character.

The once-honored, and very valuable, practice of Scripture memorization is now almost a forgotten discipline, and one reason for this must be the confusion over which version to memorize. After all, why should one commit to memory a particular verse of Scripture if even the authorities don't agree on what the verse says?

Furthermore, many of the translators of these modern versions have been men who were not themselves committed to faith in the full verbal inspiration of the Bible. No matter how thorough their knowledge of the original languages and of the Biblical manuscripts may have been, their low view of Scriptural infallibility and perspicuity is bound to be reflected in a certain looseness and subjectivity of translation, which will inevitably corrupt the divinely intended revelation. The translators of the King James Version, on the other hand, were not only scholars of equal calibre to any in the modern era, but also men who regarded the Scriptures as profoundly sacred, with every word placed in the original text exactly as intended by God. This reverence for the text is obvious in the high degree of faithfulness to the original Greek and Hebrew which is characteristic of the King James. It is also reflected in the use of italics in the translation wherever words were added in the English which were not specifically present in the Greek or Hebrew, a practice regrettably not followed in modern versions.

Furthermore, the English of the King James is not nearly so archaic or difficult to follow as its critics allege. In fact, it is in general written in a much simpler vocabulary, with a higher percentage of one- and two-syllable words, than almost any of the modern translations. The honest reader will find it at least as easy to understand as any other. Most of the truly archaic expressions were modernized in a late eighteenth-century revision, in fact, so that the language as found in the King James actually is quite characteristic of the vocabulary of the late colonial period while still retaining the beauty and power of expression of the English of the Elizabethan era.

The King James Version, in fact, is almost universally acknowledged as the greatest of all masterpieces of English literature. To a considerable extent it has, in fact, formed the English language as we know it, because of its wide reading and usage by almost all English-speaking people for more than a dozen generations. Its beauty and majesty are without parallel in our literary heritage, and its phrases abound even in our every-day speech and writing today.

Even its so-called archaic words and forms are instructive. The "th" endings on certain verbs, the pronouns "thee" and "thou," and similar usages all were employed for valid reasons in the Shakespearean English of the day, permitting much finer distinctions as to person, tense, and other grammatical niceties than does the decadent English of our modern speech.

Finally, the King James New Testament, alone of all the English translations, is based on the Greek text known as the Textus Receptus, which is the Greek New Testament used during the spiritual awakenings of the Reformation period. Before the invention of printing, of course, the Scriptures were transmitted by hand copying and circulation. The generally acknowledged and accepted manuscripts were, of course, widely used and so wore out fairly quickly and had to be continuously re-copied on fresh papers or parchments. Great numbers were always current, however, and there was thus a continual self-checking process going on, securing the text against any significant accumulation of copyists' errors. It was from this source that the Greek New Testament known as the Textus Receptus ("Received Text") was compiled. The great majority of the surviving manuscripts agree with this so-called "Byzantine" text, as preserved through the early centuries of Christianity by the Greek-speaking churches themselves.

When a manuscript was prepared which, either through carelessness or deliberate intent, contained significant errors or alterations, it naturally would tend to be discarded when its character was discovered. Unless it was deliberately destroyed, however, it would tend to survive longer than others, for the very reason that it was not being used. This is probably the case with the so-called Sinaitic and Vatican manuscripts, as well as certain others, which were discovered in the nineteenth century and which were older than any of the still-preserved manuscripts of the Received Text.

These manuscripts contain an amazing number of obvious and careless mistakes and probably even some deliberate alterations. Nevertheless, because of their antiquity, they were accepted by the scholars Westcott, Hort, Nestle, and others as the basis for their Greek New Testaments, which were published in the nineteenth century and which have in turn served as the basis for all the subsequent modern-English translations.

Thus there is good reason to believe that the King James Version is still the most accurate and reliable translation we have. In view of the other considerations noted above, there is certainly as yet no good reason to replace it with some ephemeral modern translation.

Chapter II

THE FACT OF GOD

1. *Question: "How do we know that God really exists?"*

Answer: Many people today would like to escape the authority of God and therefore have tried to convince themselves and others that science has done away with God and creation. Men would like to believe that they are accountable only to themselves, and therefore they seek either to reject God altogether or else to relegate Him to some intangible, impersonal role in the cosmos, of no direct concern to themselves. Communism, which has already enslaved half the world and is well along in its struggle for the rest of it, is founded squarely on the religion of atheism and evolutionism. Even in Christendom, so-called, although God is still recognized in a nominal way, He is largely ignored in the political and scientific and educational realms, where His authority ought to be most clearly recognized and His guidance most carefully sought and followed.

Yet the evidence for God is so clear and certain that the Psalmist could exclaim: "The fool hath said in his heart, There is no God!" (Ps. 14:1).

The very essence of the scientific method, in common with all human experience, involves the basic principle of Cause and Effect. That is, no effect can be greater than its cause. "From nothing, nothing comes!" There must therefore be a First Cause of all things which has at least all the characteristics which are seen in the universe which has been produced by it.

Thus, the First Cause must have intelligence, because there are intelligent beings in the universe, and the universe itself is intelligible, capable of being studied and described intelligently. It is an "effect" which must have an adequate "cause," and such a cause must therefore have intelligence in such a high degree as practically to be called "omniscient."

Similarly the First Cause must have emotional attributes, since such things as emotions are surely present in the world. The highest

14

and noblest emotion, most men would agree, is that of love, and thus the Cause of love must itself be One who possesses love in a very high degree.

Furthermore, the attribute of "will," or volition, is very prominent among men, and, since it did not produce itself, the great First Cause must also possess a sovereign will.

Then there are tremendous reservoirs of power and energy in the universe, spread over innumerable suns and inconceivable distances, and the original Cause of such vast sources of power must itself have even more power and therefore be, as far as we can judge, omnipotent. Since space and time are also real "effects," and since our scientific studies have been unable to place finite limits on either space or time, their original Cause surely must be both omni-present and eternal as well.

Finally, since moral and spiritual realities are not self-produced and since all men are aware of such entities, it is certain that the First Cause must be both moral and spiritual in an exceedingly high degree. Furthermore, although we may not understand just how "evil" could be permitted in a moral universe, it is surely significant that men everywhere recognize that "good" is better than "bad" and that "right" is better than "wrong." They intuitively know there is a difference between right and wrong, even though they may not always agree as to the precise definitions thereof.

This moral consciousness can be explained only in terms of a great First Cause with a moral consciousness.

Thus, merely by application of the basic scientific law of Cause and Effect, we can deduce that the First Cause must almost certainly be One who is eternal, omnipotent, omnipresent, omniscient, volitional, loving, and righteous. The Cause is therefore a great Person, and is exactly such a person as the God revealed in the Bible, the One who created and upholds all things, and to whom every man must account in the Last Day.

Some would claim that there was no First Cause—that the universe never had a beginning. But this is precluded by the Two Laws of Thermodynamics, which are the most basic and best-proved of all scientific laws and which control all known events and processes in the universe.

The First Law is that of Conservation of Mass-Energy, and it assures us that the universe is not creating itself, since nothing can ever be truly created by conservative, non-creative processes.

The Second Law is that of Increasing Disorder, and it says that

15

the universe is running down and wearing out. All processes tend toward a state of decay and ultimate death. Eventually, if present processes continue, the universe will die. And, since it has not yet died, it cannot be infinitely old and must have had a beginning at some time in the past.

The universe is not creating itself in the present, but must have been created in the past by a great First Cause, and that Cause must have been a Person! This is the most reasonable possible conclusion of true science and of all knowledge and experience.

Therefore, men who reject or ignore God do so, not because science or reason requires them to, but purely and simply because they want to! As the Scripture says, "They did not like to retain God in their knowledge" (Rom. 1:28). "Professing themselves to be wise, they became fools, and changed the glory of the uncorruptible God into an image made like unto corruptible man" (Rom. 1:22, 23).

For those who really desire to know God, however, He has revealed Himself perfectly through His Son, the Lord Jesus Christ. "No man hath seen God at any time; the only begotten Son, which is in the bosom of the Father, he hath declared him" (John 1:18). Jesus Christ is God incarnate—the God-man. The perfection of His life and teachings, His atoning death, the certainty of His bodily resurrection, and the glorious life imparted to each one who receives Him by faith as Lord and Saviour, all unite in a perfect testimony to the reality of the true God.

2. Question: "How can one God be three persons?"

Answer: The doctrine of the Trinity—that God the Father, God the Son, and God the Holy Spirit are each equally and eternally the one true God—is admittedly difficult to comprehend, and yet is the very foundation of Christian truth. Although skeptics may ridicule it as a mathematical impossibility, it is nevertheless a basic doctrine of Scriptures, as well as profoundly realistic in both universal experience and in the scientific understanding of the cosmos.

Both Old and New Testaments teach both the Unity and the Trinity of the Godhead. The fact that there is only one God, who created all things, is repeatedly emphasized in such Scriptures as Isaiah 45:18: "For thus saith the Lord that created the heavens; God himself that formed the earth and made it; . . . I am the Lord; and there is none else." A New Testament example is James 2:19: "Thou believest that there is one God; thou doest well; the devils also believe, and tremble."

16

The three persons of the Godhead are, at the same time, noted in such Scriptures as Isaiah 48:16: "I have not spoken in secret from the beginning; from the time that it was, there am I: and now the Lord God, and his Spirit, hath sent me." The speaker in this verse is obviously God, and yet He says He has been "sent" both by the Lord God (that is, the Father) and by His Spirit (that is, the Holy Spirit). The New Testament doctrine of the Trinity is evident in such a verse as John 15:26, where the Lord Jesus said: "But when the Comforter is come, whom I will send unto you from the Father, even the Spirit of Truth, which proceedeth from the Father, he shall testify of me." And of course there is the baptismal formula: ". . . baptizing them in the name of the Father, and of the Son, and of the Holy Ghost" (Matt. 28:19). One name—yet three names!

That Jesus, as the only-begotten Son of God, actually claimed to be God, equal with the Father, is clear from numerous Scriptures. For example, He said: "I am Alpha and Omega, the beginning and the ending, saith the Lord, which is, and which was, and which is to come, the Almighty" (Rev. 1:8).

The Holy Spirit is sometimes thought to be an impersonal divine influence of some kind, but the Bible teaches that He is a real person, just as are the Father and the Son. Jesus said: "Howbeit when he, the Spirit of truth, is come, he will guide you into all truth: for he shall not speak of himself; but whatsoever he shall hear, that shall he speak: and he will shew you things to come" (John 16:13).

The teaching of the Bible concerning the Trinity might be summarized thus. God is a Tri-unity, with each Person of the Godhead equally and fully and eternally God. Each is necessary, and each is distinct, and yet all are one. The three Persons appear in a logical, causal order. The Father is the unseen, omnipresent Source of all being, revealed in and by the Son, experienced in and by the Holy Spirit. The Son proceeds from the Father, and the Spirit from the Son. With reference to God's creation, the Father is the Thought behind it, the Son is the Word calling it forth, and the Spirit is the Deed making it a reality. We "see" God and His great salvation in the Son of God, the Lord Jesus Christ, then "experience" their reality by faith, through the indwelling presence of His Holy Spirit.

Though these relationships seem paradoxical, and to some completely impossible, they are profoundly realistic, and their truth is engrained deep in man's nature. Thus, men have always sensed first the truth that God must be "out there," everywhere present and the First Cause of all things. But this intuitive knowledge of the Father

17

men have corrupted into pantheism and ultimately into naturalism. Similarly, men have always felt the need to "see" God in terms of their own experience and understanding, but this knowledge that God must reveal Himself has been distorted into polytheism and idolatry. Men have thus continually erected "models" of God, sometimes in the form of graven images, sometimes in the form of supposed written descriptions and false scriptures, sometimes even in the form of philosophical systems purporting to represent ultimate reality. Finally, men have always known that they should be able to have communion with their Creator and to experience His presence "within." But this deep intuition of the Holy Spirit has been corrupted into various forms of false mysticism and fanaticism, and even into spiritism and demonism. Thus, the truth of God's tri-unity is engrained in man's very nature, but he has often distorted it and substituted a false god in its place.

Furthermore, the truth of the tri-une nature of the Creator is clearly implied by the profoundly tri-une nature of the Creation. Thus the physical cosmos is clearly a tri-universe of Space, Matter, and Time, and each of these is co-extensive with the entire universe. Space is the omnipresent background of all physical reality, Matter (or "Mass-Energy") is that which is everywhere observed in Space, and Time is the ever-flowing but invisible agent through which we can actually experience the phenomena of Matter and Energy.

Each of these three entities is also itself a tri-unity. Thus, Space is three-dimensional, with each dimension comprising the entire space. Space is measured in terms of one single dimension (e.g., the foot, meter, etc.), but can be seen in only two dimensions and "lived in" in three dimensions. Just as the "reality" or volume of space is obtained by multiplying the three dimensions together, so one might say the mathematics of the Trinity is not 1 plus 1 plus 1 equals 1, but rather 1 times 1 times 1 equals 1.

Similarly Time is a tri-unity of Future, Present, and Past time. The Future is the unseen source of Time, becoming visible moment-by-moment in the Present, and then passing into the realm of the "experienced" Past. Each is the whole of Time, yet each is distinct and necessary for the understanding of Time.

Finally those phenomena and processes which take place in Space, through Time, which men call Matter, also constitute a remarkable tri-unity. Energy is the unseen source, manifesting itself in Motion, and then experienced in a particular process or phenomenon. Everything that "happens" in Space and Time is measured in terms of its particular rate or motion—how much time to move through a unit of space. But the particular Motion is inseparably linked with the particular kind of Energy which caused it on the one hand, and the particular kind of phenomenon which it produces on the other. The tri-unity of Matter thus is that of Energy continually producing and revealing itself in Motion, which is then experienced through associated phenomena.

The physical universe is thus fundamentally a Trinity of Trinities! Everywhere we look we see this universal tri-unity of Cause, Event, and Consequence—of Source, Manifestation, and Meaning. It is therefore not at all mathematically unreasonable, but rather intensely realistic, to believe that the Creator of this Tri-universe is a Tri-une God.

3. Question: "What is the Holy Spirit?"

Answer: The Holy Spirit is not simply the spirit, or influence, of God, in an impersonal sense, as the above question implies. Rather, He is a real person, just as real as God the Father and as the Lord Jesus Christ, who is God the Son. He is one of the three divine Persons of the Holy Trinity—one God in three persons.

The mystery of the Trinity is beyond the capacity of our very finite and limited minds to comprehend in its fullness. God the Father is the invisible, omnipresent Source of all being—the God "out there." God the Son, as manifest bodily in Jesus Christ, is God as revealed to His creature man—the God-man, Immanuel ("God with us"). God the Holy Ghost is again invisible and multi-present— taking the things of God and making them real and meaningful in human experience—the God "within."

Although beyond the ability of the human mind to comprehend by reason, the tri-une nature of God can easily be understood in the heart by faith. As noted in the previous section, men have always sensed that God must be everywhere in and beyond the universe. Sadly, however, they have often corrupted this truth of God as eternal and omnipotent Father into the false and inadequate philosophies of deism or pantheism. Similarly they have always felt that God must be capable of being seen or heard by man, but this truth of God as Logos—the Word, the Son—has been grossly caricatured into polytheism, animism, and idolatry.

In like manner, men have always felt that God should be experienced in a personal way, as an inner light for individual guidance. This is the truth of God as Spirit, interacting with man's spirit, but too often has this also been corrupted into mysticism and fanaticism—sometimes even into demonism.

But the fact that the Godhead has been counterfeited by Satan's deceptions, or that it is difficult to apprehend intellectually, should not deter us from believing and appropriating the glorious truth of God as revealed in Scripture. Every possible need of life is met in knowing God as Father through receiving Christ as Lord and Saviour and the Holy Spirit as Comforter and Guide.

The ministry of the Holy Spirit at the present time may be summarized in part as follows:

(1) *Restraint of evil.*—The fact that there is still much good in the world, even though the "whole world lieth in the wicked one" (I John 5:19), is because of the restraining work of the Holy Spirit, both directly and indirectly through His guidance of the lives and actions of individual Christians. When the latter are taken "out of the way" at Christ's coming, to meet Him in the air (I Thess. 4:16, 17; II Thess. 2:7-10), the world's moral and spiritual state will rapidly decay to its lowest state since the days of Noah.

(2) *Conviction of sin.*—Jesus said, concerning the Holy Spirit: "When he is come, he will reprove the world of sin, and of righteousness, and of judgment" (John 16:8). By various means—conscience, the Scriptures, the testimony of Christian friends, the preaching of the gospel—the Holy Spirit convicts men that they are lost sinners, facing the judgment of God and in urgent need of a Saviour.

(3) *Regeneration.*—When a person responds to the convicting of the Spirit, and believes on the Lord Jesus Christ as personal Saviour, then the Spirit imparts a new spiritual life to that person, and he is "born again," "Not by works of righteousness which we have done, but according to his mercy he saved us, by the washing of regeneration and [i.e., 'even'] the renewing of the Holy Spirit" (Titus 3:5).

(4) *Baptism into Christ.*—"For by one Spirit are we all baptized into one body" (I Cor. 12:13). The Holy Spirit, as He regenerates the new believer, simultaneously places him into the spiritual body of Christ, of which he thenceforth is a member. This is symbolized by his baptism in water and his uniting with a local church.

(5) *Indwelling the believer.*—When a believer has received Christ

20

by faith, the Holy Spirit in some special way indwells his very body from that moment on. "What! know ye not that your body is the temple of the Holy Ghost which is in you, which ye have of God, and ye are not your own? For ye are bought with a price: therefore glorify God in your body, and in your spirit, which are God's" (I Cor. 6:19, 20).

(6) *Instruction.*—It was by the Holy Spirit that the Scriptures were inspired (II Peter 1:21) when they were first written by the prophets and apostles. The unregenerate man cannot truly understand and appreciate the Scriptures (I Cor. 2:12-14), but the one who has been born again finds a new love for the Bible, and it begins to open up to him in a new way. This is because of the illumination of his spiritual mind by the divine Teacher, the Holy Spirit. "Howbeit when he, the Spirit of truth is come, he will guide you into all truth. . . . He shall glorify me [i.e., Christ]" (John 16:13, 14).

(7) *Guidance and comfort.*—Primarily through the Scriptures, but also, as need be, through both external circumstances and inner conviction, the Holy Spirit will lead the believer in the way of God's will in all things. He will not compel him, of course, but will guide in the way of greatest blessing if the Christian will only allow Him to do so. "Walk in the Spirit, and ye shall not fulfill the lusts of the flesh" (Gal. 5:16).

> "Now the God of hope fill you with all joy and peace
> in believing, that ye may abound in hope, through the
> power of the Holy Ghost" (Rom. 15:13).

4. Question: "What was God doing before He created the universe?"

Answer: It is interesting to note that only the Biblical revelation, out of all the world's religions, speaks about a special creation of all things in the beginning, out of nothing. All of the other religions and philosophies of men, both ancient and modern, have been evolutionary systems, starting as they do with eternally pre-existing matter.

The Bible, uniquely among the sacred writings of mankind, begins with an eternal, omnipotent, personal God, Who brought all things into being, not out of primeval chaos or eternal matter, but out of nothing! Special creation is a concept absolutely unique to the Bible. To the ancient Israelites, accustomed as they were to thinking in terms of the evolutionary cosmologies of the Egyptians and the

Canaanites, this was a radically new idea. The writer of Genesis therefore had to be quite clear and emphatic in his account of creation, in order to keep them from reading their evolutionary preconceptions into it.

This is why the first chapter of Genesis teaches so plainly and definitely that all things—"the heavens and the earth and all the host of them"—were spoken into existence and brought into their finished perfection directly by God alone. He was not in any way dependent upon pre-existing matter or upon natural processes in this accomplishment. Thus there was nothing at all before the creation period—only God.

Our minds cannot really grasp the idea of an eternal God, existing independently of the universe which He created. But, for that matter, neither can they comprehend the idea of eternal chaotic matter, or an infinite chain of secondary causes extending back to eternity. Our minds are finite and are bound by the framework of the space-mass-time universe in which they function. They cannot successfully comprehend infinity and eternity or any kind of existence outside of and prior to space and time.

But what we cannot comprehend, we can believe. Millions of people through the ages have found mental and spiritual rest through simple faith in an eternal Creator, revealed and incarnate in Jesus Christ.

The special creation of our space-mass-time universe is declared by the introductory statement of the Word of God. "In the beginning [Time] God created the heavens [Space] and the earth [Matter]." The tri-universe thus spoken into existence reflects the tri-une nature of its Creator. The tri-une God—Father, Son, and Holy Spirit—is thus the great First Cause, the source of all meaning and reality.

Skeptics sometimes attempt to ridicule the Biblical chronology by saying: "But if the creation took place only six thousand years ago, what was God doing before that?" One can surely see, however, that is the same question as: "What was God doing prior to the hypothetical creation of the universe five billion years ago?" Infinity minus six thousand is exactly the same as infinity minus five billion.

In either case, there is only one way in which we could possibly learn anything whatever about events prior to the Creation. We can only know what God has been pleased to reveal in His Word. And there are a few such glimpses given us in the Holy Scriptures.

We are given an insight into the heart of God when we hear Christ pray to the Father: "Thou lovedst me before the foundation of the world" (John 17:24). The three persons of the Godhead apparently shared a mutual love and fellowship in their eternal counsels.

In these counsels, we are told that somehow the Tri-une God made plans for the history of the universe and its inhabitants prior to the creation. "Known unto God are all his works from the beginning of the world" (Acts15:18). "Being predestinated according to the purpose of him who worketh all things after the counsel of his own will" (Eph. 1:11).

And then we learn that a certain body of people would be created who, before they even existed, were "chosen in him before the foundation of the world" (Eph. 1:4). Furthermore, a "book of life" was prepared in which their names were written, although there would be many born in the future world "whose names were not written in the book of life from the foundation of the world" (Rev. 17:8).

But God, knowing that man would choose to rebel against His will and thereby deserve nothing but punishment and separation from Him, undertook also to work out a marvelous plan of salvation for those whom He had chosen. It was agreed that God's eternal Son would become a man and would endure the punishment and separation from God which men deserved. He was "foreordained before the foundation of the world" (I Peter 1:20) to be "the Lamb slain from the foundation of the world" (Rev. 13:8).

On the basis of this great sacrifice, God could then "promise eternal life, before the world began" (Titus 1:2) to all who would come to God's Son, believing that promise. The marvelous redemption thus planned by the Tri-une God was thus "the hidden wisdom, which God ordained before the world unto our glory" (I Cor. 2:7).

Finally, having planned and provided all details, God then could proceed to the actual work of creation of the universe and its inhabitants, thence to the work of redemption, and finally to the effectual calling and salvation, through the preaching of the gospel, of all those whom He had chosen in Christ.

Thus, it is God, and He alone, "who hath saved us, and called us with an holy calling, not according to our works, but according to his own purpose and grace, which was given us in Christ Jesus before the world began" (II Tim. 1:9).

5. Question: "Why did God create the universe?"

Answer: It is of course presumptuous for man to think he could ever fully understand the mind and purposes of God. "For who hath known the mind of the Lord?" (Rom. 11:34). "Shall the thing formed say to him that formed it, Why hast thou made me thus?" (Rom. 9:20).

On the other hand, there is no doubt that the mind of man, which itself was created by God, seems intuitively to raise such questions and this could mean that God actually has placed these very thoughts deep in man's heart. It is certainly true that one of man's most fundamental needs is to have a purpose in life, to know why he was placed here and what his life is all about. The question of God's purpose in creation is therefore of profound importance, and it is reasonable to believe that God would make His purpose known to those who seek it in humility and faith.

It is not presumptuous to consider this question, therefore, unless one does it apart from God's revelation in His Word. Human philosophical speculations, on such subjects as this, should be rejected out of hand, but to seek this information in the Holy Scriptures is both reverent and relevant.

For example, consider the magnificent song of testimony at the throne of God, recorded in Revelation 4:11. "Thou art worthy, O Lord, to receive glory and honour and power: for thou hast created all things, and for thy pleasure they are and were created." Here is conveyed the remarkable news that it gave pleasure to God to create the universe!

But in what way could the creation of the physical universe bring pleasure to its Creator? Certainly it was not just in the abstract contemplation of its vastness and intricacy. "For thus saith the Lord that created the heavens; God himself that formed the earth and made it; he hath established it, he created it not in vain, he formed it to be inhabited" (Isa. 45:18).

His purpose in creating the earth, therefore, was that it might "be inhabited." Its living creatures would be His pleasure.

But it was not just the wonderful ordered complexity of living things that pleased him. "He delighteth not in the strength of the horse: he taketh not pleasure in the legs of a man" (Ps. 147:10). But, then, on the other hand: "The Lord taketh pleasure in them that fear him, in those that hope in his mercy" (Ps. 147:11).

Now we begin to glimpse the answer to our question. It was only man who was "created in the image of God" (Gen. 1:27) and who therefore could "hope in his mercy." All other things were created for man's use and control. "Thou madest him to have dominion over the works of thy hands; thou hast put all things under his feet" (Ps. 8:6).

We see, therefore, that the physical and biological creations were made for the service of man. Even angels themselves were created as "ministering spirits, sent forth to minister for them who shall be heirs of salvation" (Heb. 1:14).

It may be noted in passing that this fact points up one of the many absurdities of the evolutionary theory. Since the creation was entirely for man's dominion, it is incredible that the Creator would have forced the earth and its other organic inhabitants to endure a five-billion-year preamble of confused and meaningless existence before its master was ever present to try to comprehend and order it.

Thus, as the Bible says: "The Lord hath made all things for himself" (Prov. 16:4). More directly, all things were made for man, and man for God. "I have created him for my glory, I have formed him; yea I have made him" (Isa. 43:7).

Man's chief purpose, therefore, is to glorify God and to bring Him pleasure, to "fear him" and to "hope in his mercy." But then here is another problem. This kind of response from man is not forced upon him by God. If it were forced, it could not be genuine. Enforced "love" is a contradiction in terms, and so are mandatory "hope" and required "faith."

Man was consequently created with moral freedom. But freedom to love and trust God necessarily also means freedom to hate and reject God. The Creator, therefore, knew before He created man, that man would sin and thus bring the curse of death into the world (Rom. 5:12). And surely the agony of the ensuing millenniums of suffering and death in a groaning creation (Rom. 8:22) does not bring pleasure to God. "As I live, saith the Lord God, I have no pleasure in the death of the wicked" (Ezek. 33:11).

Nevertheless, God has permitted man's age-long rebellion, because even this has its purpose in His divine economy. "Surely the wrath of man shall praise thee: the remainder of wrath shalt thou restrain" (Ps. 76:10). God not only is Creator; He also is Redeemer. He permits the effects of man's sin and rebellion to extend only so far and to endure only so long. Furthermore, He Himself has paid the price for man's redemption and restoration. He has "made peace through the blood of his cross, by him to reconcile all things unto himself . . . whether they be things in earth, or things in heaven" (Col. 1:20).

Any man who, despite his human sin and failure, still desires to know and love and serve God is thus now free to come and be reconciled to Him, through simple faith in His Son, the Lord Jesus Christ. God is revealed to him, not only as the great Creator, but also as the loving and merciful Saviour. "God commendeth his love toward us, in that, while we were yet sinners, Christ died for us" (Rom. 5:8). And here, finally, God experiences the divine pleasure for which He created the universe: Jesus said, "Joy shall be in heaven over one sinner that repenteth" (Luke 15:7). "He shall see of the travail of his soul and shall be satisfied" (Isa. 53:11). He, "for the joy that was set before him, endured the cross" (Heb. 12:2).

There are those, however, who regard this divine desire for personal pleasure as unworthy of an infinite God. Some have even charged Him with selfishness and egotism, with a morbid craving for love and worship from His creatures.

God's "pleasure" from those that "hope in his mercy," however, is not a selfish pleasure, but is infinitely unselfish. Because He is "the God of all grace" (I Peter 5:10), it is His nature to be gracious. He has created man, and redeemed man for the very reason that He possesses infinite love.

After this brief interruption of an age of sin and suffering, and after He has "restored all things" (Acts 3:21; Rev. 21:5), then all who have been saved will know Him in the fulness of both His creative power and His redeeming grace. His full purpose in creation will thereafter be displayed eternally. "God, who is rich in mercy, for his great love wherewith he loved us, Even when we were dead in sins, hath quickened us together with Christ, . . . That in the ages to come he might shew the exceeding riches of his grace in his kindness toward us through Christ Jesus" (Eph. 2:4, 5, 7).

Chapter III

JESUS CHRIST

1. *Question:* *"Isn't it idolatrous for Christians to worship Jesus as God?"*

Answer: It would indeed be the height of foolishness and blasphemy for people to worship any mere man, because true worship belongs only to God Himself. Man seemingly has a perverse streak in himself which is continually manifesting itself in some form of idolatry. Actually, by worshiping an image of his own making—whether it be the wooden idol of the pagan or the mental "model" of cosmic law constructed in the imagination of the philosopher—he is fundamentally worshiping himself.

This is why history has seen over and over again the phenomenon of multitudes of people actually worshiping some man, receiving his words as absolute truth and his commands as absolute law. Even in our enlightened twentieth century, millions have worshiped such men as Hitler, Stalin, Mao-tse-Tung, Father Divine, Hirohito, Nkrumah, and even Elijah Muhammad! The Bible says there is a time that is coming when there will be a great world government and a tremendously powerful and attractive man at the pinnacle, and that "all that dwell upon the earth shall worship him, whose names are not written in the book of life of the Lamb, slain from the foundation of the world" (Rev. 13:8). By worshiping a great superman, one thus actually rejects his Creator and worships a creature (Rom. 1:25), subconsciously worshiping himself. And this is the greatest and worst form of idolatry.

When people claiming to be Christians regard Jesus as merely a great human teacher and example and then proceed to sing songs of praise to Him and to pray in His name, such a religion is indeed absurd and even blasphemous. If Jesus is only a man, He certainly should not be worshiped.

As a matter of fact, if He is merely a man, He does not even deserve to be honored, because He then must have been either a lying deceiver or a crazy fanatic, and thus not even a good man! This conclusion follows inescapably from the fact that He claimed again and again to be God's only and unique Son, and to have rights and powers which belong only to God.

Consider, for example, a few of His remarkable claims: "I am the light of the world; he that followeth me shall not walk in darkness, but shall have the light of life" (John 8:12). "Heaven and earth shall pass away, but my words shall not pass away" (Matt. 24:35). "I am the way, the truth and the life; no man cometh unto the Father except by me" (John 14:6). "The Son of man hath power upon earth to forgive sins" (Luke 5:24). "All power is given unto me in heaven and in earth" (Matt. 28:18). "For the Father judgeth no man, but hath committed all judgment to the Son" (John 5:22). "Ye shall see the Son of man sitting on the right hand of power, and coming in the clouds of heaven" (Mark 14:62).

These and many other like claims were made by Christ Himself. If such statements were ever made by any other man, he would immediately be branded as either a lunatic or a charlatan. But from the lips of Jesus Christ they sound appropriate and prophetic. For two thousand years, He *has* been the Light of the world, and His words have *not* passed away! Millions of people of all times and cultures, and of all degrees of wealth and education, have accepted Him as Saviour and Lord, and have invariably been satisfied that His claims were vindicated and His promises were true.

Finally, He alone, of all men who ever lived, conquered death itself. By all rules of evidence, His bodily resurrection from the grave can be adjudged the best-proved fact of all history. "I am the resurrection and the life," He said; "Because I live, ye shall live also" (John 11:25; 14:19).

Thus, although Jesus was certainly a true man—indeed the one perfect Man in all history—He was also God, the second Person of the eternal Trinity. It is completely wrong, even idolatry, to worship Him while believing He is only a great man. But it is perfectly fiittng to bow down and worship Him as our "great God and Saviour, Jesus Christ" (Titus 2:13). Indeed, such acceptance and worship of Him, recognizing Him as Creator and Redeemer, is, as He said, the one and only way to forgiveness and salvation and eternal life.

2. Question: "How do we know that Jesus was the Messiah?"

Answer: The word "Messiah" means "Anointed One," the name given to the promised Deliverer who would some day come to the people of Israel as their great Saviour and Redeemer, "anointed" as Prophet, Priest, and King by God Himself. Some, of course, are still looking for the fulfillment of these Old Testament promises in the future, when the "Messiah" will come to establish a world kingdom of peace and justice centered around the chosen nation, Israel.

On the other hand, the group of Jewish believers who became the first founders of Christianity were convinced that Jesus of Nazareth was their promised Messiah. The name "Christ" is the Greek equivalent of "Messiah," so that the name Jesus Christ really means "Jesus the Messiah," or "Jesus the Anointed." They preached this truth with such conviction and power that not only many Jews but, later, a still greater host of Gentiles, believed on Jesus, both as the Christ and also as the Lord and Saviour of all men.

And indeed they had good reason for such faith. The Old Testament messianic prophecies were found to be uniquely fulfilled in the Lord Jesus Christ. There are hundreds of these prophecies, so that the possibility of their accidental convergence on any ordinary man is completely ruled out by the laws of probability.[1]

Some of the prophecies are so framed, in fact, as to preclude their fulfillment by anyone living after the first century A.D. For example, the patriarch Jacob said, in Genesis 49:10, "The sceptre shall not depart from Judah, nor a lawgiver from between his feet, until Shiloh come." The name "Shiloh" is a title of the Messiah, and the prophecy states that Judah's tribe would remain the chief tribe in Israel, in particular providing their kings, until Messiah would come. The prophecy must have been fulfilled prior to the destruction of Judah and Jerusalem in A.D. 70, by which time certainly all semblance of a sceptre had departed from Judah.

Similarly the promise was given to King David that the Messiah should be one of his descendants, as the King eternal, the one of whom God said, "I will stablish the throne of his kingdom for ever" (II Sam. 7:13). Isaiah said, "There shall come forth a rod out of the stem [literally 'stump'] of Jesse [that is, David's father], and a Branch shall grow out of his roots" (Isa. 11:1). This is another name of the Messiah, and indicates that, even after it would appear that the family tree of Jesse has been cut down, yet one Branch will grow out of the stump. Evidently the very last one who could be known to

[1] It has been shown that the probability of the chance fulfillment of only forty-eight of these messianic prophecies by one person is only one chance as against 10^{181} chances against it, which is the same as saying that it is absolutely certain that they were *not* fulfilled accidentally by chance, but rather by divine omniscience. See *The Bible and Modern Science*, by H. M. Morris (Chicago: Moody Press, 1968), p. 120.

have come of this lineage would finally prove to be the promised Messiah!

This was fulfilled uniquely in Jesus. His foster father, Joseph, was in the royal line from David and thus held the legal right to the throne (Matt. 1:1-16). His mother, Mary, was also a descendant of David, as shown by her genealogy in Luke 3:23-31. But ever since the time of Jesus, it would be quite impossible to establish the legal or biological lineage of any pretender to David's throne, as all the ancient genealogical records were destroyed soon after that.[2]

An even more striking prophecy is given in Daniel 9:24-27. There Daniel was told explicitly that Messiah would come 69 "sabbaths" (that is, 69 sabbatical years—a total of 483 years) after the decree was given to rebuild Jerusalem, which at that time lay in ruins after Nebuchadnezzar, king of Babylon, had destroyed it.

Such a decree was given later by the Persian emperor. Although the exact date of the decree is somewhat uncertain, the termination date of the prophecy must have been some time in the first century A.D. In fact, it must have been before the destruction of the city and the temple by the Romans in A.D. 70, because the prophecy said quite explicitly: "After [the 483 years] shall Messiah be cut off, but not for himself: and the people of the prince that shall come shall destroy the city and the sanctuary" (Dan. 9:26). Not only must Messiah come before this destruction, but He was also to be "cut off," rejected and killed, before it came.

It is obvious that no one but Jesus could have fulfilled these prophecies. The prophecies absolutely preclude any still future Messiah, except that even that hope also will find its fulfillment in the second coming of Christ.

And then, of course, there are still hundreds of other prophecies all of which were fulfilled by Jesus Christ: His virgin birth (Isa. 7:14); His birth in Bethlehem (Micah 5:2); His sacrificial death (Isa. 53:5); His crucifixion (Ps. 22:14-18); His bodily resurrection (Ps. 16:10); and many others unite in their witness that "Jesus is the Christ, the Son of God" (John 20:31).

The probability that hundreds of such specific predictions, each quite independent of the others, could all be fulfilled concurrently in one individual, is unlikely in the highest degree, especially in view

[2] The apparent discrepancies in the genealogies of Jesus in Matthew and Luke are removed when it is realized that Luke is actually giving Mary's family tree. Thus, Luke 3:23 could legitimately be rendered as "Jesus . . . the son of Joseph, which was (the son-in-law) of Heli."

of the miraculous nature of many of them (e.g., the virgin birth, the resurrection, etc.). No rational conclusion seems possible except that Jesus is all He claimed—Messiah, Saviour, Lord, and God.

3. Question: "What did Jesus look like?"

Answer: One of the most remarkable features of the gospel records is that they give no information whatever about the physical appearance of the Lord Jesus Christ. Whether He was tall or short, lean or heavy, dark or light in complexion, bearded or clean-shaven—no one knows. The only real information we have about Christ and His life is in the four Gospels—Matthew, Mark, Luke, and John—and these writers simply do not say one word about His appearance! This in itself is evidence of divine inspiration. They wrote in considerable detail about His words and deeds, and it would seem almost certain that any writer dealing specifically with such biographical material would include some kind of physical description of the one of whom he was writing. But these writers were all constrained somehow not to do so.

We do not even know that His features were "Jewish" in character. Although He was born in the family of David, it must be remembered that neither of His earthly parents was connected with Him genetically. He was "conceived by the Holy Ghost" and simply placed in the womb of the Virgin Mary.

Now, since the Holy Spirit, in His work of inspiring the Holy Scriptures, has carefully refrained from satisfying our curiosity about Jesus' human appearance, it is utterly futile for men to speculate about this matter. The commonly accepted representation of His features, as expressed in countless paintings and images over the centuries, thus has no basis in fact and is quite misleading. Certain supposed verbal descriptions of Him that have come from extra-Biblical sources are likewise generally known to date from long after the apostolic period.

There is a very good reason for this divine reticence about the physical aspects of Jesus. He is the Son of man—the representative Man, the divine Substitute for all men of all times and places. If we knew that He had been a tall man, for example, then we would subconsciously sense that God preferred tall men and that it was somehow a mark of God's disfavor for a man to be small in stature. The same sense of pride or resentment would tend to attach itself to the possession or lack of any other specific physical characteristic known to be a part of Christ's human aspect.

A second reason for the Lord's refusal to allow a description of Himself in the Scriptures is man's perverse tendency to idolatry. Man is continually "changing the glory of the uncorruptible God into an image made like to corruptible man, and to birds, and fourfooted beasts, and creeping things" (Rom. 1:23). Because of the root sin of pride and unbelief in his soul, he rebels at the thought of submitting himself in faith to his Creator, and instead desires to submit himself to a god of his own making, one he has either constructed in his mind (the mental "model" of ultimate meaning postulated by the philosopher) or else constructed with his own skills (the brazen "model" of God in the pagan temple or even the canvas "model" of the Son of God that human artists have contrived). The Apostle Paul has warned: "We ought not to think that the Godhead is like unto gold or silver, or stone, graven by art and man's device" (Acts 17:29). The last words of the Apostle John in his epistle were: "Little children, keep yourselves from idols" (I John 5:21).

John the Baptist, as he introduced Christ in his message, said: "No man hath seen God at any time; the only begotten Son, which is in the bosom of the Father, he hath declared Him" John 1:18). The invisible God is seen, therefore, not in the bodily incarnation of Himself in Christ, but rather through Christ's "declaration" of His character in His words and deeds. The human body of Christ finally was offered up as a sacrifice, to suffer and die in the bitterest agony, ". . . his visage so marred more than any man, and his form more than the sons of men: . . ." (Isa. 52:14), in order that sinful and hell-deserving men might be redeemed as He died in their place.

We are not, therefore, to continually think of Jesus as He once was, but rather to worship Him as He now is, the risen Lord of life, who rose from the dead and ascended back to heaven. We must forever praise and thank Him for His unspeakable gift of salvation, in living as our perfect Example and dying as our all-sufficient Saviour, but we must also believe His Word and obey Him as our eternal Lord. Some day, probably very soon, we shall ourselves be made like Him, ". . . for we shall see him as he is" (I John 3:2).

In the meantime, we do have one description of His visible appearance in the Bible, not as He was when He walked in Galilee, but rather as He is now, in heaven. John saw, in his great vision of the return of the Lord, ". . . one like unto the Son of man, clothed with a garment down to the foot, and girt about the breast with a golden girdle. His head and his hairs were white as snow; and his eyes were as a flame of fire; and his feet like unto fine brass, as if they burned in a furnace; and his voice as the sound of many waters. And he had in his right hand seven stars: and out of his mouth went a sharp two-edged sword: and his countenance was as the sun shining in his strength" (Rev. 1:13-16).

This is the Lord Jesus Christ as we shall see Him some day, either to "rejoice at his coming" (I Thess. 2:19), if we now trust Him as our Lord, or else to cry out to "hide us from the face of him that sitteth on the throne" (Rev. 6:16), if we have rejected Him and His Word.

4. Question: "Could Jesus have sinned?"

Answer: That Jesus was truly a man, and not a super-human angelic being of some kind, is evident from many passages of Scripture. "For verily he took not on him the nature of angels; but he took on him the seed of Abraham. Wherefore in all things it behooved him to be made like unto his brethren, that he might be a merciful and faithful high priest in things pertaining to God, to make reconciliation for the sins of the people" (Heb. 2:16, 17).

As a true man, He was subject to all the physical infirmities of human flesh, such as hunger, fatigue, pain, and finally death. On the other hand, He was not genetically connected by direct heredity to His parents, since He was miraculously placed in an embryonic form into Mary's womb by the Holy Spirit, thus entering the world by virgin birth. A perfect human body was created for Him, and thus the eternal "Word was made flesh" (John 1:14). "Wherefore when he cometh into the world, he saith . . . a body hast thou prepared me" (Heb. 10:5).

The question now at hand is whether, in His perfect humanity, He could have yielded, not only to the physical infirmities of human flesh (as He actually did when he died on the cross) but also to the temptations of sinful flesh. There is no doubt that God sent His own Son "in the likeness of sinful flesh" (Rom. 8:3), but could He actually have sinned?

We know He did *not* sin, of course. This was the uniform testimony of all who knew Him. Those who were His closest companions, who knew Him best of all, and who therefore would be best acquainted with His weaknesses, agree completely on this. John, the closest of the apostles to Jesus, said, "In him is no sin" (I John 3:5), and Peter, the spokesman for the apostles, said, "He did no sin, neither was guile found in his mouth" (I Peter 2:22).

Not only His close friends, but even His enemies, those who hated

Him and finally caused His death, agreed on His moral sinlessness. The one who betrayed Him, Judas, cried out in remorse, "I have betrayed innocent blood" (Matt. 27:4). The governor who condemned Him to be executed, Pilate, said, "I find in him no fault at all" (John 18:38). The charge against Him by the priests that led to His condemnation was solely that of blasphemy. "The Jews answered him, We have a law, and by our law he ought to die, because he made himself the Son of God" (John 19:7). Though blasphemy is indeed a grievous sin, Jesus was, of course, not really guilty of it, because He *was* truly the Son of God as He claimed.

Thus He was absolutely sinless in every respect, the only man who ever lived who never sinned: "Wherefore, as by one man [i.e., Adam] sin entered into the world, and death by sin, and so death passed upon all men, for that all have sinned" (Rom. 5:12). Every man other than Jesus Christ was under God's condemnation because of sin; Christ alone was fully righteous and thus was able to become a perfect sacrifice for sin. "For he hath made him to be sin for us, who knew no sin; that we might be made the righteousness of God in him" (II Cor. 5:21).

This would, of course, have been impossible had Jesus Himself become a sinner. If He had ever sinned, in the very least degree, He also would have fallen under the just condemnation of God, and thus could never have died in substitution for the sins of others. All men would then have died with no further hope of salvation. If God Himself, incarnate in His only Son, could not measure up to the standard of His own holiness, then it is utterly futile to search elsewhere for meaning and salvation in the universe.

Since it is impossible that the omnipotent God could be fully defeated in His own purpose for the world and mankind, however, and since the consummation of that purpose required the offering of a perfect sacrifice for sins in the person of His own eternal Son, it is therefore completely impossible that Jesus could ever have sinned. He was the "Lamb without blemish and without spot, . . . foreordained before the foundation of the world" (I Peter 1:19, 20).

Though He was completely man, He was also completely God. "The Word was with God, and the Word was God" (John 1:1). He is "the great God and our Saviour Jesus Christ" (Titus 2:13). By very definition, what God does is right; God therefore cannot sin, and Jesus Christ is God! "God cannot be tempted with evil." (James 1:13).

Jesus is not half God and half man, but fully God and fully man.

34

Neither is He man part of the time and God part of the time. The divine and human natures are united in Him in perfect unity, forever.

Although He had (and has) a human nature, it must be remembered that He has a perfect human nature! He is Man as God intended man to be. The perfection of His human nature was assured by the miraculous conception, so that He did not in any wise inherit a fallen, sinful nature from Adam, as have all other men.

Because He possessed a perfect human nature from the very beginning, He did not need to be "converted," as do other men. He told Nicodemus, the most moral and religious man of his day, "Ye must be born again." He was as perfectly sinless in His human nature then as He is now. "Jesus Christ, the same yesterday, today and forever" (Heb. 13:8).

What does the Scripture mean, then, when it says, "He was tempted in all points like as we are, yet without sin? (Heb. 4:15). How could there be real temptation, if it was impossible for Him to sin? He was, in fact, "forty days tempted of the devil" (Luke 4:2), and this temptation was undoubtedly the most severe temptation to which any man was ever subjected. But how could He really be "tempted" if it was not at all possible for Him to yield to any temptation?

The really essential aspect of a temptation, however, is that of a "testing," and only secondarily need it involve a "solicitation to do wrong." A test may be quite real and valuable, *even though there is no possibility of failure*, because it *demonstrates* to the skeptical observer the invulnerability of the object tested. Thus the perfect holiness of Jesus Christ was openly demonstrated to men and angels and devils, when He was tempted (that is, "tested") in all things, yet without sin.

Furthermore, because He has personally experienced the whole gamut of Satanic testing, He perfectly understands every temptation and trial to which we may ever be subject. Therefore He is able to provide perfect comfort and deliverance in all things. "For in that he himself hath suffered being tempted, he is able to succour them that are tempted" (Heb. 2:18). "Let us therefore come boldly unto the throne of grace, that we may obtain mercy, and find grace to help in time of need" (Heb. 4:16).

5. Question: "Must a Christian accept the doctrine of the Virgin Birth?"

Answer: For some reason both ancient and modern skeptics have based much of their attack on Christianity on the Biblical teaching that Jesus was born of the Virgin Mary. The Virgin Birth, of course, in addition to requiring a biological miracle, would also imply that Jesus Christ was absolutely unique among men and would be consistent with His later claims that He was the only begotten Son of God. These claims are repugnant to the natural man, and therefore men have sought to destroy them by first attacking their foundation, namely, the doctrine of the Virgin Birth.

It is not surprising that materialists would reject this teaching, but it is sad in our modern era to see so many liberal religious leaders doing the same thing. The latter tend to regard it as unimportant, not affecting the idea of the incarnation or the spiritual meaning of the birth of Christ.

Nevertheless the Biblical record does lay great stress on the literal Virgin Birth of Christ, making it an integral part of the whole plan of God to redeem and save lost men. Immediately after man first sinned, and God placed the Curse on man and his dominion, the first promise of the coming Redeemer was given. Of this One God said, in effect, "The seed of the woman shall crush the head of the serpent" (Gen. 3:15). Thus the coming Deliverer, who would vanquish Satan, would be, not of man's seed (though, biologically speaking, all people are normally of the seed of the male) but of the woman's seed.

This prophecy was clarified, much later, in the prophecy of Isaiah 7:14. "Therefore the Lord himself shall give you a sign; Behold, the virgin shall conceive, and bear a son, and shall call his name Immanuel." The definite article ("the" virgin), which is in the original text, indicates that a very specific virgin was in mind; most logically this refers to the "woman" of Genesis 3:15. The birth was to be unique, since it was a "sign" from the "Lord himself" (hardly applicable therefore to an ordinary birth) and was to bring forth One who would be "Immanuel" (which means, "God with us").

The Hebrew word for "virgin" which is used here occurs only six other times in the Bible. Although its exact meaning has been debated, its usage is always consistent with the meaning "virgin," and in some cases this is the only possible meaning. The scholars who translated the Old Testament into the Greek Septuagint version used the standard Greek word for "virgin" in translating Isaiah 7:14. So did Matthew when he quoted this prophecy (Matt. 1:23) as being fulfilled in the Virgin Birth of Christ.

Isaiah 9:6, 7 speaks of the "child born" as One who is also "The Mighty God." Micah 5:2 says that the One who would be born in Bethlehem would also be One "Whose goings forth have been from

36

everlasting"! Such prophecies surely require an absolutely unique kind of entry into the human family.

It was promised that the coming Redeemer would be a descendant of Shem (Gen. 9:26), then of Abraham (Gen. 22:18), then Isaac (Gen. 26:4), Jacob (Gen. 28:14), Judah (Gen. 49:10), and finally David (II Sam. 7:12, 13). The line of Judah's kings extended from David through Jechonias (also called (Coniah), but the extreme wickedness of the latter led God to pronounce judgment: "No man of his seed shall prosper, sitting upon the throne of David and ruling any more in Judah" (Jer. 22:30), and yet God also promised that, "David shall never lack a man to sit upon the throne of the house of Israel" (Jer. 33:17).

The Bible's seeming contradictions and paradoxes are always harmonious and satisfying upon deeper study. This one finds its solution in another superficial discrepancy, the apparently contradictory genealogies of Christ in Matthew 1:6-16 and Luke 3:23-31. Matthew gives the legal and royal lineage from David through Solomon and Jechonias (the last man to occupy Judah's throne) to Joseph, the foster father of Jesus. Luke gives the true biological line from David through Nathan to Heli, the father of Mary. To have the legal right to the throne of David, Jesus must be the legal son of Joseph, but he could not be the true son of Joseph because of God's judgment on Jechonias. And yet he must be actually of the "seed of David" to occupy that throne. The Virgin Birth resolves this impasse.

There is no reason, except naturalistic prejudice, for anyone to doubt the birth narratives of Matthew and Luke, and these make it very plain that Mary was still a virgin when she brought forth her firstborn son. The Gospel of John further makes the profound statement that the eternal "Word," which "was God," "became flesh and dwelt among us" (John 1:1, 14). This is an implicit reference to the prophesied coming of "Immanuel." It seems far more difficult to believe that the God of eternity would become a man by natural human procreative processes than to believe that He would be miraculously conceived and virgin-born!

There are many other references in the gospels and epistles from which the Virgin Birth, even though not explicitly mentioned, is clearly inferred. For example, Paul says: "When the fulness of time was come, God sent forth his Son, made of a woman" (Gal. 4:4).

The objection of the modern liberal that such an event would be impossible because it is contrary to biological law is quite vacuous. This is the whole point—the Virgin Birth was a mighty miracle and was accomplished directly by the power of God Himself! To say that such a miracle is impossible is to deny the existence of God or else to deny that He can control His creation.

Not only is the Virgin Birth true because it is clearly taught in the Bible, but also because it is the only type of birth consistent with the character and mission of Jesus Christ and with God's great plan of salvation for a lost world. It is altogether fitting that the One who performed many miracles during His life, who offered Himself on the cross as an atoning sacrifice for the sins of men, and who then rose bodily from the dead in vindication of all His claims, should have begun such a unique life by a unique entrance into that life.

If He is truly our Saviour, He must be far more than a mere man, though also He is truly the Son of man. To die for our sins, He must Himself be free from any sin of His own. To be sinless in practice, He must first be sinless in nature. He could not have inherited a human nature, bound under the Curse and the bondage of sin as it must have been, as do all other sons of men. His birth, therefore, must have been a miraculous birth. The "seed of the woman" was implanted in the virgin's womb when, as the angel said: "The Holy Ghost shall come upon thee, and the power of the Highest shall overshadow thee; therefore also that holy thing which shall be born of thee shall be called the Son of God" (Luke 1:35).

The first Christmas (meaning "Christ-sent") thus climaxed the greatest event in all history since the creation itself. Certainly true Christians must believe and rejoice in the historical fact of the Virgin Birth of their Lord and Saviour.

Chapter IV

THE WORK OF CHRIST

1. Question: "Was Jesus a revolutionary?"

Answer: One of the strangest of the revolutionary doctrines of the so-called "new left" movement is the notion that Jesus and the early Christians were actually revolutionaries. Modern hippies like to point out the similarity of their long hair, their "Jesus shoes," their nomadic life style, their persecution by the "establishment," and other such things, to analogous aspects in the life of Christ. They maintain that they, like Christ, are opposed to the society of their day and seek to bring in a better social order.

Actually, this idea (like all the other ideas of the "new" left) is not new at all. Socialists and Communists have been claiming for more than a hundred years that Jesus was a true socialist and that the early church was really a communist society. Much stranger and more disturbing than the claim itself, which has, of course, been refuted many times over the past century, is that it is now being echoed by many supposed Christians in their rather wistful desire to be "relevant" in this supposedly revolutionary age.

Even evangelical churches and youth organizations in many cases have adopted this technique, thinking somehow that calling Jesus a revolutionary[1] will entice modern young people to accept Him! They forget that "preaching another Jesus, whom we have not preached" (II Cor. 11:4) is not really preaching Christ at all, but rather a self-manufactured pseudo-Christ, in whom is no true salvation.

The image of Jesus as a revolutionary is not at all the picture given in the New Testament Scriptures. In the first place, His clothing and physical appearance were no different from those of the other people of His time. He and His disciples did not try to set themselves apart from the rest of society in this respect, as do the

---

[1] What some mean by this, of course, is that Jesus "revolutionizes" one's life. But the term itself is misleading, since it conveys an entirely different meaning to the very young people they are trying to win. Anyway, the Lord Jesus does not really reform or revolutionize the life; rather He transforms and regenerates it.

hippies of today. The length of His hair is completely unknown to us (despite the supposed portraits of Him painted during the Middle Ages which picture Him with long hair), but it was certainly short enough to distinguish Him clearly as a man, rather than a woman. The Bible says, "The woman shall not wear that which pertaineth unto a man, neither shall a man put on a woman's garment: for all that do so are an abomination unto the Lord thy God" (Deut. 22:5). Furthermore, it says: "If a man have long hair, it is a shame unto him" (I Cor. 11:14). The Lord Jesus came "not to destroy God's law but to fulfill it" (Matt. 5:17).

It is true that He was persecuted by the religious and political leaders, but this was hardly because He was a radical or rebel! As a matter of fact, the Jewish leaders themselves were anxious to throw off the Roman rule and were thus the real revolutionists of the day. The history of the time indicates a complex network of plots and abortive revolutions, but Christ and His followers had no part in any of this.

On the contrary, He continually urged His listeners to be good citizens, submitting to the government and obeying the law. "Render to Caesar the things that are Caesar's," He said (Matt. 22:21).

Rather than demanding their "rights," He instructed His followers: "Give to every man that asketh of thee; and of him that taketh away thy goods, ask them not again. . . . But love ye your enemies, and do good, and lend, hoping for nothing again" (Luke 6:30, 35). He lived in a time and place where slavery itself was a significant social institution, but He never spoke against it. Later many of the early Christians were from the slave population, and, rather than counselling agitation and rebellion, the Apostle Paul said: "Let as many servants as are under the yoke count their own masters worthy of all honour" (I Tim. 6:1). Slavery eventually was abolished through the moral influence of Christianity, not by means of civil disobedience and revolution stirred up by the Christians.

Though Jesus was surely concerned with man's physical needs as well as his spiritual needs, He knew that the latter were infinitely more important and that in this present world, controlled as it is by sinful man and by Satan himself, neither poverty nor war could ever be eliminated. He counselled the rich young ruler, for example, to "sell whatsoever thou hast, and give to the poor" (Mark 10:21), but He also cautioned that "the poor always ye have with you" (John 12:8). Thus, while Christian charity to the deserving needy (note II Thess. 3:10—". . . if any would not work, neither should he eat") is commanded, yet He recognized that state-enforced welfare projects would always be futile.

Similarly, though He warned "all they that take the sword [that is, in aggression, either in warfare or for personal gain] shall perish by the sword" (Matt. 26:52), He also said: "When ye shall hear of wars and rumours of wars, be ye not troubled: for such things must needs be" (Mark 13:7).

Thus, although the Lord Jesus Christ did not at all approve or condone the evils of this present world, not one time did He ever suggest either violent or non-violent rebellion against it! He said rather, at the very time when this world-system was actually condemning Him to death: "My kingdom is not of this world: if my kingdom were of this world, then would my servants fight" (John 18:36).

He came, in fact, "not to condemn the world, but that the world through Him might be saved" (John 3:17). He came not to provide "bread and circuses" for the world's peoples, but rather salvation from sin and hell. "I am the living bread which came down from heaven: if any man eat of this bread, he shall live forever: and the bread that I will give is my flesh, which I will give for the life of the world" (John 6:51).

And ultimately, because He died and rose again, the world itself shall be transformed! When the Lord Jesus, now in heaven, comes back again, then "the creation itself also shall be delivered from the bondage of corruption into the glorious liberty of the children of God" (Rom. 8:21). Christ came, not to stir up rebellion and revolution, but to bring salvation and regeneration to all who put their trust in Him!

2. Question: "If Jesus was God, how could He die?"

Answer: The mystery of the divine-human nature of Christ is beyond our finite understanding. As the Son of man, He was subject to His parents as a youth, engaged in the carpenter's trade, had to eat and sleep like other men, and was subject to pain and suffering, and finally to death, like other men.

But as the Son of God, He was born of a virgin mother, performed mighty miracles of creation, even controlling the wind and the sea, and finally conquered death itself when He left the empty tomb! As man He was "tempted in all points like as we are" (Heb. 4:15), but as God, He "knew no sin" (II Cor. 5:21). As man, He was unjustly "crucified and slain by wicked hands," but as the Lamb of God, He was "delivered" [to be put to death] by the determinate counsel and foreknowledge of God" (Acts 2:23).

The Bible simply presents as fact the great truth that Jesus Christ was both God and man. It does not try to explain how this could be, because it is inexplicable. It must be apprehended on faith alone, and true Christians have always found full rest and peace in this reality. Those of a skeptical and rationalist bent, however, have always made this doctrine a stumbling block. The first heretics, the Gnostics, said that Christ was only divine, rejecting His humanity. Modern-day skeptics, on the other hand, reject His deity. The former said that, since He was God, He never really died on the cross. The latter say that, since He died, He could not have been God. But the Bible says that He was God and that He died!

One should remember, of course, that physical death is not the end of existence. When Christ's body died, God did not die in the sense that He ceased to exist. In the Spirit, He was intensely active (note I Peter 3:18; Eph. 4:9, etc.). The death of His physical body (and even this was only for three days) was merely a change of state, as it were, from the limitations of the flesh to the freedom of the spirit. When He returned to His body, triumphant over death and hell (Rev. 1:18), He empowered even His physical body with full freedom from the limitations imposed by time and space, and the principle of decay and death, so that He now lives forever in His glorified body.

However, the most important aspect of the death of the Son of God was not His physical death, but His spiritual death, which was fully accomplished on the cross before He ever "yielded up the ghost" (Matt. 27:50) physically. For three awful hours darkness engulfed the whole land during the very middle of the day, as "He who knew no sin was made sin for us, that we might be made the righteousness of God in him" (II Cor. 5:21). Although He "did no sin, neither was guile found in his mouth," nevertheless, "He bore our sins in his own body on the tree" (I Peter 2:22, 24). He became the very personification of evil, bearing the guilt of all the sins of all men of all time, enduring the punishment of the outraged holiness and perfect justice of the Creator of every man. Though He had always been in perfect communion with His Father, He now had to be utterly forsaken by God (Matt. 27:46), and allowed to drink to the very dregs the awful "cup" (Matt. 26:39) of God's infinite wrath.

This, of course, is the essence of what hell will be—that is, the state of being utterly forsaken by God. Those who reject the offer of forgiveness through the atoning death of Christ, and who thus continue to retain the guilt of their own sins, will finally be separated forever from the presence and power of God (II Thess. 1:8, 9). Hell is an eternal existence far removed from all evidences of God's presence—an eternity of darkness, wickedness, turmoil, pain, and wretchedness, the just destiny of those who willfully reject God's gift, in Christ, of light, holiness, peace, immortality, and joy.

In the most real sense, therefore, the Lord Jesus endured hell itself as our substitute, when He was forsaken by God for those three terrible hours on the cross. Thus, He could give the great victory cry: "It is finished!" (Luke 23:46; John 19:30), just before he dismissed the spirit, from His tortured body, back to the presence of His Father.

Here, once again, we confront the mystery of the divine-human nature of Christ, the "hypo-static union," as theologians have called it. Christ, as man, suffered and died, "more than any man" (Isa. 52:14), but as God He could endure infinite and eternal punishment in a finite time and specific place, thus satisfying forever the righteousness of God and manifesting to perfection His redeeming love.

Though the "hypostatic union" is a mystery and a paradox, there is more mental, as well as spiritual, rest in accepting it by faith than there is in trying to explain away the overwhelming evidences of both His deity and His humanity. Similar paradoxes, of course, abound in His creation, perhaps even intentionally, as a reflection of their Creator.

Thus, "Space," like Christ, is both finite and infinite. "Time," like Christ, is both temporal and eternal. "Matter" is related to "Energy" in terms of the motion of Light, through Space, in Time, and "light" is both a "wave" motion and a "particle" motion. The processes of nature seem both "deterministic" in terms of natural laws and yet "indeterministic" in their ultimate nature, paralleling the paradox of "predestination" versus "free choice and responsibility" in human experience. All of these and similar paradoxes we accept in terms of experience, even though we can't reconcile them with our limited capacity of understanding.

Thus, too, the Christian believer, though he doesn't understand it all, can rejoice in the historical and experimental reality that God Himself, in Christ, has died for his sins and now lives forever as his eternal Saviour.

3. Question: "Who was responsible for the death of Christ?"

Answer: The crucifixion of Jesus Christ, by normal human standards of right and wrong, seems to have been the greatest miscarriage of justice in all the history of the world. In spite of the fact that He was guilty of no crime, against either individuals or society, and was in fact absolutely sinless even in the sight of God Himself, He was nevertheless subjected to an increasing crescendo of indignities and tortures, and finally to the most agonizing and cruel form of capital punishment ever invented by man. Surely, if there is such a thing as reason and morality in the universe, those responsible for such a crime ought to be recognized and brought to account.

A popular myth among many nominal "Christians," for two thousand years, has been that the Jews were responsible, and this has served as one excuse for many of the waves of persecution which the Jews have endured over the centuries. And indeed the leaders and representatives of the Jewish nation at the time of Christ did play a very definite part in the proceedings, though this is certainly no justification for charging a whole people with "deicide." The "chief priests and the scribes and the chief of the people sought to destroy him" (Luke 19:47). They arranged for His betrayal and arrest (Luke 22:2-6, 52) and called the Sanhedrin together for a mock trial to condemn Him (Mark 14:53-64). Not having authority to enforce the death penalty themselves, they persuaded the Roman governor, Pilate, to send Him to be crucified (Mark 15:14). When he demurred, they threatened to accuse him as an enemy of Caesar and palliated his conscience by saying, "His blood be on us, and on our children" (Matt. 27:25).

Though the Jewish leaders instigated the murder, it was, after all, the Gentiles who actually carried it out. Pilate "delivered him to be crucified" (Matt. 27:26), and the Roman soldiers drove the spikes and thrust the spear. These were the official representatives of the greatest Gentile nation in the world at that time, the mighty Roman Empire. Thus both Jewish and Gentile officialdom are directly involved in the crucifixion of Christ, even though this in itself does not directly implicate either Jews or Gentiles as individuals.

There were also spiritual beings involved. "Then entered Satan into Judas" (Luke 22:3). The Evil One not only possessed and controlled Judas the betrayer, but undoubtedly also was behind the scenes in many of the other activities of that last week. Surrounding the cross itself were the principalities and powers of darkness (Luke 22:53; Col. 2:14, 15).

But even this is not the whole picture. Jesus said to Pilate: "Thou couldest have no power at all against me, except it were given thee from above" (John 19:11). The whole power of the Jewish and

Gentile worlds, and even the might of Satan himself, could not suffice to place Jesus on the cross had not God Himself ordained it! The early church, in its confession to God, said: "For of a truth against thy holy child Jesus, whom thou hast anointed, both Herod and Pontius Pilate, with the Gentiles, and the people of Israel, were gathered together, For to do whatsoever thy hand and thy counsel determined before [that is, literally, 'predestinated'] to be done" (Acts 4:27, 28).

Thus, although the Jews and the Gentiles, as well as the hosts of Satan, were directly responsible for the death of Christ, yet His heavenly Father was the One who permitted and, indeed, ordained it!

But even this is not all. The Lord Jesus was not forced by His Father, any more than He was forced by His enemies, to go to the cross. When His disciples tried to prevent His capture in the garden, He said: "Thinkest thou that I cannot now pray to my Father, and he shall presently give me more than twelve legions of angels? But how then shall the Scriptures be fulfilled, that thus it must be?" (Matt. 26:53, 54). He said: "No man taketh [my life] from me, but I lay it down of myself. I have power to lay it down, and I have power to take it again" (John 10:18).

It seems therefore that, in the final analysis, Christ Himself was responsible for His own death. He deliberately chose to suffer and die—and to rise again!

Now, He is Himself perfect wisdom, and in this great sacrifice of Himself is bound up all the meaning of life, as well as all the holiness and justice and love of God. "But God commendeth his love toward us, in that, while we were yet sinners, Christ died for us" (Rom. 5:8). "Christ crucified" is, to them who believe, "the power of God, and the wisdom of God" (I Cor. 1:23, 24).

"Christ died for our sins, according to the Scriptures" (I Cor. 15:3). He "tasted death for every man" (Heb. 2:9). The Apostle Paul said: "I am crucified with Christ: nevertheless I live: . . . I live by the faith of the Son of God, who loved me and gave himself for me" (Gal. 2:20).

Thus it finally comes to this: each one of us, individually, is responsible for the death of Christ. It was the sins of each man that nailed Him to the cross. Each of us has sinned willfully, in greater or lesser degree, against the God of creation and holiness, and therefore each of us deserved to die and spend eternity away from God in hell. But the Lord Jesus loved us so much that He was willing— even anxious—to suffer the judgment of death and hell as our substitute, in order that we might be saved. And God the Father was willing to offer His only begotten Son as the sacrifice for our sins, in order to satisfy both the demands of perfect justice and the compulsions of perfect love.

The forgiveness and peace, both temporal and eternal, thus purchased for us by Christ on His cross are now available freely and fully to each one who will acknowledge and receive Him, by simple trust, as his personal Lord and Saviour.

4. Question: "How do we know Christ really rose from the dead?"

Answer: The bodily resurrection of Jesus Christ from the dead is the central fact of the Christian faith. As Paul wrote: "If Christ be not raised, your faith is vain; ye are yet in your sins" (I Cor. 15: 17). The entire structure of Christianity—and indeed of any hope for eternal life and for any meaning to human existence—stands or falls with Christ's resurrection.

Death is man's greatest enemy, and every man, no matter how great, eventually dies. The whole world—physical, biological, and social—is under the reign of death, imposed by God's Curse on man's dominion when he first rejected God's Word and brought sin into the world (Gen. 3:17). But Jesus Christ, the eternal Son of God and the world's promised Redeemer, has conquered death, bearing the Curse Himself (Gal. 3:13), and thus opening the way to God and everlasting life.

The fact of His resurrection is the most important event of history and therefore, appropriately, is the most certain fact in all history. It is supported by a wider variety of testimonial and other evidence than any other historical event that has ever taken place since the world began. It is therefore mandatory that every individual must face the issue of the claims of Christ on his own life and service.

The very fact of Christianity is proof in itself. The preaching of the apostles (note Acts 2:22-36; 3:14-15; 4:10-12; 10:36-43; 13: 26-39; 17:31; 26:22, 23; etc.) always centered on the resurrection. "With great power gave the apostles witness of the resurrection of the Lord Jesus" (Acts 4:33), and this was the message that won thousands to faith in Christ and indeed, as their enemies alleged, "turned the world upside down" (Acts 17:6). The first Christians were devout Jews, accustomed to worshiping the Lord faithfully on the seventh day of the week, but now they began meeting instead on the first day, because that was the day of the resurrection. Similarly, their greatest annual observance was the Passover, but this soon became Easter for them, when they realized that Christ had fulfilled the Passover, dying as the Lamb of God, and then rising again from the dead. These institutions—observance of the Lord's Day and Easter, as well as the Lord's Supper, and even the Christian Church itself—can be traced back to the apostolic period, and only the fact of the resurrection can account for them.

There can be no doubt whatever that the apostles and early Christians, by the tens of thousands, believed and preached the resurrection. Is it possible they could have been wrong and that their faith was based on some wicked deception or some fanatical delusion?

They certainly had every reason to consider this possibility. Most of them suffered severely for their faith, losing their possessions and often their lives in the great Jewish and Roman persecutions of the first century. They would hardly have persisted in their testimony unless they had been firmly persuaded, after thorough consideration of all the facts, that their Saviour had conquered death!

They had the witness of the apostles, of course, and also of the "five hundred brethren at once" (I Cor. 15:6), all of whom had seen the Lord Jesus after His resurrection, and they were convinced their testimony was true.

Some have suggested that these post-resurrection appearances of Christ were only visions or hallucinations, or perhaps a case of mistaken identity. But visions and hallucinations don't occur repeatedly like this, to individuals and to groups, indoors and outdoors. And certainly the disciples could recognize the One who had been with them every day for more than three years!

As a matter of fact, when they saw Him in the upper room after the resurrection, they themselves first "supposed that they had seen a spirit" (Luke 24:37). But then He invited them to touch Him and especially to note the nail scars in His hands and feet. Then He ate dinner with them, and they could no longer doubt that it was Jesus Himself, in the same body, as they had always known Him.

Some have suggested that He never really died, but only fainted, on the cross, thus illustrating the absurd lengths to which men will go to avoid facing facts. The Roman soldiers pronounced Him dead, the mixture of blood and water had poured forth from His wounded side, He was wound in a great weight of grave clothes, and was sealed in a tomb for three days. A grievously wounded and weakened, almost-dead Jesus could never have inspired His disciples to the heights of courage and power which they soon began to manifest.

Even if He had only swooned on the cross, He must have died soon after as a defeated and now-impotent leader.

In addition to the ten or more post-resurrection appearances of the Lord, there is the evidence of the empty tomb. The tomb had been sealed with the Roman seal and was guarded, under pain of death, by a detachment of Roman soldiers, and a great stone was rolled in front of its entrance. Nevertheless on the first Easter morning, the soldiers fled in terror as a mighty angel rolled away the stone, and the body had vanished from the grave, with the grave clothes still as they had lain before it had passed out of them.

The empty tomb has never been explained, except by the bodily resurrection. If the body actually were still there, or in any other place still accessible to the Jews or Romans, they would certainly have produced it as a sure means of immediately quenching the spreading flame of the Christian faith. If the apostles or other friends of Jesus somehow had the body themselves, and thus knew He was dead, they could never have preached His resurrection as they did, knowing it would surely mean persecution for them and possibly death. No man will willingly sacrifice his life for something he knows to be a lie!

Thus we have the certain testimony of the empty tomb and the many appearances of Christ after His resurrection, further supported by the uniform teaching of Scripture, innumerable references to it in the non-Biblical literature of the early Christians, the institutions of the Church, the Lord's Day and Easter, the promises and prophecies of the Old Testament, as well as the very necessity to bring real meaning and confidence into human life, all as proof of the fact of the bodily resurrection of Christ from the dead.

There is no other fact of history supported by such an array of evidence as this! And the final evidence is the experimental reality of the assurance of salvation and eternal life, enjoyed by each person who has ever placed his personal faith in the living Christ. "If thou shalt confess with thy mouth the Lord Jesus, and shalt believe in thine heart that God hath raised him from the dead, thou shalt be saved" (Rom. 10:9).

5. Question: "Where is Jesus now?"

Answer: Jesus is not, like other men who lived in the past, somewhere in a grave. He is unique among men, in that, though He died and was buried, He rose again! His resurrection was not in any sense a spiritual resurrection, because His spirit never died! It was His body that was raised, leaving an empty tomb. "Handle me and see," He told His astonished disciples; "a spirit hath not flesh and bones, as ye see me have" (Luke 24:39).

His resurrection body, though truly a physical body, was also a spiritual body, controlled and activated by His spirit, no longer subject to the infirmities and limitations of the flesh. He could now instantly transport Himself to any place directed by His spirit— even from earth to heaven (John 20:17).

After clearly demonstrating the fact of His resurrection to His disciples, "to whom he showed himself alive after his passion by many infallible proofs, being seen of them forty days," He ascended up to heaven (Acts 1:3). "And while they looked stedfastly toward heaven as he went up" (Acts 1:10), they received a promise from angels standing by. "This same Jesus, which is taken up from you into heaven, shall so come in like manner as ye have seen him go into heaven" (Acts 1:11).

Thus, since He ascended bodily *into* heaven, He will some day return bodily *from* heaven. This can only mean that He is now bodily *in* heaven!

And this in turn means that heaven is a real, physical place, existing somewhere in this physical universe. Jesus, in fact, had said: "I go to prepare a place for you" (John 14:2). The place which He is now preparing is described in Revelation 21:2. "I John saw the holy city, new Jerusalem, coming down from God out of heaven, prepared as a bride adorned for her husband." This passage is not a description of heaven; rather it describes a city coming down *out of* heaven, to the earth. God's throne is itself in the midst of the city. "And there shall be no more curse: but the throne of God and of the Lamb shall be in it" (Rev. 22:3).

Somewhere, right now, far out beyond the starry heavens, too far to be observed by man's puny telescopes or space vehicles but quite real nonetheless, exists a "city which hath foundations, whose builder and maker is God" (Heb. 11:10). In this city are abiding the departed spirits of all those whose bodies are "asleep in Christ" in their graves. These are the ones who are now "absent from the body and present with the Lord" (II Cor. 5:1).

Some day, probably very soon, the Lord Jesus will once again leave His throne in the heavenly Jerusalem and return to earth. This "coming of our Lord Jesus Christ" will be "with all his saints" (I Thess. 3:13). When He "shall descend from heaven," the "dead in Christ shall rise first," then "we which are alive," and all—both the reunited spirits and bodies of those resurrected from the graves, and the immortalized bodies of those then living, will "meet the Lord in the air" (I Thess. 4:16, 17). They will all then "appear before the judgment seat of Christ" (II Cor. 5:10). This judgment throne may well be the same as the "throne being set in heaven" (that is, now, the atmospheric heaven)[2] of Revelation 4:2, indicating that the holy city may then have come down to a point near the earth itself, there to remain as a sort of a stationary (or orbiting) satellite until the end of the great tribulation (Rev. 7:14), the millennium (Rev. 20:6), and the renovation of the earth and its atmosphere (Rev. 21:1). Finally, it will descend to the new earth itself, there to remain forever (Rev. 22:5).

At this moment, therefore, the Lord Jesus is in the heaven of God's throne, a real physical place somewhere in His created universe, but "far above all heavens" (Eph. 4:10), also called "the third heaven" and "paradise" (II Cor. 12:2, 4).

In numerous Scriptures, in fact, Jesus is said now to be "sitting on the right hand of God" (Col. 3:1). In fact, there are no less than 21 distinct references in the Bible to the presence of Christ at the right hand of the Father! This remarkable fact has great significance, and a study of the passages will show that they are delineating two important aspects of Christ's present activity in this location.

The first[3] such occurrence is in Psalm 16, the great psalm of Christ's resurrection, where Christ speaks prophetically: "In thy presence is fullness of joy; at thy right hand there are pleasures for evermore" (Ps. 16:11). In this passage obviously the emphasis is on the access and joyous fellowship which presence at the Father's right hand entails.

The second occurrence is in Psalm 110:1. "The Lord said unto my Lord, Sit thou at my right hand until I make thine enemies thy footstool." This chapter speaks of the invincible power to be wielded over His enemies because of His position at God's right hand.

All the other occurrences of this phrase are in the New Testament, and all emphasize one or both of these two aspects of Christ's present position. Thus, He is "the Son of man sitting on the right hand of power" (Mark 14:62), able to exercise all necessary power on behalf of His own. "That ye may know . . . the exceeding greatness of his

[2] The Bible uses the term "heaven" to refer both to the atmospheric heaven and to the starry heaven, as well as to the "third heaven," where God's throne is at present. The context determines which is meant in each particular case.

[3] The first occurrence of any important word or theme in Scripture will almost invariably be found to be of determinative significance with respect to the development of that theme in all the rest of Scripture.

50

power to us-ward who believe, according to the working of his mighty power, which he wrought in Christ, when he raised him from the dead, and set him at his own right hand in the heavenly places, Far above all principality and power, and might, and dominion" (Eph. 1:18-21).

But His presence at the Father's right hand is also a token of perfect fellowship and immediate access to the Father, and it is there that He continually intercedes for those who trust Him. "It is Christ that died, yea rather, that is risen again, who is even at the right hand of God, who also maketh intercession for us" (Rom. 8:34). "If any man sin, we have an advocate with the Father, Jesus Christ the righteous" (I John 2:1).

For all who have received Him by faith as Lord and Saviour, therefore, Jesus Christ is "such an high priest, who is set on the right hand of the throne of the Majesty in the heavens" (Heb. 8:1), who is "able also to save them to the uttermost that come unto God by him seeing he ever liveth to make intercession for them" (Heb. 7:25).

Chapter V

THE WAY OF SALVATION

1. *Question: "What must I do to be saved?"*

Answer: This is undoubtedly the most important of all the questions that a person could ask in relation to his own personal life. To be "saved," in Biblical terminology, means to be saved from sin and death and hell, and to be saved unto righteousness and heaven and everlasting life. Salvation has past, present, and future aspects: we are saved from the penalty of past sin through Christ's atoning death on the cross, from the power of sin through the presence of the Holy Spirit in our lives right now, and ultimately from the very presence of sin in heaven.

This question was asked by the Philippian jailer in Acts 16:30, and was forthrightly and simply answered by the Apostle Paul when he said: "Believe on the Lord Jesus Christ and thou shalt be saved" (Acts 16:31). Jesus Himself said: "For God so loved the world, that he gave his only begotten Son, that whosoever believeth on him should not perish, but have everlasting life" (John 3:16).

Thus, personal faith in Jesus Christ as the Son of God and the victorious Saviour from sin and death is the means by which salvation is received. The substitutionary death of Christ for our sins is the basis on which God is justified in saving us through faith, and this is demonstrated and guaranteed in the victorious bodily resurrection of Christ from the grave.

But the natural man is proud and tends to resist the idea that there is nothing he can do to save himself and that he must trust in Christ to do it all. Accordingly he has invented many substitutes for this simple way of salvation, and these substitutes have led multitudes down the road to eternal destruction. Biblical refutations of some of these false ideas about salvation are outlined below:

(1) One cannot be saved simply by believing and sincerely practicing any religion he chooses. "Neither is there salvation in any other; for there is none other name under heaven given among men, whereby we must be saved" (Acts 4:12).

52

(2) We are not saved by keeping God's laws, for no one can keep them perfectly. "Cursed is everyone that continueth not in all things which are written in the book of the law to do them" (Gal. 3:10). "There is none righteous, no, not one" (Rom. 3:10).

(3) No one can be saved through doing good works. "Not by works of righteousness which we have done, but according to his mercy he saved us, by the washing of regeneration, and renewing of the Holy Ghost" (Titus 3:5).

(4) Baptism is not the means of salvation. Paul said: "For Christ sent me not to baptize, but to preach the gospel" (I Cor. 1:17). The gospel, by definition, is the "good news" of Christ's atoning death and resurrection, and it is by believing the gospel, not by baptism, that men are saved (I Cor. 15:1-4). The thief on the cross was saved, but never baptized (Luke 23:42, 43).

(5) We are not saved by joining a church. There are multitudes of unsaved church members. To the members of the church in Laodicea, for example, Christ said: "Because thou art lukewarm, and neither cold nor hot, I will spue thee out of my mouth" (Rev. 3:15).

There are numerous other false ideas about salvation that are prevalent, but all of them, like the above, consist in man's doing something which he feels will help earn his salvation. Thus they all contribute to the upbuilding of human pride and the downgrading of God's marvelous gift in the Lord Jesus Christ. The Bible says: "For by grace are ye saved through faith; and that not of yourselves; it is the gift of God; Not of works, lest any man should boast" (Eph. 2:8, 9).

It is certainly true that a person who has been genuinely saved, through faith in Christ and His work, will gladly do the above and other good works. He will follow the Lord in baptism, be a faithful church member, seek to obey God's laws, and do works of righteousness and try sincerely to live a consistent Christian life in every way. If he refuses or neglects to do these things, there is reason to doubt the genuineness of his salvation. "And hereby we do know that we know him, if we keep his commandments" (I John 2:3).

But it is extremely important to do these things with the right motive. If the unsaved man does them to earn salvation, he is deceiving himself and "frustrating the grace of God" (Gal. 2:21).

The true Christian does these and other good works out of love and gratitude to the Lord Jesus for saving him. "For the love of

Christ constraineth us; because we thus judge, that if one died for all, then were all dead; . . . that they which live should not henceforth live unto themselves, but unto him which died for them, and rose again" (II Cor. 5:14, 15).

2. Question: "What do Christians mean when they say they have been 'born again'?"

Answer: This is essentially the same question that Nicodemus, the great Jewish teacher, asked Jesus one night long ago. Jesus had just said: "Except a man be born again, he cannot see the kingdom of God" (John 3:3). Nicodemus replied: "How can a man be born when he is old? Can he enter the second time into his mother's womb, and be born?"

Jesus, of course, was referring to a spiritual birth, and He made this clear by saying: "Except a man be born of water and the Spirit, he cannot enter into the kingdom of God" (John 3:5). This can better be translated "water, even the Spirit." That is, the waters of baptism, which symbolize the entrance of a believer into the Christian life, are representative of the spiritual birth that takes place when a person passes out of the old life, and is baptized by the Spirit of God into a new life in Christ.

Every individual, once he reaches an age where he knows right from wrong, soon becomes a conscious sinner, and therefore a guilty sinner, in the sight of an all-holy God. Although he may do many good things and may even be a religious person, he is nevertheless a sinner. Both Scripture and universal experience unite in their testimony that "there is not a just man upon earth, that doeth good, and sinneth not" (Eccles. 7:20).

God's moral law is a unit and is "holy, and just, and good" (Rom. 7:12). To break any part of His law is to break all of it. "For whosoever shall keep the whole law, and yet offend in one point, he is guilty of all" (James 2:10). A man who is proud, or selfish, or who distorts the truth, or neglects the Sabbath, or uses profanity or vulgarity in his speech, is as much a lost sinner in God's sight as the thief, or adulterer, or murderer. Sins of omission also are evil. "Whosoever, therefore, knoweth to do good, and doeth it not, to him it is sin" (James 4:17).

The Bible, in fact, teaches that all men are "dead in trespasses and sins" (Eph. 2:1). Since men are all in a state of spiritual death in their natural condition, separated from God and out of fellowship with Him, it is no wonder that Jesus said: "Ye must be born again" (John 3:7).

The Bible also teaches that men, in their natural state, are "children of wrath" (Eph. 2:3). They are "children of the devil" (I John 3:10) and "children of disobedience (Eph. 5:6). The popular notion that all men are fundamentally "children of God" is an utterly false and dangerous idea, completely without any basis in Scripture.

It is therefore clear that every man urgently needs to be born again, to become a "child of God" rather than a "child of the wicked one," to have spiritual life rather than to continue in a state of spiritual death. But the great question is still, as Nicodemus asked, "How can these things be?"

The only solution is found in Christ Himself. Since each ordinary man is already dead in sins, he cannot bring himself to spiritual life by his own power. He must receive such regenerative power from the Holy Spirit, and this can only be given if his sins are first forgiven and washed away. But "without shedding of blood is no remission of sins" (Heb. 9:22), for "the wages of sin is death" (Rom. 6:23).

Jesus Christ is the sacrificial "Lamb of God, which taketh away the sin of the world" (John 1:29). He was offered up for our sins, "that he by the grace of God should taste death for every man" (Heb. 2:9). He explained it thus to Nicodemus: "As Moses lifted up the serpent in the wilderness, even so must the Son of man be lifted up." That is, He must be lifted up to die on the cross. "For God so loved the world that he gave his only begotten Son, that whosoever believeth on him, should not perish, but have everlasting life" (John 3:14, 16).

Now, therefore, when an individual sees the sinfulness of his own life for what it really is, deserving nothing from God but eternal separation in hell, but then also truly sees and believes that Christ loved him and suffered and died to save him from his sins, his heart is thereby made ready for the marvelous miracle of regeneration. In response to his repentance and faith, the Holy Spirit—that is, God Himself—enters his heart and imparts His own eternal spiritual life to the new believer. His sins are charged to Christ's account, and Christ's perfect righteousness is placed to his own account (II Cor. 5:21). The indwelling Holy Spirit gives him a new nature, new motives, new goals, new understanding, and new power. "Therefore, if any man be in Christ, he is a new creature; old things are passed away; behold, all things are become new" (II Cor. 5:17). "To as

55

many as received him, to them gave he power to become the sons of God, even to them who believe on his name" (John 1:12).

3. Question: "Can a person really know that he is saved?"

Answer: It is certainly possible for a person to know that he is saved and is ready to meet God. In fact, God intends and desires us to have this assurance.

First, however, we should realize that trying to live a Christian life is not sufficient. As the Apostle Paul says, "For I know that in me [that is, in my flesh] dwelleth no good thing: for to will is present with me; but how to perform that which is good I find not. For the good that I would I do not; but the evil which I would not, that I do" (Rom. 7:18, 19). If such a man as Paul found it impossible to live as he should, in spite of his sincere desire to do so, then this will certainly be true of the rest of us.

But what Paul could not do himself, Christ accomplished in him. "I am crucified with Christ: nevertheless I live; yet not I, but Christ liveth in me: and the life which I now live in the flesh I live by the faith of the Son of God, who loved me and gave himself for me" (Gal. 2:20).

Just as Paul did, when one believes in his heart that Christ gave Himself for *him*—that is, He suffered and died as his substitute, bearing God's judgment for his sins—then he can know the real joy and peace of all sins completely forgiven. Since he was thus judged by God to be dead because of sin, he is then also reckoned by Him to be raised from the dead, to a new life in Christ. He thenceforth, as it were, lives in and through the believer, and His power and guidance will enable that one to live a true Christian life.

Having been thus "born again" (note John 3:3), he can then claim all the Bible's gracious promises of assurance of salvation, some of which are as follows:

These things have I written unto you that believe on the name of the Son of God; that ye may know that ye have eternal life (I John 5:13).

For I know whom I have believed, and am persuaded that he is able to keep that which I have committed unto him against that day (II Tim. 1:12).

Whoso keepeth his word, in him verily is the love of God perfected; hereby know we that we are in him (I John 2:5).

The Spirit himself beareth witness with our spirit, that we are the children of God (Rom. 8:16).

We know we have passed from death unto life, because we love the brethren (I John 3:14).

These and many other Scriptures show that a person may rightly claim that he knows that he is saved, provided that he has been born into a new life through faith in Jesus Christ as the Son of God and his personal Saviour from sin. The reality of this faith and his new life in Christ will be shown, both to him and to others, by his love and respect for the Word of God and for his fellow Christians, and will be confirmed in his own heart by the witness of the Holy Spirit, who has come to indwell him. Therefore, if one is really a Christian in the true sense, he should have genuine assurance that he is in full possession of God's great salvation.

4. Question: "Can a person receive Christ as his Saviour without accepting Him as Lord?"

Answer: The doctrine of the Lordship of Christ is an integral part of the "doctrine of Christ." As pointed out later,[1] the doctrine of Christ is really the entire system of Christ's teachings. These can be conveniently grouped under the categories: teachings concerning His person, His work, and His relationship to us as Lord.

The Scripture says that whosoever "abideth not in the doctrine of Christ hath not God" (II John 9). This obviously implies far more than a mere spoken or ritualistic assent to certain historical facts. To "believe," in the Biblical usage, means to "trust completely," to "rely fully." One must come to Christ under the conviction that he is unable to help himself in any way, absolutely "dead in trespasses and sins" (Eph. 2:1). He must recognize and accept Jesus as the only begotten Son of God, who died on the cross in payment for his sins, both satisfying the justice of God and manifesting the love of God. He must believe that Christ, raised from the dead and with all power, is able and willing to save him, forgiving his sins and assuring him of eternal life.

But he cannot come to Christ in a bargaining posture, willing to accept Him as Saviour provided he does not have to accept Him as Lord. If he must first be assured that he can retain certain pet beliefs or practices before he will commit himself to Christ, he will never be saved. He is "dead in sins," and a dead man does not make conditions or bargains.

It is clear from the Scriptures that true conversion makes Christ the

---

[1] See Section IX-3.

57

Lord of one's life as well as his Saviour from the penalty of sin. "Believe on the LORD Jesus Christ (not just believe on Jesus), and thou shalt be saved" (Acts 16:31).

Similarly, "If thou shalt confess with thy mouth Jesus as LORD, and shalt believe in thine heart that God hath raised him from the dead, thou shalt be saved" (Rom. 10:9). Also, "no man can say that Jesus is the LORD but by the Holy Ghost" (I Cor. 12:3). Jesus said to His disciples: "Ye call me Master and Lord: and ye say well: for so am I" (John 13:13).

It is interesting and significant that, in the four Gospels, none of the disciples ever addressed the Lord Jesus by His given name, "Jesus." Normally they addressed Him as "Lord," occasionally as "Master." In the narrative portions of the Gospels, statements about His activities do frequently use His human name "Jesus," but His disciples always addressed Him as "Lord," and this is what we should do as well. "God hath made that same Jesus, whom ye have crucified, both Lord and Christ" (Acts 2:36). To us, therefore, He is "the Lord Jesus Christ," and it is most appropriate for us normally to speak of Him this way.

Of course, it is hypocritical and meaningless to call Him "Lord" unless He really is the Lord of our lives. "Why call ye me, Lord, Lord, and do not the things that I say?" (Luke 6:46). "Not everyone that saith unto me, Lord, Lord, shall enter into the kingdom of heaven; but he that doeth the will of my Father which is in heaven" (Matt. 7:21).

Christ must be our Lord in reality as well as in name. This means that we are His servants and that we obey His commandments. Similarly, He is our Master (literally "teacher") and we are His disciples (literally "learners"), so that we also believe His words. Thus, the doctrine of His Lordship involves our acceptance of His absolute authority, both in belief and in practice. "Ye are not your own . . . For ye are bought with a price: therefore glorify God in your body, and in your spirit, which are God's" (I Cor. 6:19, 20).

Acceptance of Christ's Lordship, for example, certainly entails acceptance of the Bible as the fully inspired, fully authoritative, inerrant Word of God. He said, for example, "The Scriptures cannot be broken." With respect to the Pentateuch, He said: "For had ye believed Moses, ye would have believed me: for he wrote of me. But if ye believe not his writings, how shall you believe my words?" (John 5:46, 47). It is obviously impossible to believe truly in Christ as Lord if we reject any of His own beliefs or teachings.

Similarly, if He is really our Lord and we are His servants (literally "bond-slaves"), we will earnestly try to understand and obey all His commands—beginning with baptism and then all the rest. "He that hath my commandments, and keepeth them, he it is that loveth me" (John 14:21).

Thus the "doctrine of Christ" is not some emasculated, least-common-denominator, non-controversial preaching of "another Jesus, whom we have not preached" (II Cor. 11:4), such as is becoming very common today, even in evangelical churches and fellowships. Rather it is "all the counsel of God" (Acts 20:27), the entire body of "the faith once-for-all delivered unto the saints" (Jude 3), and one cannot safely reject or ignore any part of it. One who truly is saved, and who therefore loves the Lord Jesus Christ, even though in this life he may be unable to understand completely and obey all His words, will surely believe them and, by His grace, seek to follow them as the Lord reveals them to him through the Scriptures.

5. Question: "How can we be saved by faith alone? Doesn't the Bible teach that faith without works is dead?"

Answer: Those who wish to find contradictions in the Bible often point to the supposed conflict between Paul and James. James does say, "Ye see then how that by works a man is justified, and not by faith only" (James 2:24). Paul says, on the other hand, "For by grace are ye saved through faith, and that not of yourselves: it is the gift of God, not of works, lest any man should boast" (Eph. 2:8, 9).

However, there are no real contradictions in the Bible. The Bible is God's Word, and God cannot contradict Himself. One should remember that "a text without a context is a pretext," and always carefully study both the immediate context and the broader context when dealing with any verse which seems to entail some kind of difficulty.

In the context, James is concerned with "justification" (that is, "declaring righteous") by man, whereas Paul is talking about being justified by God. Man necessarily must judge by what he sees, and he cannot look into man's heart to ascertain whether he really has saving faith or not. So, James says, "I will show thee my faith by my works" (James 2:18).

Paul does not contradict this at all, but is fully in agreement with the principle that genuine faith will inevitably and necessarily manifest itself in works. In the verse immediately following the passage quoted above (Eph. 2:9), in which he strongly emphasizes that works do not contribute in any way to salvation, he then says, "For we are his workmanship, created in Christ Jesus unto good works, which God hath before ordained that we should walk in them" (Eph. 2:10).

Thus "good works"—that is, a "walk" in obedience to God's Word—will certainly be a result of a faith which is truly genuine. This, of course, will be observed by other people, and such a man will therefore be "justified" in their sight. A faith which fails to produce such works is a spurious faith. James asks the rhetorical question, "Can that faith save him?" And the answer, of course, is "Faith without works is dead" (James 2:14, 20).

But it is not these, or any other works, which actually save the individual, and it is extremely important that we realize this. "Knowing that a man is not justified by the works of the law, but by the faith of Jesus Christ, even we have believed in Jesus Christ, that we might be justified by the faith of Christ, and not by the works of the law: for by the works of the law shall no flesh be justified" (Gal. 2:16).

If a person is depending in any way upon his own righteousness or good works to earn his salvation, he may very well not be saved at all, since basically he is trusting in himself and what he is doing, rather than in Christ and what He has done.

It is interesting to note that every human religion, except Biblical Christianity, is a religion of salvation by works. Each does involve faith, of course—that is, faith in the particular founder, or god, or system associated with that religion. But each also involves a certain set of good works which must be accomplished before salvation is merited.

Invariably, however, this standard is capable of attainment by human effort. This proves it to be a man-made standard, since no man or group of men would ever institute a set of requirements for salvation which they could never reach. Thus every religion, with the exception of genuine Christianity, is a religion of salvation through both faith and works, with both specified as necessary, and with both well within the capabilities of man to attain.

On the other hand, the Biblical standard is one of absolute perfection, a character of holiness equal to that of God Himself! Any lapse whatever is fatal. "For whosoever shall keep the whole law, and yet offend in one point, he is guilty of all" (James 2:10). "As it is written, There is none righteous, no, not one" (Rom. 3:10). Thus, James and Paul are in complete agreement that no one is sufficiently righteous to merit salvation by his works.

Many people today have the vague notion that salvation is a simple matter of arithmetic, and will be awarded by some cosmic bookkeeper if one's good deeds outnumber his bad deeds. And, of course, since each person feels he has the right to decide himself what is good and what is bad, he naturally is confident that he is on the right side of the ledger.

But this popular delusion is deadly foolishness, and comes from the age-old lie of the serpent himself. "Ye shall not surely die" (Gen. 3:4). No one will ever be saved who is relying on his own good works, or his family, or his church, or his education, or his wealth, or any other human factors whatever, for that salvation. In fact, pride and unbelief are the most deadly sins of all, and these characteristically afflict those persons who, by ordinary human criteria, have attained the highest status in society.

Thus, eternal life is not something to be earned by good works, or even something to be maintained by good works, because no one is able to meet God's standard of absolute holiness of heart and life. But that which could never be earned, our God of all grace gives as a free gift to everyone who will accept it. "For the wages of sin is death, but the gift of God is eternal life, through Jesus Christ, our Lord" (Rom. 6:23).

One should not minimize the value of this gift, however. Although free to the recipient, it is infinitely costly to the Giver, "Who bore our sins in his own body on the tree" (I Peter 2:24). Every sin each man has ever committed—even the sin of unbelief—was laid on the Son of man, as He suffered the agonies of the cross and even the depths of hell itself in our place. "He who knew no sin was made sin for us, that we might be made the righteousness of God in Him" (II Cor. 5:21).

When, through faith, we believe in Jesus Christ as our Lord and Saviour, accepting His gracious offer of pardon and salvation, then it is that our characters are so transformed, and the whole direction and motivation of our lives so revolutionized, that we are, in fact, "born again" (John 3:3). We must, and will, thenceforth seek to live unto Him in all things, not in the hope of earning salvation, but in gratitude and love to Him who purchased it with His own blood and has freely given it to us. We can then say with Paul, "I am crucified with Christ, nevertheless I live; yet not I, but Christ liveth in me: and the life which I now live in the flesh, I live by the faith of the Son of God, who loved me, and gave himself for me" (Gal. 2:20).

Chapter VI

THE BIBLE AND SCIENCE

1. *Question: "Has modern science discredited the Bible?"*

Answer: Probably the most basic reason for the modern widespread rebellion against traditional values in every realm—social, moral, political, educational, religious—is the widespread impression that Biblical principles have been outdated by the discoveries of modern science. Our constitution and our entire American culture were permeated in their origins with a strong national faith in God and His Word. The gradual undermining of confidence in the Scriptures, resulting from the rise of uniformitarianism and evolutionism in the nineteenth century, inevitably was followed by a revolt against the social and political institutions erected on that faith. It is no accident that religious liberals are almost always moral and political liberals, and vice versa.

The fact is, however, that true science has always confirmed the Bible! It is not science but scientism (that is, the extension of scientific theories to a supposedly complete philosophy of life and meaning) that has attacked the Bible.

"Science" means "knowledge" and therefore includes only that which we actually know, by direct observation and experience. It is the organized body of factual knowledge and relationships. The "scientific method" necessarily involves experimental reproducibility and verification. Thus science, in its proper sense, can deal only with the processes of the world as they now exist. It can tell us nothing for certain about prehistoric events and processes, nor can it predict future events and processes with certainty.

Many scientists (not science as such, but scientists—men who are just as biased, fallible, sinful, and human as any other men) have assumed that these present processes are eternal processes, and therefore that they can explain everything that ever has been or ever will be in terms of what exists now! This is the philosophy of "uniformitarianism" and is the ruling philosophy in the modern scientific establishment. It necessarily leads to "evolutionism," which seeks to explain the origin and development of all things in terms of present natural processes.

But this assumption itself violates the two most fundamental laws of science, the First and Second Laws of Thermodynamics! These laws deal with the all-embracing entity known as "energy," which includes all the phenomena of the physical universe. All processes are basically interchanges of energy—even matter itself is fundamentally a type of energy, which can, under the right circumstances, be converted into other forms. The First Law is the Law of Energy Conservation, which states that nothing is now being created or destroyed. The Second Law is the Law of Energy Decay, which states that in all real processes there is a net loss of energy available for further work. All natural processes, without any exception whatever, operate within the framework of the Two Laws.

Thus all processes are conservative and disintegrative, not creative and integrative.

The Bible, instead of being discredited by science, has actually anticipated modern science. The Two Laws were stated in the pages of the Scriptures thousands of years before their recognition by nineteenth-century scientists. In fact, the institution of the First Law by God is commemorated every Sabbath Day. "For in six days the Lord made heaven and earth, the sea, and all that in them is, and rested the seventh day" (Ex. 20:11). All of His "works were finished from the foundation of the world" (Heb. 4:3). He is now "upholding all things by the word of his power" (Heb. 1:3). Thus, He is not now creating anything, but neither is He allowing anything to be annihilated.

The Second Law expresses in a formal way the fact that something is intrinsically wrong with the world. Everything gets old, wears out, runs down, and finally dies. In all processes, some energy becomes degraded to low-level heat energy and can no longer be used. Every ordered system, left to itself, tends to become disorganized. Complex structures tend to break up and become simpler. The "entropy" (that is, the disorder, or randomness) of a system tends to increase, and this tendency can only be superseded, locally and temporarily, if there is an excess supply of ordering energy brought in from outside the system.

In the Bible, this Law is called the "bondage of corruption" (literally, "decay") under which the "whole creation is groaning" (Rom. 8:21, 22). It is nothing less than God's primeval Curse on man and

63

his entire dominion (Gen. 3:17), which God invoked when man first brought sin into God's originally perfect creation.

This Second Law teaches that, unless God Himself intervenes, the universe is proceeding inexorably toward an ultimate "heat death," when all available energy will have been degraded to low-level heat and no more work can be done. Since this state has not yet been reached, the universe is not infinitely old and thus must have had a definite beginning!

The First Law states that, since all present processes are conservative, not creative, the beginning of all things required by the Second Law must have been accomplished by means of creative processes which are not now in existence.[1] Therefore they are inaccessible to science, and anything we are ever to learn about them must come by revelation from the Creator Himself.

Thus the basic framework of science, confirmed by Biblical revelation, leads us inexorably and irrefutably to the first words ever written and the most profoundly important truth ever comprehended: "In the beginning, God created the heavens and the earth" (Gen. 1:1).

2. Question: "Do miracles such as we read about in the Bible still occur today?"

Answer: The standard belief of the scientific establishment today is that miracles are impossible and that genuine miracles have never occurred, either in Biblical days or in our own day. It is usually claimed that supposed miracles can always be explained in terms of natural laws in one of the following ways: (a) the witnesses, under the excitement of the moment, may have been mistaken in what they claimed to have seen; (b) with the advance of scientific knowledge, more and more phenomena, once thought to be supernatural, are found to have a purely naturalistic explanation; (c) every natural process is known to vary statistically about some typical method and rate of operation, and thus a supposed miracle may really be only a rare, but not impossible, variation in the particular process.

Undoubtedly many so-called miracles can actually be explained by such means. God is the Creator and Sustainer of the universe, and His laws are exceedingly reliable. If it were not so, our world would be a chaos, and science and technology would be impossible.

On the other hand, since He established the laws, He is also able

---

[1] The Biblical, theological, and scientific implications of the First and Second Laws are treated more fully in the author's book, *Biblical Cosmology and Modern Science* (Nutley, N. J.: Craig Press, 1970), pp. 111-139.

to change them if He so wills. To say that miracles are impossible is actually to deny that God exists. The question, therefore, is not whether miracles *can* happen, but whether they *do* happen. And this depends merely upon whether God has adequate reason for superseding His ordinary laws or not, and also upon whether there is adequate evidence that He has done so.

These two conditions are abundantly satisfied with respect to all the Biblical miracles, and we are quite justified in believing that they really happened and that they were really miracles. Here it will be helpful if we note that there may actually be two different kinds of miracles.[2]

The first type is what we might call a miracle of creation. This involves actual creative activity on the part of God Himself. We know scientifically that there are just two basic laws controlling all natural phenomena, as discussed in the preceding section. The First Law is the Law of Energy Conservation, and this law states that nothing is now being created in the physical universe so far as science can tell. The Second Law is the Law of Energy Degradation, and this law states that everything is moving toward a state of disorder and ultimate death. Every natural process—that is, everything that happens in the known universe—obeys these two basic laws.

Therefore, if a particular event involves a new act of creation—of matter, or energy, or order—then it is a genuine miracle which only the power of God Himself can accomplish, since He alone is the Creator. Such miracles are exceedingly rare, but they have occurred. For example, the great "signs" recorded in the Gospel of John, such as the turning of water into wine, the feeding of the five thousand, and the raising of Lazarus from the dead, were all creative miracles, and thus unite in their testimony that "Jesus is the Christ, the Son of God, and that, believing, ye might have life through his name" (John 20:31).

One special miracle of creation is actually very common, even today. This is the miracle of regeneration, whereby, "if any man be in Christ, he is a new creation; old things are passed away; behold, all things are become new" (II Cor. 5:17). When a person truly believes on the Lord Jesus, he is "born again," receiving assurance of forgiveness and everlasting life, and a transformed attitude, with purpose and meaning in his life as never experienced before. This is a true miracle in the fullest sense of the word.

[2] See *ibid.*, pp. 35-45, for a more complete discussion of this subject.

The second type of miracle is a miracle of providence. This does not involve a divine intervention in the two basic laws, but rather a special ordering of the manner or time of occurrence of a particular process. Such a miracle was the Philippian earthquake (Acts 16:26), the 3½-year drought of Elijah (I Kings 17), and many other Biblical miracles. Often God uses his angels to accomplish miracles of this kind (note Dan. 6:22; Ps. 34:7; Heb. 1:14, etc.).[3]

Providential miracles still occur today. Every believing and practicing Christian knows from personal experience that God does answer prayer, often in unlikely and remarkable ways. True answers to Christian prayer, in the providential ordering of circumstances, will, of course, always be in conformity with Biblical revelation and will honor the Lord Jesus Christ.

3. Question: "How could Moses have written Genesis when writing was unknown in his day?"

Answer: This is an ancient criticism which is still voiced frequently today. The answer is, first, that writing was known and widely used long before Moses' time and, second, that he quite possibly compiled and edited the book of Genesis, rather than writing it himself.

There is no doubt whatever that writing was practiced long before Moses was born. For example, archaeologists have unearthed an ancient library in the city of Ur containing thousands of stone "books." It will be recalled that Ur of the Chaldees was Abraham's home before he migrated to Canaan, and these stone books were written even before Abraham's day. Many of them constituted records of a most mundane sort, which indicates that not only scholars but also ordinary tradesmen could read and write.

Whether writing was invented by the Sumerians, as many scholars believe, or by still earlier peoples, it is quite certain that Moses, educated in the palace of the Egyptian emperor as he was, was fully competent to write the Pentateuch (the first five books of the Bible). It is significant that Christ Himself accepted and confirmed the universal belief of the Jews that Moses wrote these books, frequently quoting from them as of Mosaic authorship. In fact, He taught that

---

[3] However, one should also be aware that Satanic angels exist and are capable of producing unusual phenomena of this kind on occasion. All such supposedly supernatural phenomena should be carefully evaluated in terms of their fidelity to God's Word and their testimony to Jesus Christ as the Incarnate Lord and Saviour (I John 4:1-3).

belief in the divine authority of Moses' writings was prerequisite to recognition of His own authority. "If ye believe not [Moses'] writing," said He, "how shall ye believe my words?" (John 5:47). Those who profess allegiance to Christ, while denying the reliability and historicity of the book of Genesis, for example, would do well to ponder such statements as these.

But now an interesting fact appears. Although the New Testament writers quoted from Genesis at least 60 times and include it under the general category of the Mosaic writings, they never cite any of these quotations as of specific Mosaic authorship. Moses is referred to at least 80 times, however, in connection with references or quotations from the other four books of the Pentateuch.

This circumstance is best explained by the assumption that Moses *edited* the writings that now constitute the book of Genesis, rather than authoring them himself. He then brought them together in a collection with his own writings (Exodus, Leviticus, Numbers, Deuteronomy) to formulate the Torah, the "Law" of God. This explanation is also consistent with the fact that the events in Genesis all took place before Moses was born, whereas those in the other four books start with his birth and end with his death (the last chapter of Deuteronomy, describing Moses' death, was probably written by Joshua, although Moses, of course, could have written it prophetically).

The question then arises as to who originally wrote the book of Genesis. By far the most plausible answer to this is that many different men wrote it, each narrating those events which he himself had seen or investigated. This type of origin, in fact, is implicit in the very structure of Genesis, which breaks down most naturally into the ten divisions marked off by the recurring phrase: "These are the generations of. . . ."

It has been noted by archaeologists that ancient records, especially in Babylonia, were kept on stone tablets, which were commonly identified by the author's name as a subscript at the end of the narrative on the tablet.

This fact provides an exciting key to the probable origin of the original documents of Genesis. Each division can be understood as terminating with the subscript of its author. "These are the generations [that is, 'records of the generations'] of [author's name]." It is significant to note that the actual events thus recorded in each division occurred within the lifetime of the individual so named, and thus were directly accessible to his observation or interrogation. The importance of this recurring formula is indicated by the fact that the very name "Genesis" was derived from the Greek word used to translate the Hebrew word for "generations" in the ancient Greek Septuagint translation of the Old Testament.

Thus, the division from Genesis 2:4b to Genesis 5:1 ends with the statement: "This is the book of the generations of Adam." (Note that it was a "book," therefore an actual written document of some kind.) This division narrates those events with which Adam, and only Adam, could have been familiar—the description of the garden of Eden, the manner of his own creation, as well as that of Eve, the temptation and fall, God's curse on him and his dominion, the expulsion from Eden, and the history of Cain and Abel.

A similar analysis could be made of each of the other divisions. All of this leads to the significant conclusion that the events of the very earliest ages of the history of man and his world were written by eye-witnesses of the events! We are not at all dependent upon age-long traditions, handed down with continuing embellishment by word-of-mouth, but rather on direct, first-hand observations and reliable records, recorded originally on stone tablets by the ancient patriarchs themselves. These were transmitted down through the line of patriarchs from Adam to Noah, then to Shem, Abraham, and finally to Moses. The latter then brought them all together with appropriate editorial transitions and explanations into the book of Genesis as we now have it. And, of course, assuring the absolute accuracy and integrity of the entire work was the guiding inspiration of the Holy Spirit.

It is noteworthy that the very first of the divisions, Genesis 1:1 - 2:3, describing the work of the six days of creation, does not name a human author in its subscript. Instead it says: "These are the generations of the heavens and the earth, when they were created" (Gen. 2:4a). Obviously no human writer, not even Adam, was present to observe most of the great events of the six days. This record could only have come by direct revelation from God Himself, who was the only one there. Perhaps it was even written on stone by the very "finger of God," as was later true with the Ten Commandments (Ex. 31:18). In either case, this marvelous first chapter of the Bible was written in a more direct way by God Himself than probably any other portion of Scripture. It is thus absolutely true in its facts and clear in its meaning, and men who reject it or "explain" it away, or ignore it, are presumptuous in the highest degree before God.

4. Question: "How does the Bible explain the origin of different races?"

Answer: The concept of "race" is biological, not Biblical. There is no mention of different races, as such, in the Bible, nor even of the very concept of a "race." Evidently, there is no Biblical or theological meaning to the term, and we must conclude, therefore, that races are purely arbitrary entities invented by man for his own convenience in biological and anthropological studies.

Biologically a race is generally thought of as a variety, or subspecies, within a given species. In terms of evolutionary philosophy, it may represent a stage in the evolution of a new species. Thus different sub-species within a species may vary in their respective degrees of evolutionary advance over the ancestral species, depending upon the relative efficiencies with which the postulated evolutionary mechanisms of mutation, segregation, natural selection, etc., have been functioning in each case.

This leads to the observation that racism, in the sense of struggle between races and the conviction that one race is superior to others, must be based on evolutionism, not on theism. Evolutionary scientists may not all be "racist" in their personal or political philosophies. Nevertheless, the various philosophies that have promoted racism have, quite understandably, used the supposed universal evolutionary process as their intellectual framework for such a position. Nazism and Marxism are two notable examples.

The testimony of the Bible, however, is that all men who have ever lived in the world are descendants of Adam and, therefore, are of essentially the same race—the human race. "God hath made of one blood all nations of men for to dwell on all the face of the earth" (Acts 17:26). Furthermore, all men in the present world are also descendants of Noah, after the great Flood. Before the Flood, God had said: "The end of all flesh is come before me; . . . behold, I will destroy them with the earth" (Gen. 6:13). Then, later the Bible says: "All flesh died that moved upon the earth . . . and every man" (Gen. 7:21). After the Flood, "God blessed Noah and his sons, and said unto them, Be fruitful and multiply and replenish the earth" (Gen. 9:1). Finally the Bible says: "And the sons of Noah, that went forth of the Ark, were Shem, and Ham, and Japheth: . . . and of them was the whole earth overspread" (Gen. 9:18, 19).

Now although the Scriptures do not mention races, they do have a great deal to say about nations and languages. These distinctions are even noted in heaven. In Revelation 7:9, the vision of the heavenly throng was given as of "a great multitude, of all nations, and kindreds, and people, and tongues." The description of the eternal city includes this remarkable statement: "And the nations of them which are saved shall walk in the light of it: and the kings of the earth do bring their glory and honour into it" (Rev. 21:24). Thus, in some sense, national identities are to be retained, even in the ages to come.

The most distinctive characteristic, and the most divisive, possessed by various groups among men, is not skin color or physical size, or some other physical trait, but language. Communication is of paramount importance for understanding and harmony, and language is certainly the most basic element in communication.

The origin of human language, and especially of the tremendous diversity of human languages, is as yet quite inexplicable to the evolutionist. There is nothing even remotely comparable to such an ability among the higher animals. That human speech and language are divine creations is by far the most reasonable explanation. Furthermore, the fact that the great variety of languages reflects a divine judgment on early man, as the Bible teaches, is also the most reasonable explanation we have.

After the Flood, when "the whole earth was of one language and one speech" (Gen. 11:1), men disobeyed God's command to scatter and fill the earth, preferring to remain together and erect a single great world empire, with its capital at the first Babylon, and centered in the worship of the "host of heaven." For this purpose they erected a gigantic temple tower, or ziggurat, at whose apex was a shrine dedicated "unto heaven," undoubtedly inscribed with the signs of the Zodiac and other astrological emblems. The "host of heaven," frequently mentioned in the Bible, refers both to the stars and to the angelic and demonic hosts identified with the heavenly bodies. The great Tower of Babel, therefore (part of which is evidently still standing in the ruins of Babylon), was essentially a temple dedicated to Satan worship and evolutionary pantheism.

God's judgment on this great rebellion was to "scatter them abroad from thence upon the face of all the earth," through "confounding their language, that they may not understand one another's speech" (Gen. 11:7, 8). This must have been some kind of physiologic miracle, an instant change in those centers of the brain controlling speech, so that each family suddenly found itself identifying different sounds with various objects and actions than other families used. The confusion and incoherent arguments finally led each family to go its own way and eventually to establish its own national and linguistic identity.

Since physiologic changes were necessarily involved in this sudden confusion of tongues, it may well have been that still other physiologic changes were also induced by God at the same time, in order to hasten the establishment of each group as a distinct national entity. Whether or not this is the case, it is certainly true that the development of specific national, or even what we call "racial" traits, could not take place as long as men lived together and intermarried freely. A certain amount of isolation and national inbreeding is genetically essential for the establishment of particular characteristics in a nation or race. Thus these could not have developed until after mankind was dispersed from its first post-diluvian home in Babylon.

Even apart from the miraculous changes suggested above, such characteristics could have developed quite rapidly, assuming that the different genetic factors (for skin color, stature, hair texture, and the like) were present in the ancestral stock, and that isolation and selection pressures of some kind—whether climatic or social or others— operated in favor of certain characteristics in each tribe. These, however, are all basically superficial and could never result in a new "kind" of man.

All nations are alike before God in that all are in need of a Saviour, and in that all can come to the Saviour if they will. "For God so loved the world, that he gave his only begotten Son, that whosoever believeth on him should not perish, but have everlasting life" (John 3:16).

5. *Question: "Was the long day of Joshua a fact of history or only a legend?"*

Answer: The account of the "long day," as found in the tenth chapter of Joshua is certainly one of the most remarkable records in the Bible. That a day could actually have been extended, even through the length of another whole day, as indicated in Joshua, seems impossible and unbelievable.

And yet it is found in the Word of God! Furthermore it is found in the context of the other events in Israel's conquest of Canaan, the general outline of which has been remarkably confirmed by archaeological discoveries in recent years. Dr. Nelson Glueck, probably the greatest living Palestinian archaeologist, president of the Hebrew Union College, has written: "As a matter of fact, it may be stated categorically that no archaeological discovery has ever controverted a Biblical reference. Scores of archaeological findings have been made which confirm in clear outline or exact detail historical statements in the Bible."[4]

According to the narrative, God caused the day to be lengthened in order that the army of Israel could complete the conquest of the Amorite forces before they could escape and re-group under cover of darkness. This was a key battle in the Canaanite campaign, and its outcome would determine whether or not Israel could win the promised land.

Thus the integrity of God's promises was at stake here, as well as the vindication of His moral law. He had, at one time, delayed the occupation of the land by Abraham's descendants, because, as He said, "the iniquity of the Amorites is not yet full" (Gen. 15:16). But by Joshua's time, their wickedness and degeneracy were so pervasive and irreversible (a fact increasingly being confirmed by archaeological research into their cultures) that considerations of mercy, for their neighbors and even for their own descendants, dictated their removal.

There was thus adequate reason for God to intervene in any way appropriate to accomplish His purposes—first, in the destruction of Amorite power and influence and second, in the fulfillment of His promises to the seed of Jacob. The reason for using the sun in such an unusual way to do this, quite possibly, was because the Amorites were sun-worshipers. For the chief object of their worship to be used as an agent in their defeat must have implied that the God of Israel was the true God, not only to the Amorites themselves but also to the other peoples of the region who had been intimidated by them.

It is noteworthy that the Bible is not the only ancient record of the long day. As a matter of fact, traditions of a long day (or of a long night, among the American Indians and the South Sea Islanders) are quite common among early nations and tribes. Immanuel Velikovsky, in his book *Worlds in Collision*,[5] gives abundant documentation of this fact, as have many other writers. It is difficult to account for the widespread incidence of such an unlikely narrative unless it is based on an actual fact of early human history. Whatever the cause, the event itself seems really to have occurred.[6]

---

[4] *Rivers in the Desert*, p. 31.

[5] *Worlds in Collision* (New York: Doubleday, 1950), 401 pp.

[6] Recent widely circulated reports that computer calculations made in connection with the space program had turned up a missing day in astronomic history are, unfortunately, not factual. The nature of the phenomenon would preclude its identification by such means as this, regardless of whether or not it actually occurred.

72

One common criticism of the Biblical record of the long day is that its language is unscientific. It says, for example, that "the sun stood still in the midst of heaven, and hasted not to go down about a whole day" (Josh. 10:13). Critics say that the earth, rather than the sun, would have to "stand still" for the day to be prolonged, since normally its axial rotation controls the length of the day.

But such a criticism itself is unscientific! All motion is *relative* motion, and the sun is moving as well as the earth. No one knows where in the universe there may be a fixed point of zero motion. That being so, all velocities must necessarily be measured with respect to some arbitrarily assumed fixed reference point. The proper point to choose is normally the one which is most convenient to the observer. In the case of the relative motion of the sun and the earth to each other, it is almost always most convenient (and therefore most "scientific") to consider the earth as fixed and the sun as moving around it. Joshua's language, therefore, is perfectly modern and correct.

As a matter of fact, since the account says that the moon also stood still (Josh. 10:13), it may be that the entire solar system stopped in its tracks for a day, with all relative positions and motions simply suspended. This seems no more difficult to believe than that only the earth stopped rotating.

The natural reaction to the idea of a "long day" is one of incredulity, of course. It would certainly constitute an amazing miracle. The Bible itself says "there was no day like that before it or after it" (Josh. 10:14).

But to deny the possibility of the miraculous (and, after all, how do we measure the dynamics of one miracle as against another?) is to deny the existence of God. That the earth should stop rotating on its axis for a time is no more inexplicable than that it should start rotating in the beginning. The Creator who started it could also stop it if He so desired. The question is not whether an alleged miracle *could* occur, but whether it *did* occur. The testimony of Scripture, as well as the many supporting traditions, confirms that it did.

There was presumably a gradual deceleration of the motions, rather than instantaneous, so that no catastrophic geologic or geographic changes need have been caused by the long day. However, the circulation of the atmosphere and the hydrologic cycle are both controlled to some extent by the earth's rotation, so that such an event would undoubtedly disturb the atmosphere to a profound degree. This is indirectly confirmed by the devastating hailstorm which accompanied the long day as recorded in the Bible (Josh. 10:11) and by the many evidences of atmospheric violence noted by Velikovsky in his collection of ancient traditions of the miracle.

Although no amount of evidence could prove a miracle to someone who does not want to believe they can occur, there is certainly adequate reason for the Bible-believing Christian to accept Joshua's long day as a real fact of history.

6. Question: "How could Jonah survive three days and three nights in the belly of a whale?"

Answer: This is one of the Bible stories most ridiculed by people who consider themselves sophisticated and intellectual. Skeptics say that no whale could swallow a man in the first place, and, even if he did, the man would certainly never survive three days and three nights in his belly, as the Bible claims.

"Christian liberals" have attempted to avoid this problem by saying that the story of Jonah was only an allegory and was never meant to be understood as actual history. However, whenever the Bible writers used allegories or parables or other symbolic stories, they always either said so or else made it evident in the context. The book of Jonah is certainly written as though it were actual history. Jonah was a real prophet and is mentioned also in II Kings 14:25. None of the ancient Jews or early Christians ever doubted the authenticity and historicity of the book of Jonah and its story.

Most importantly, the Lord Jesus Christ accepted the account as true. He said that Jonah was a prophet (Matt. 12:39) and that the people of Nineveh repented of their sins as a consequence of his preaching (Matt. 12:41). He even said: "For as Jonah was three days and three nights in the whale's belly; so shall the Son of man be three days and three nights in the heart of the earth" (Matt. 12:40). Thus Christ actually compared Jonah's experience to His own coming death and resurrection, pointing out the miraculous nature of both. One cannot deny the factuality of Jonah's experience, therefore, without charging the Lord Jesus Christ with either deception or ignorance, either of which is equivalent to denying His deity.

There is little question that the event was a miracle, but this fact certainly does not disprove it! The account in fact says as much: "Now the Lord had prepared a great fish to swallow up Jonah. And Jonah was in the belly of the fish three days and three nights" (Jonah 1:17). Later it says: "And the Lord spake unto the fish, and it vomited out Jonah upon the dry land" (Jonah 2:10). God was certainly able to accomplish this if He wished; to deny the possibility of miracles is atheism. The actual occurrence of this particular miracle is adequately attested by the very fact of its record in the Holy Scriptures, and is doubly confirmed by the testimony of Christ.

The "great fish" may have been either a whale or a shark or even a fish specially prepared by the Lord for this purpose. (The Hebrew and Greek words that are used merely mean "a great aquatic animal.") Some species of whales and some species of sharks are quite capable of swallowing a man whole. Among these are the sperm whale, the white shark, and the whale shark, all of which have been found with whole animals as large or larger than a man in their stomachs.

As a matter of fact, there are some cases recording in whaling history even of *men* swallowed whole by these great animals! In at least two well-documented cases, the men were later rescued and survived.

As to whether a man could survive "three days and three nights" under such conditions, there are three possible answers that could be suggested in defense of the Biblical narrative. In the first place, it has been well established that the phrase "three days and three nights" in ancient Hebrew usage was an idiomatic expression meaning simply "three days," and was applicable even if the beginning and ending days of the period were only partial days. Thus it could refer to a period as short as about 38 hours. At least one man in modern times (James Bartley, in 1895) is known to have survived a day and a half inside a whale before being rescued. There is always some air in the whale's stomach, and, as long as the animal it has swallowed is still alive, digestive activity will not begin. Thus Jonah's experience could possibly have happened entirely within the framework of natural law.

It is much more likely, however, that the event involved a divine miracle, as the Scripture strongly implies. The "great fish" was prepared and sent by God, as was the intense storm that threatened the ship on which Jonah was traveling. The storm ceased as soon as Jonah was cast overboard (Jonah 1:4, 15). In like manner, it was quite probable that God preserved Jonah's life miraculously all through the horrifying experience.

A third possibility is that Jonah actually suffocated and died in the great fish and then God later brought him back from the dead. There are at least eight other such "resuscitations" recorded in the

Bible, as well as the glorious bodily resurrection of Christ—of which Jonah's experience in particular was said by Christ to be a prophetic sign.

This is implied also by Jonah's prayer, when he said: ". . . out of the belly of hell [i.e., "sheol," the place of departed spirits] cried I, and thou heardest my voice" (Jonah 2:2). In any case, it was a mighty experience, evidently well known and certified in his day, probably contributing in significant degree to the fact that all the people of Nineveh repented and turned to God (Jonah 3:5) when Jonah returned "from the dead," as it were, to preach to them.

Even in Jesus' day, it was so well known that He could use it as a "sign" of His own impending death and resurrection, which were to constitute God's crowning proof of the deity of His Son and the great work of salvation which He would accomplish on the cross for all who would receive Him. "God now commandeth all men everywhere to repent: Because he hath appointed a day, in the which he will judge the world in righteousness by that man whom he hath ordained; whereof he hath given assurance unto all men, in that he hath raised him from the dead" (Acts 17:30, 31).

7. Question: "Are there intelligent beings on other planets?"

Answer: It is impossible to prove a universal negative, but there is not as yet even the slightest evidence, either Biblical or scientific, that there are men like us inhabiting other planets or star systems. There is an abundance of pseudo-scientific speculation of this sort, but the hard evidence is against it.

Life, at least such as we know it, requires a very complex combination of environmental factors to be possible, and only this planet, so far as is known, provides this combination. Water must be abundant, for example. Little if any water exists on the moon, or Mars, or Venus, or the other planets, certainly not in liquid form. The temperatures on all the other known planets are either too cold or too hot for life in any higher form comparable to the earth's human life.

In addition, many complex chemicals must be present in abundance in order to support life processes. An atmosphere essentially like our own would also have to be present. In general, life in any form comparable to human life would require a planet essentially the same as our own planet in every respect. There is no evidence, however, other than speculation, that such a planet exists anywhere else in the universe.

The main reason that men keep wishfully searching for evidence of extraterrestrial life is that this would give support to their evolutionary philosophy. That is, if life is just a product of natural chemical developments here on the earth, as the leaders of evolutionary thought insist, then the same chance developments should also have taken place in other places in the universe, they feel, in view of the almost infinite number of other stars. Nevertheless, the actual evidence remains massively negative.

As far as the Scriptures are concerned, they teach unequivocally that the earth is uniquely the abode of man. "The heaven, even the heavens, are the Lord's; but the earth hath he given to the children of men" (Ps. 115:16). "God hath made of one blood all nations of men to dwell on all the face of the earth, and hath determined the times before appointed, and the bounds of their habitation" (Acts 17:26).

It was to this earth, alone among all the uncounted billions of heavenly bodies, that God Himself, in Jesus Christ, came down to suffer and die for man's salvation. "And no man hath ascended up to heaven, but he that came down from heaven, even the Son of man, which is in heaven" (John 3:13). The earth may not be the center of the universe (though no one knows, of course, where such a center might be), but it is certainly the center of interest of the universe! "In this was manifested the love of God toward us, because that God sent his only begotten Son into the world, that we might live through him" (I John 4:9). It seems grotesque and blasphemous to suggest that the tragedy of Calvary's cross should be repeated on millions of other planets, for the benefit of other unknown and hypothetical members of God's creation.

The earth, as the astronauts observed, is uniquely beautiful and uniquely equipped as man's home. Though it is small, it is of infinitely more complex organization and variety than even the largest stars, composed as they are mostly of the simplest elements, hydrogen and helium.

Since the sun and moon were made specifically to "give light upon the earth" (Gen. 1:15), it may be possible that the moon, and even the solar system, were within the "dominion" which man was commissioned by God ultimately to "subdue," by his science and technology (Gen. 1:28). This is uncertain, but it is at least clear that the other stars, the nearest of which is four light-years away, are well beyond man's power ever to explore directly, or to control, in the present order of things.

Why, then, did God create them? What is the purpose, in God's wisdom, for the tremendous number and variety of stars, and perhaps a still greater number of planets' (though the existence of these is speculative, based only on analogy with the solar system) throughout the vast universe?

We can only give tentative suggestions, of course, but it is well to remember that God is still the Creator, and there are endless ages of eternity ahead of us. Even though, for the moment, the only obvious function of the stellar heavens is to reflect the infinite power and grandeur of their Creator, it may well be that they are awaiting more specific uses by Him in the ages to come, after the completion of His redemptive program for the earth and men.

It is also possible that, even now, they have some relationship to the angels of God. This may be implied by the fact that angels are often called "stars" in Scripture (e.g., Job 38:7; Isa. 14:12, 13; Rev. 12:4, 9; 9:1; etc.) and that the phrase "host of heaven" is applied both to the stars and to the angelic hosts (e.g., Jer. 33:22; II Chron. 18:18). The worship of the stars, which has always been a characteristic of polytheism, has, in reality, been a worship of angels (or "gods"), especially those angels who have followed Satan in his great rebellion against the true God (note II Kings 17:16; Col. 2:18; I Cor. 10:20, etc.). It seems possible, at least, that this frequent identification of stars and angels is more than mere poetic imagery; possibly angels, who are mighty spiritual beings created by the "Lord of hosts," have their primary sphere of operations in the heavens, in the stars. The Bible says "[He] maketh his angels spirits, and his ministers a flaming fire" (Ps. 104:4; Heb. 1:7), and it also says there is "an innumerable company of angels" (Heb. 12:22) that "do his commandments" (Ps. 103:20).

Thus, although it is all but certain that no other man-like creatures inhabit other worlds, it is true that in God's universe, and possibly on the stars themselves, there exists a vast host of intelligent and powerful beings, the angels of God. Though it is futile to try to establish contact with them by such devices as space-ships and radio telescopes, we can communicate with God Himself through prayer and through His Word, by faith, and the angels then are "sent forth to minister for them who shall be heirs of salvation" (Heb. 1:14).

Chapter VII

CREATION AND EVOLUTION

1. Question: *"Should a Christian believe in evolution?"*

Answer: This is a very common question, frequently asked by young people who are being indoctrinated with evolutionary concepts in the public schools or universities.[1] The answer depends on what is meant by the term "evolution." If it is defined simply as "change" (for example, the growth of a baby into an adult, the production of hybrids and other new varieties of plants or animals through scientific breeding processes, or the development of the various types of dogs or cats from one original dog or cat "kind"), then no one would argue this question at all.

However, the prevalent theory of evolution today is far broader in scope than this. The leading evolutionists consider it as a basic principle of continual development, of increasing order and complexity throughout the universe. The complex elements are said to have developed from simpler elements, living organisms to have evolved from non-living chemicals, complex forms of life from simpler organisms, and even man himself to have gradually evolved from some kind of ape-like ancestor. Religions, cultures, and other social institutions are likewise believed to be continually evolving into higher forms.

Thus, evolution is actually a complete world-view, an explanation of origins and meanings without the necessity of a personal God who created and upholds all things. Since this philosophy (one might even say this "religion") of universal evolutionary progress is so widely and persuasively taught in our schools, Christians are often tempted to accept the compromise position of "theistic evolution," according to which evolution is viewed as God's method of creation.

---

[1] For a brief treatment of the so-called evidences of evolution and their Biblical implications, written specifically for young people, see H. M. Morris, *Evolution and the Modern Christian* (Nutley, N. J.: Presbyterian and Reformed Publishing Co., 1967), 72 pp.

However, this is basically an inconsistent and contradictory position. Some of its fallacies are as follows:

(1) It contradicts the Bible record of creation. Ten times in the first chapter of Genesis, the inspired writer tells us that God created plants and animals to reproduce "after their kinds." The Biblical "kind" may have been broader than our modern "species" concept, but at least it implied definite limits to variation. The New Testament writers accepted the full historicity of the Genesis account of creation. Even Christ Himself quoted from it as historically accurate and authoritative (Matt. 19:4-6).

(2) It is inconsistent with God's methods. The standard history of evolution involves the development of innumerable misfits and extinctions, useless and even harmful organisms. If this is God's "method of creation," it is strange that He would use such haphazard, inefficient, wasteful processes. Furthermore, the idea of the "survival of the fittest," whereby the stronger animals and races eliminate the weaker in the "struggle for existence" is the essence of Darwin's theory of evolution by natural selection, and this whole scheme is flatly contradicted by the Biblical doctrine of love, of unselfish sacrifice, and of Christian charity. The God of the Bible is a God of order and of grace, not a God of confusion and cruelty.

(3) The evolutionary philosophy is the intellectual basis of all the anti-Christian and anti-God systems that have plagued mankind for centuries. It served Hitler as the rationale for Nazism and Marx as the supposed scientific basis for communism. It is the basis of the various modern methods of psychology and sociology that treat man merely as a higher animal and which have led to the mis-named "new morality" and ethical relativism. Its whole effect on the world and mankind has been harmful and degrading. Jesus said: "A good tree cannot bring forth evil fruit" (Matt. 7:18). The evil fruit of the evolutionary philosophy is evidence enough of its ultimate origin in Satan's age-long rebellion against his Creator.

(4) It is contradicted by the basic laws of science. Evolution teaches that "creation" is continually being accomplished by nature's evolutionary processes, but the most basic law of science, the Law of Energy Conservation, states that nothing is now being created or destroyed. Evolution teaches that there is a universal process of development and increasing order and complexity in the universe, but the Second Law of Thermodynamics (which is

a basic law of nature, with no exceptions known) states that all systems tend to become disordered and simpler. All things tend to grow old, wear out, run down, and die. Evolution involves universal change "upward" whereas the real processes of nature involve a universal change "downward." The concept of special creation of all the basic "kinds" of plants and animals, with provision for ample variation within the kinds, is much more in accord with the actual facts and laws of science than is the speculative philosophy of universal evolutionary development.

Thus, evolution is not really a science but a religious philosophy. Although it may be the religion of many scientists, this is not because of the actual data of their science, but because of their intellectual and moral preference for this kind of faith. The faith of Biblical Christianity is diametrically opposite to that of evolution, but is fully supported by all the real facts of life.

2. Question: "Is the creation story in Genesis meant to be taken literally or was it written in figurative language?"

Answer: Just as any building is only as strong and as safe as its foundation, so the doctrines of the Bible and of Christianity rest on the foundation doctrine of creation and are bound to fall if the foundation is undermined. All Biblical doctrines have their foundations laid in the book of Genesis, and the book of Genesis itself is founded on the events of its first chapter. Therefore it is extremely important that we understand exactly what is revealed by God in this all-important chapter of the Bible, and that we believe it wholeheartedly.

Many critics have maintained that Genesis is mainly an old legend, and that it is filled with scientific and historical errors. However, the writers of the New Testament frequently quoted from Genesis and obviously regarded it as historically accurate and as divinely inspired. If they were wrong about Genesis, they were probably wrong about other things and are thus not really dependable guides at all. Jesus Christ Himself specifically quoted from Genesis 1 and 2 (in Matt. 19: 4-6), accepting it as historically accurate and divinely authoritative. Thus, even Christ may not really be believed, if Genesis 1 and 2 are not true.

It is not surprising that the earlier widespread rejection of Genesis and its account of creation has been followed by the present-day rejection of the teachings of Christ and His apostles and especially by the almost universal rejection of the doctrines of sin, salvation, redemption, and regeneration. If Christ is not even a reliable teacher, then He can hardly be trusted as Saviour and Lord of one's life!

Some Bible teachers have suggested that the author of Genesis wrote in terms of creation, rather than evolutionary development, because the primitive Hebrews for whom he was writing could not have comprehended such a sophisticated concept as evolution. He thus supposedly wrote in this figurative language merely as an accommodation to the naive culture and mentality of the people of that day.

This notion is quite unsound, however. All of the ancient religions and philosophies were evolutionary systems, regarding matter as eternal and the earth as extremely old and developing into its present form through many ages or cycles. This was true in particular of the ancient Egyptians and Babylonians with whom the Israelites had most frequent contact.

The concept of special, recent creation, by an eternal, all-powerful, personal God is unique in the Bible! It was a radically new revelation to a people surrounded by pagan evolutionary speculations. In order to be understood at all, it thus had to be simple, clear, and direct, not mystical and vague.

Therefore, the Genesis record of creation was meant by its author to be a sober, straightforward, historical record of the actual events of creation. It is God's revelation to man of that which he could never discover for himself. "All things were created by him, . . . and by him all things consist" (Col. 1:16, 17). Since He is our Creator, He is also our Judge. For those who are willing to believe and trust Him, He can also be personal Saviour and Lord.

3. Question: "Is evolution a scientific fact?"

Answer: Evolution is accepted as fact by a majority of scientists, but one should remember that scientific principles are not established by majority vote. There is a significant minority of scientists today (undoubtedly numbering in the thousands) who either reject the theory altogether or who regard it as a still unsettled issue. Even those who do accept it, in many cases, do so not because of the actual scientific evidence (with which even most scientists are only superficially familiar), but because they have been intimidated by the myth that all scientists accept evolution!

As a matter of fact, no theory of origins—evolution or special creation or anything else—can possibly be scientific. "Science" means "knowledge" and by definition means that which we actually *know* concerning the facts of nature and their inter-relationships. The very heart of the "scientific method" is the reproducibility of experiments. That is, if a certain process is observed and measured today, and then the experiment is conducted again in the same way tomorrow, the same results should be obtained. In this way, by experimental repetition and verification, a scientific description of the process is eventually developed.

Since it is impossible for us to repeat the supposed evolutionary history of the world and its inhabitants, and since no human observers were present to observe and record the supposed evolutionary changes of the past, it is clear that evolution in the broad sense is beyond the reach of the scientific method. The theory of evolution is, therefore, not science at all.

The actual processes of nature as they occur today are conservative and decay processes, rather than creative and developmental. That is, all processes (and this includes biological and geological processes) operate within the framework of the First and Second Laws of Thermodynamics, which are beyond question the two best-proved facts of science. The First Law is the Law of Mass-Energy Conservation and states that nothing in the observable universe is now being created or annihilated. The Second Law is the Law of Increasing Entropy, which says that the entropy (that is, the disorder or disorganization) of every observable system in the universe tends to grow. Thus the basic structure of the universe is not one of continuing "creation" but rather of "conservation." The basic law of change in the universe is not one of evolutionary development upward but rather of "devolutionary" change downward.

These facts are so common to every-day experience that it is amazing that anyone has ever suggested anything else. We do see much biological variation, of course, but always within definite limits. No two individuals are exactly alike, even when born of the same parents. New varieties or species are occasionally developed, either by artificial breeding techniques or by natural selection in response to environmental changes, but these are always still of the same basic "kinds."

That is, there are many varieties of dogs and many varieties of cats, but never any kind of new animal intermediate between a dog and a cat! Or between a horse and an elephant, or an ape and a man. If evolution were really true, it should be quite impossible for biologists to develop any kind of classification scheme (that is, division into species, genera, families, etc.), because there would be everywhere a continuous intergrading of all forms of life. As a matter of fact, since all living plants and animals supposedly have arisen by gradual modification from a common ancestor, in the same world, it stands to reason that they all ought to be exactly alike!

Nor does it help any to attribute these changes all to the prehistoric past, the world of the fossils, because the same great "gaps" exist between basic kinds in the fossil world that exist in the modern world. There are new varieties of dogs and new varieties of cats found in the fossil world, but still nothing between a dog and a cat! The "missing links" are still missing, despite the innumerable fossils of animals and plants that have been excavated over the centuries.

Special creation by a divine Creator can account for the actual observed facts of nature much better than a hypothetical process of development in the past which is contrary to basic known scientific law in the present. It is more reasonable that "similarities" be explained in terms of a common Designer, who created similar structures for similar functions, rather than by assumed ancestral relationships. Furthermore, creation accounts for the differences as well as the similarities, which evolution cannot do.

In addition, it is reasonable that God would have made for each basic "kind" a genetic system which would permit ample variation in response to environmental changes, even though it must basically continue to "bring forth after its kind" (Gen. 1:11, etc.). Biochemists are only now beginning to unravel the marvelously complex genetic code, which assures that characteristics transmitted to the progeny will be those already present in the parents, even though much variation is possible within those limits.

Occasionally so-called "mutations" occur. These are sudden changes in the genetic structure brought about by penetration of the germ cell by short-wave-length radiation or some other disorganizing medium. Evolutionists believe that if these mutations turn out to be helpful to the individual (or population of individuals) in the natural environment, they will be preserved and transmitted to the descendants by natural selection. This is believed by most evolutionists to be the chief mechanism by which evolution occurs.

The trouble with this idea is that practically all mutations (even leading evolutionists acknowledge this to be true of at least 99.9% of all known mutations) are harmful, rather than helpful, in the supposed struggle for existence. Mutant varieties thus almost always die out if left to themselves, or else revert back to the ancestral types. This, of course, is in perfect accord with the Second Law of

Thermodynamics. A mutation is a random change in a highly organized system. In accordance with statistical thermodynamics, a random change in an ordered system will almost certainly decrease the order therein. But if, by infinitesimal chance, the order is accidentally raised, then the chance that another mutation would improve the system still farther is even smaller. The probability of an increased order arising by random variation decreases as the degree of order of the system increases.

Thus evolution, if it occurs on any broad scale, requires at every step an almost magical manipulation of the basic laws of nature as they are known to function at present.[2] It is a religious philosophy, held by faith, and propagated by the missionary zeal of its leaders. This is still a free country, and men are free to advocate any religion they choose. But the actual data support the faith of the creationist far better than that of evolutionist.

4. Question: "Can the theory of evolution be harmonized with the Second Law of Thermodynamics?"

Answer: One of the arguments which creationists have used effectively against evolution is that the evolutionary hypothesis of the development of the cosmos and of the present organic world is contradicted by the entropy principle, the Second Law of Thermodynamics. Evolutionists, however, sometimes argue that there is no contradiction and that both can be true. It is well to let two leading evolutionists define the two concepts. Sir Julian Huxley, probably the world's greatest living evolutionist, has defined evolution as follows:

> Evolution in the extended sense can be defined as a directional and essentially irreversible process occurring in time, which in its course gives rise to an increase of variety and an increasingly high level of organization in its products. Our present knowledge indeed forces us to the view that the whole of reality is evolution—a single process of self-transformation.[3]

Thus evolution encompasses all reality: particles evolve into atoms and atoms into molecules and molecules into worlds and stars and galaxies; inorganic compounds evolve into living materials and these into more and more complex plants and animals and finally into man, who now presumably can intelligently control all future evolution.

[2] For a documented treatment of evolution in its religious aspects, see the author's book, *The Twilight of Evolution* (Grand Rapids: Baker Book House, 1964), 103 pp.
[3] In *What Is Science?* (New York: Simon & Schuster, 1955), p. 278.

The Second Law of Thermodynamics is also known as the Law of Increasing Entropy. The outstanding Princeton bio-chemist, Harold Blum, describes this law in the following way:

> The Second Law of Thermodynamics has as one of its consequences that all real processes go irreversibly. Any given process in this universe is accompanied by a change in magnitude of a quantity called the entropy. . . . All real processes go with an increase of entropy. The entropy also measures the randomness or lack of orderliness of the system, the greater the randomness the greater the entropy.[4]

Thus, according to Huxley, evolution is a universal law requiring that all processes lead irreversibly toward an "increase of order." According to Blum, the entropy principle is a universal law requiring that all processes lead irreversibly toward a "decrease of order." Each is exactly the converse of the other! It seems obvious, therefore, that one of them must be wrong. Since the Second Law of Thermodynamics is universally accepted as a basic principle governing all processes, has been verified experimentally thousands of times, and is consistent with all experience, there can be no doubt whatever that, if there is such a thing as a scientific law at all, this is it! The evolutionary philosophy therefore, creationists insist, must simply be wrong.

However, evolutionists can point to two possible ways out of this difficulty. One is to deny the universality of the entropy principle. Since man is quite limited in knowledge, and since he is able to make observations on only a very small part of the vast universe, he cannot be certain that the Second Law applies everywhere in time and space. Empirical measurements can never establish universal certainty.

This stricture is philosophically valid, of course. However, wherever and whenever the entropy principle has been subjected to scientific test, it has always worked, with no exception. Though we cannot be absolutely sure that the total entropy of the whole universe is increasing, we can say that, wherever it can be scientifically tested, the entropy in *any given portion* of the universe is increasing. Universal evolution, on the other hand, requires that the degree of order of *at least most portions* of the universe must be increasing, but no scientific experiments have given any quantitative confirmation of this at all!

The other possible escape from the evolutionist's dilemma is to say that the Second Law only applies to so-called "isolated systems." There may well be an increase of order in an "open system." Thus, a

---

[4] "Perspectives in Evolution," *American Scientist*, October, 1955, p. 595.

baby grows into an adult, two animals may multiply into a population of thousands, man's store of acquired knowledge accumulates to tremendous proportions. Even in the inorganic realm, simple elements may combine naturally to form complex compounds, and molecules may grow into crystals of beautiful complexity. All of these are open systems and their increased organization is derived from a source outside themselves.

The evolutionist correctly points out that the earth itself is an open system, continually receiving energy from the sun, and that this can provide the basic source of power for maintaining the evolutionary process and the ever-increasing order which it entails. The same argument could be extended to the entire solar system and presumably to any finite part of the universe. Since the Second Law of Thermodynamics applies only to isolated systems, there is no reason why evolution cannot take place in an open system such as the earth. This, in fact, is the device Blum himself uses for reconciling evolution and entropy.

The creationist answers, of course, that although this is possible philosophically, it still is *contrary to all actual scientific measurements*. Although it is true that the Second Law has to be formally defined in terms of an idealized isolated system, it always has to be *tested* on open systems, because there is no such thing in nature as a truly isolated system! And wherever it is tested, it always works.

The entropy law therefore applies to open systems as well as isolated systems. This is why no machine or process is 100 percent efficient and why perpetual motion machines are impossible. This is why everything eventually wears out, runs down, and dies. Even those systems which seem to show increasing order for a time eventually lose out to the principle of decay. The crystal finally disintegrates, the adult finally dies, the population eventually stabilizes and finally disappears, the species becomes extinct, even great civilizations sooner or later perish as the result of outside conquest or famine or, perhaps, a nuclear holocaust. Thus, every apparent increase of order and complexity is, at best, only local and temporary, and at the cost of greater disorder to the environment from which it extracts its ephemeral ordering energy.

And even such a local and temporary increase of order can be accomplished only by means of some intricate process provided for the system for this purpose. The remarkable process of photosynthesis enables plants to utilize the sun's energy and thus to grow. The fantastic processes of blood circulation, digestion, respiration, and others

87

of similar complexity enable animals and men to grow. And both plant and animal life require the intricate coding and template structure of the genetic system for the maintenance of the species itself.

The infinitely greater increase of order implied in the evolutionary process must obviously require a far more wonderful and complex mechanism than any of these if it is to be even temporarily successful. But even after a hundred years of intensive study by thousands of scientists spending millions of dollars of research grants, the mechanism of evolution is still elusive.

The pathetic suggestion of mutation (basically a disordering mechanism operating in full accordance with the Second Law) and natural selection (a conservative principle which tends to maintain the status quo in nature) as the driving mechanisms for the organic phase of evolution illustrates the desperate extreme to which men will go to escape the clear and satisfying evidence, both in nature and in Scripture, of the fact of a completed creation.

Thus evolution can be defended against the Second Law of Thermodynamics by metaphysical speculations, but all the solid scientific evidence, as well as the testimony of the Word of God, is against it.

5. Question: "How long ago did Adam live, and where does he fit into the theory of human evolution?"

Answer: According to Biblical chronology, as found especially in Genesis 5 and 11, Adam was created only a few thousands of years ago and was definitely the first man. Acts 17:26, for example, says that "God hath made of one [man] all nations of men," and I Corinthians 15:45 speaks of "the first man Adam." Jesus himself, quoting from the story of Adam and Eve, said that "God made them in the beginning male and female" (Matt. 19:4). According to Scripture, Adam was originally without sin and lived in a perfect environment (Gen. 1:31), but rebelled against God and thus brought God's curse on the world (Gen. 3:17). Since that time, the "whole creation has been groaning and travailing together in pain until now" (Rom. 8:22).

The popular evolutionary history, however, speculates that the common ancestor of apes and men developed about 60 million years ago and that modern man appeared well over a million years ago. Evolutionary anthropologists are currently arguing over the exact line of descent, and it should be realized that there is no real fossil evidence of the innumerable missing links in human evolution, including the hypothetical common ancestor from which man and the apes originally diverged.

The study of population statistics indicates that the Biblical chronology is much more realistic than the evolutionary chronology. The human population must have started originally from the first pair, and the question is whether that pair was Noah and his wife 4,300 years ago (the time of the worldwide Flood according to the Ussher chronology of the Bible) or the first "dawn-man" and his mate a million years ago.

The present rate of population increase in the world is more than two percent per year, and the population is now over three billion. However, the average rate would only have to be one half of one percent per year to produce the present world population in 4,300 years. To put it another way, an average family size of only 2½ children per family would suffice to develop the present population in just the length of time since Noah, even with an average life-span of only about 40 years per person. These figures are very reasonable, and in fact extremely conservative, showing that the Biblical chronology is quite plausible in every way.

On the other hand, this same very conservative rate of population growth (only one fourth what it is at present), if continued for a million years, would have produced a present population infinitely greater than could be packed into every cubic foot of the entire universe! This fact alone proves that the supposed million-year history of man on the earth is completely absurd, whereas the Biblical chronology is perfectly reasonable. All of this can be proved by simple and straightforward mathematical calculations.[5]

Even if, by some miracle, the population growth rates were slowed down sufficiently to produce a population of only the present figure of three billion people after one million years of human life on earth, this would still mean that over 3,000 billion individual people had lived and died during that period of time. It is therefore passing strange that it is so difficult to find human fossils! It would seem rather that human remains ought to be extremely abundant everywhere. And this should be even more true of the pre-human ape-men that were supposedly evolving into men during 60 or 70 million years of pre-history! But all of the latter that have ever been found are a handful of doubtful bits and pieces of widely scattered bone fragments that have been variously interpreted by various professed experts on human evolution to be various uncertain links in the uncertain evolutionary chain.

[5] See *Biblical Cosmology and Modern Science*, pp. 72-84, for the full derivations of these quantities.

Evolution is thus not only anti-Biblical and anti-Christian, but is utterly unscientific and impossible as well. But it has served effectively as the pseudo-scientific basis of atheism, agnosticism, socialism, fascism, and numerous other false and dangerous philosophies over the past century. For anyone who respects the Bible as the Word of God, there is certainly no reason to reject the historical accuracy of the account of Adam, confirmed as it was by Christ Himself, in favor of the self-serving speculations of evolutionary philosophers.

6. Question: "Can the geological ages be understood as occurring in a 'gap' between the first two verses of Genesis?"

Answer: It is widely known that historical geologists think the earth originated about five billion years ago, whereas the Bible indicates that "in six days the Lord made heaven and earth, the sea, and all that in them is" (Ex. 20:11). Furthermore, the chronological data of Genesis 5 and 11 indicate that this all took place only a few thousand years ago. This obvious discrepancy is undoubtedly the most serious problem in the continuing warfare between Biblical Christianity and modern evolutionism.

It is obviously impossible to *prove scientifically* that the earth is older than the four or five thousand years for which we have actual written historical records. Science as such necessarily involves experimental observation and measurement, and no "observers" were on hand to record what may or may not have taken place in earlier times. The use of various physical processes to estimate past geologic time involves many unprovable, and in fact unreasonable, assumptions. Nevertheless, the pressures of evolutionary speculations have been so heavy during the past century that many Bible scholars have felt it desirable to reinterpret Genesis in some way that would accommodate the supposed geologic ages.

Two such theories have been advanced, one placing the geologic ages "during" the six days of creation (thus making the "days" into "ages"), and the other placing the ages "before" the six days (thus making them days of "re-creation" following a great cataclysm which had destroyed the primeval earth). The "day-age theory" is discussed in the next section and will be shown to be an impossible compromise, both Biblically and scientifically.

The "gap theory" has been advocated by many sincere Bible-teachers, but actually involves numerous serious fallacies. The geologic ages cannot be disposed of merely by ignoring the extensive fossil record on which they are based, which is what the theory tries to do. These supposed ages are inextricably involved in the entire structure of the evolutionary history of the earth and its inhabitants, up to and including man. The fossil record is the best evidence for evolution (in fact, the only such evidence which indicates evolution on more than a trivial scale). Furthermore, the geologic ages are recognized and identified specifically by the fossil contents of the sedimentary rocks in the earth's crust. The very names of the ages show this. Thus, the "Paleozoic Era" is the era of "ancient life," the "Mesozoic Era," of "intermediate life," and the "Cenozoic Era" of "recent life." As a matter of fact, the one primary means for dating these rocks in the first place has always been the supposed "stage-of-evolution" of the contained fossils.

Thus acceptance of the geologic ages implicitly involves acceptance of the whole evolutionary package. Most of the fossil forms preserved in the sedimentary rocks have obvious relatives in the present world, so that the "re-creation" concept involves the Creator in "re-creating" in six days many of the same animals and plants which had been previously developed slowly over long ages, only to gradually become extinct or else finally to perish violently in the great pre-Adamic cataclysm. The theory must include the concept of "pre-Adamic man" also, since many fossils of hominid forms have been dated at vastly greater ages (up to two million years or more) than the Bible chronology can accommodate.

The gap theory therefore really does not face the evolution issue at all, but merely pigeonholes it in an imaginary gap between Genesis 1:1 and 1:2. It leaves unanswered the serious problem as to why God would use the method of slow evolution over long ages in the primeval world, then destroy it, and then use the method of special creation to re-create the same forms He had just destroyed.

Furthermore, there is no geologic evidence of such a worldwide cataclysm in recent geologic history. Advocates of the gap theory have often identified it with the glacial age, but the latter was hardly a worldwide cataclysm, since the ice sheets only extended into the middle latitudes, and certainly did not destroy all previous life.

There is no Biblical evidence of such a worldwide pre-Adamic cataclysm either. A few texts, isolated from their contexts, may possibly be interpreted to fit in with the gap theory, but nowhere in the Bible is there a clear, straighforward account of the supposed primeval creation and the character of the hypothetical pre-Adamic cataclysm. This is strange in light of the importance which this theory has come to hold in the theologies of many Bible teachers and in the much-too-easy answers which they offer for this basic issue in the foundational history of the cosmos.

Probably the greatest problem with the theory (and over 20 others could be listed[6] if necessary) is that it makes God the direct author of evil. It implies that He used the methods of struggle, violence, decay, and death on a worldwide scale for at least three billion years in order to accomplish His unknown purposes in the primeval world. This is the testimony of the fossils and the geologic ages which the theory tries to place before Genesis 1:2. Then, according to the theory, Satan sinned against God in heaven (Isa. 14:12-15; Ezek. 28:11-17), and God cast him out of heaven to the earth, destroying the earth in the process in the supposed pre-Adamic cataclysm. Satan's sin in heaven, however, cannot in any way account for the age-long spectacle of suffering and death in the world during the geologic ages which *preceded* it! Thus God alone remains responsible for suffering, death, and confusion, and without any reason for it.

But this is theological chaos! The Scripture says, on the other hand, at the end of the six days of creation, "And God saw everything that he had made [e.g., including not only the entire earth and all its contents, but all the heavens as well—note Gen. 1:16; 2:2, etc.] and, behold, it was very good" (Gen. 1:31). Death did not "enter the world" until man sinned (Rom. 5:12; I Cor. 15:21). Evidently even Satan's rebellion in heaven had not yet taken place, because everything was pronounced "very good" there too.

The real answer to the meaning of the great terrestrial graveyard— the fossil contents of the great beds of hardened sediments all over the world—will be found neither in the slow operation of uniform natural processes over vast ages of time nor in an *imaginary* cataclysm that took place before the six days of God's perfect creation. Rather, it will be found in a careful study of the very *real* worldwide cataclysm described in Genesis 6 through 9 and confirmed in many other parts of the Bible and in the early records of nations and tribes all over the world, namely, the great Flood of the days of Noah. These matters are discussed in Chapter VIII, Question 4.

7. *Question: "Do the six days of creation in Genesis correspond to the geological ages?"*

Answer: According to the established system of historical geology, the history of the earth is divided into a number of geological

[6] *Ibid.*, pp. 62-66.

ages. The earth is supposed to have evolved into its present basic structure about five billion years ago. Certain increasingly complex chemicals in the primeval ocean, acted upon by electrical forces in the atmosphere, acquired the ability to replicate themselves perhaps about three billion years ago. For a long time only single-celled life forms existed, but about one or two billion years ago metazoan organisms began to evolve.

Since the beginning of the Cambrian period, almost a billion years ago, the developing variety of life on the earth is supposedly recognized by the fossils of organisms which have been buried and preserved in the sedimentary rocks of the earth's crust. The earliest vertebrates appeared in the Ordovician, fishes began to thrive in the Silurian and Devonian, and amphibians arose in the Permo-Carboniferous. Then, beginning about 200 million years ago, we have the Mesozoic Era, the age of the great dinosaurs. This terminated with their sudden and unexplained extinction towards the end of the Cretaceous period about 100 million years ago. Next, the Tertiary period is the age of mammals and birds. The hypothetical common ancestor of man and monkey appeared perhaps 70 million years ago. Finally man, equivalent to modern man in all essential aspects, is believed to have emerged about one or two million years ago.

In contrast to the above quite remarkable construct of the human imagination (remarkable in view of the fact that reliable written historical records extend back only four or five thousand years!), the Biblical revelation tells us that God created the entire universe in six days only a few thousand years ago. Consequently many Christian scholars have labored diligently, especially for the past century and a half, to find some way of reinterpreting Genesis to fit the framework of earth history prescribed by the geologists, not wishing to incur the easily provoked ridicule of the intellectual establishment and yet wishing to retain, somehow, faith in the integrity of the Scriptures.

The most popular of these devices has been the "day-age" theory, by which the "days" of creation were interpreted figuratively as the "ages" of geology. However, there are so many difficulties with this theory that, for most people who have held it, it has been only an escape-hatch and, quite often, only a temporary stopping-point on the road to outright rejection of the historical records in Genesis (and, eventually and inevitably, of the historical accuracy of the rest of the Bible too).

The Hebrew word for "day" is "yom," and this word can occasionally be used to mean an indefinite period of time, if the context warrants. In the overwhelming preponderance of its occurrences in the Old Testament, however, it means a literal day—that is, either an entire solar day or the daylight portion of a solar day. It was, in fact, defined by God Himself the very first time it was used, in Genesis 1:5, where we are told that "God called the light, day." It thus means, in the context, the "day" in the succession of "day and night," or "light and darkness."

Furthermore, the word is never used to mean a definite period of time, in a succession of similar periods (that is, "the first day," "the second day," etc.) or with definite terminal points (that is, as noted by "evening and morning," etc.) unless that period is a literal solar day. And there are hundreds of instances of this sort in the Bible.

Still further, the plural form of the word (Hebrew "yamim") is used over 700 times in the Old Testament and always, without exception, refers to literal "days." A statement in the Ten Commandments, written on a tablet of stone directly by God Himself, is very significant in this connection, where He uses this word and says plainly: "In six days, the Lord made heaven and earth, the sea, and all that in them is" (Ex. 20:11).

Not only is the day-age theory unacceptable Scripturally, but it also is grossly in conflict with the geological position with which it attempts to compromise. There are more than 20 serious contradictions[7] between the Biblical order and events of the creative days and the standard geologic history of the earth and its development, even if it were permissible to interpret the "days" as "ages." For example, the Bible teaches that the earth existed before the stars, that it was initially covered by water, that fruit trees appeared before fishes, that plant life preceded the sun, that the first animals created were the whales, that birds were made before insects, that man was made before woman, and many other such things, all of which are explicitly contradicted by historical geologists and paleontologists.

But the most serious fallacy in the day-age theory is theological. It charges God (the God of love, of mercy, of order, of wisdom and purpose) with the direct responsibility for five billion years of history of purposeless variation, accidental changes, evolutionary blind alleys, numerous misfits and extinctions, a cruel struggle for existence, with preservation of the strong and extermination of the weak, of natural disasters of all kinds, rampant disease, disorder and decay and, above all, with death. The Bible teaches that, at the end of the

7 *Ibid.*, pp. 58-62.

creation period, God pronounced His whole creation to be "very good," in spite of all this. It also teaches plainly that this present type of world, "groaning and travailing in pain" (Rom. 8:22) only resulted from man's sin and God's curse thereon. "By one man sin entered into the world, and death by sin" (Rom. 5:12). "God is not the author of confusion" (I Cor. 14:33).

If God's purpose in creation was the creation and redemption of man, as those who advocate this theory believe, what purpose could there have been, for example, in the age-long reign of the dinosaurs and their extermination millions of years before man appeared? Christian ethics (healing the sick, unselfish sharing, turning the other cheek, self-sacrifice) are diametrically opposed to evolutionary ethics (destruction of the unfit, aggressiveness, self-preservation).

The above are only a few of the dozens of Biblical, scientific, and theological fallacies in the day-age theory and, indeed, in any theory which seeks to accommodate the Christian faith to evolutionary faith.

Chapter VIII

THE ANCIENT WORLD

1. *Question: "When did the world begin?"*

Answer: According to Scripture, "in six days the Lord made heaven and earth, the sea, and all that in them is" (Ex. 20:11). These words were written on a tablet of stone by God Himself (Ex. 31:18), and it is therefore presumptuous for man to question it. Nor can the word "days" be interpreted as "ages." The Hebrew word (yamim") is used more than 700 times in the Old Testament and always, without exception,[1] means literal solar "days" and nothing else, as anyone can verify by consulting an exhaustive concordance of Old Testament word usage.

Nevertheless, most people today believe that it took drastically longer than a mere "six days" to make the universe. The consistent materialist, in fact, believes that matter is eternal, that the solar system is about five billion years old, that life began on earth about three billion years ago, and that modern man finally evolved about a million years ago.

This vast time span is, of course, necessary for any viable theory of evolution. And of course evolution is absolutely essential if men are going to reject the Biblical doctrine of special creation, as our modern political and intellectual Establishment has chosen to do.

Nevertheless, it should be obvious that it is quite impossible to prove, scientifically, the age of the earth or how long it took to bring it into its present form. Science is built upon direct observation of natural processes, and on experimental verification of hypotheses. Nothing is more impossible now than to observe, experimentally, the origin of the solar system or the evolution of man or the development of life over the geological ages! Consequently, speculations on these subjects are necessarily outside the scope of genuine science.

---

[1] One possible exception might be claimed, in Hosea 6:2. This passage also probably refers to literal days, but since it is a prophecy yet awaiting future fulfillment, this cannot be conclusively demonstrated either way in terms of actual history.

Written historical records (apart from those in the Bible) extend back only about four thousand years. Events which may have occurred before that time, therefore, can be verified neither by historical description nor by scientific repetition. They must be accepted on faith, and *only* on faith! That faith may be placed either in the divinely inspired Biblical record of those events or else in the uniformitarian extrapolations of modern evolutionists. This is a spiritual decision, not a scientific decision!

The Bible clearly teaches a relatively recent creation of all things, measured in thousands rather than billions of years. In order to provide the immense ages required by evolution, the principle of "uniformitarianism" is employed, according to which the entire history of the earth is to be explained in terms of the processes operating at present, and at approximately the same rates as at present.

However, even on this assumption (which is obviously a pure assumption, quite impossible to prove) there is ample reason to question the orthodox evolutionary history of the earth. Practically all of the earth's surface rocks and physiographic features (e.g., the great orogenic and tectonic movements by which mountains were formed, the tremendous volcanic terrains, the evidences of continental glaciation, the vast thicknesses of sediments in alluvial valleys and high plains, etc., etc.) must have required geophysical phenomena of character and intensity utterly beyond anything ever actually observed taking place in the present relatively inactive world.

Even the radioactivity dating techniques which are used to "prove" these vast ages are highly vulnerable[2] on a logical basis. The method of radiocarbon dating, for example, which has been widely used to "date" events over the past supposed 50,000 years, involves at least a dozen unprovable assumptions. One of these assumptions is that, on a global basis, radiocarbon has attained equilibrium with natural carbon, with as much radiocarbon now being formed in the upper atmosphere as is presently decaying throughout the world. Actual measurements, however, have indicated that such equilibrium has *not* yet been attained and that in fact the present state of non-equilibrium corresponds to a maximum age of only about 6,000 years for the beginning of the atmosphere itself! All so-called "radiocarbon ages" therefore should accordingly be drastically reduced.

[2] See *The Genesis Flood,* by John C. Whitcomb and Henry M. Morris (Nutley, N. J.: Presbyterian and Reformed Publishing Co., 1961), 518 pp., for a detailed and documented critique of uniformitarianism and geologic dating criteria.

Similarly, the widely used potassium-argon method involves many assumptions and uncertainties. In fact, it can at best be only as reliable as the uranium-lead method by which it must be calibrated.

But the uranium methods likewise involve numerous assumptions! For example, it is well known that radiogenic lead can be added to a uranium mineral system by external processes and that uranium can easily be leached out of such a system, either of which would make the "apparent age" of the system immensely greater than its "true age."

In general, it is evident that for any geophysical process to be a valid means of measuring prehistoric time, it must satisfy at least the following three conditions: (1) the relative amounts of "parent" and "daughter" products must be measured in the system at the beginning of the decay process (but this is impossible, since this was supposedly millions of years ago!); (2) the decay process converting "parent" into "daughter" must never have changed its rate (but there is no such thing in nature as an unchangeable process rate, and this is especially cogent in view of current ideas concerning geomagnetic reversals, intermittent showers of intense cosmic radiation from space, etc.); and (3) the system being used must have remained a perfectly "closed" system during all the vicissitudes of geologic history since it was first formed, unmodified by any external activities (but there is no such thing in nature as a truly closed system, and this is especially true for a geological system).

If one wants to base his evolutionary faith on such uniformitarian assumptions, this is a free country! But he should recognize that this is no more "scientific" than faith in the historical chronology recorded by divine inspiration in the Holy Scriptures.

2. Question: "Where did Cain get his wife?"

Answer: This is certainly one of the most ancient of all questions raised by Bible critics, and we can be sure that the superficial contradiction it implies did not escape notice by the original writers of the Bible. Cain was apparently the first son of Adam and Eve (Gen. 4:1) and Abel the second (Gen. 4:2).

After Cain had murdered his brother Abel (Gen. 4:8), God punished him by sending him away from his home and from God's presence forever. But then we are told that Cain was fearful of vengeance by others who might slay him (Gen. 4:14), that he knew his wife (Gen. 4:17), and even that he built a city. The descendants of Cain and the antediluvian civilization which they developed are described in Genesis 4:17-24.

Skeptics have, of course, "wondered" where all those other people came from if no one except Adam, Eve, and Cain were living at this time. The idea that there might have been in the vicinity a "pre-Adamic" race of men is clearly precluded by the unequivocal Bible teaching that Adam was the "first man" (I Cor. 15:45, etc.) and that Eve was "the mother of all living" (Gen. 3:20).

However, the real reason for this criticism is merely the evolutionary presupposition that such critics hold. They are unwilling to believe that God started the human race by special creation of one man and one woman, preferring instead to believe that man came instead as a slowly evolving population of primates which eventually acquired what we consider human characteristics about one or two million years ago.

However, the Lord Jesus Christ, who was Himself man's Creator in the beginning (note John 1:1-3; Col. 1:16, 17, etc.), taught otherwise. He said: "Have ye not read [that is, in Gen. 1:27, which He was quoting] that he which made them at the beginning made them male and female, . . .?" (Matt. 19:4). Thus the creation of Adam and Eve, as the progenitors of the human race, was "at the beginning," not after millions of years of evolution of a pre-human population of animals.

In the beginning, according to Scripture, man was created "very good" and would have lived forever had he not sinned. But, "by one man sin entered into the world, and death by sin" (Rom. 5:12). Even after the reign of decay and death entered the world at the time of God's great Curse on man's dominion (Gen. 3:17), most men did live for hundreds of years and undoubtedly had large families. Adam and Eve are said to have had both "sons and daughters" (Gen. 5:4) during the 930 years of Adam's lifetime, and the same is true of each of the other antediluvian patriarchs listed in the genealogies of Genesis 5. The average life-span of these patriarchs (excluding Enoch, who was taken out of the world before he died) is 912 years.

The question of how man was able to live to such great ages is a separate problem, which will be discussed later. Taking the record at face value, however, it is obvious that a very large population could have developed in the world before the Flood. It can be shown that, based on very conservative assumptions as to family size, average longevity, etc., there could easily have been many millions of people in the world long before Cain's death.

Since the Bible does not indicate at what period of his life he murdered his brother, took his wife, or built his city, there is obviously no contradiction in the record. Consequently, neither the original writer of Genesis 4 nor any later editors ever felt this was a problem that needed explanation.

Now, of course, at least one son and one daughter of Adam and Eve had to marry each other in the first generation after the beginning in order for the race to get started at all. There is no other possibility if all men are descended from Adam and Eve as the Bible teaches.

In later generations, brother-sister marriages would come to be recognized as genetically dangerous and would be prohibited as "incest." Not only the Bible but also most other legal codes refuse to sanction marriages of close relatives. The scientific reason for this restriction is that children of such marriages are more likely to be deformed or sickly or moronic than those of other marriages. The genetic basis for this probability is that inherited mutant genes, producing such unwholesome characteristics, are more likely to find expression in the children if they are carried by both parents.

However, there were no mutant genes in the genetic systems of Adam and Eve, as these had come directly from the creative hand of God Himself. Thus no genetic harm could have resulted had Cain or some other son of Adam married his sister. In fact, it would undoubtedly have taken many generations before enough genetic mutations (which are random, and therefore harmful, changes in the highly ordered structure of the germ cell, brought about by penetration of the cell by shortwave-length radiation or some other destructive agent) could have accumulated in the human race to make such marriages of close relatives genetically harmful.

The Bible is thus always consistent, not only with its own statements, but also with all known facts of science.

3. Question: "How was it possible for men to live hundreds of years before the Flood?"

Answer: One of the remarkable things about the record of the early chapters of Genesis is the straightforward simplicity with which the writer recorded certain amazing and almost unbelievable facts of history. One would think that if Genesis were really written in some late period in Jewish history, as critics allege, the writer would have interjected some explanatory comment or at least some expression of wonder at the uniqueness of the phenomena he was describing.

But instead he wrote the account in the most simple and straightforward way possible, as a sober historian or news reporter would do, with no attempt whatever to justify or explain events which would seem almost incredible to later generations.

Thus, in Genesis 5 appears a simple chronological and genealogical table, sketching the line of the antediluvian patriarchs from the first man, Adam, down to Noah. The age of each man at the birth of the next son in the patriarchal line is given, and also the age of each man when he died. This would all be very prosaic and uninteresting, were it not for the remarkable fact that the age of each at his death was many hundreds of years!

Adam lived 930 years, Methuselah lived 969 years, and the average age of the nine antediluvian patriarchs (excluding Enoch, who was— also matter-of-factly—taken into heaven without dying at age 365) was 912 years. The only logical explanation for reporting these amazing facts in such a mundane fashion is that, when the original writer recorded them they were not unusual at all, but common experience. As pointed out in Section VI - 3, these accounts in the early chapters of Genesis were probably eyewitness accounts, written originally on stone tablets and then transmitted down the line of the patriarchs until they finally came into Moses' possession, who collected and edited them as the book of Genesis.

That these ages are given in terms of real years, and not months as some have suggested, is evident from the ages of the fathers at the birth of their sons, ranging from 65 years in the case of Mahaleel and Enoch to 500 years in the case of Noah. Another proof of this is the fact that, after the Flood, the life-span began a slow and erratic decline from 950 years for Noah to 205 years for Terah (as recorded in Genesis 11), and eventually down to about 70 years at the time of Moses (note Ps. 90:10).

Evidently something happened at the time of the Flood that affected the human environment drastically, gradually accelerating the aging process and the onset of death. Although we cannot be sure what this was, there are certain interesting intimations in both science and Scripture which provide at least a plausible hypothesis.

No one knows, of course, even today exactly what causes death. There seems to be no necessary, innate reason why man could not live hundreds of years. As a matter of fact, he was originally created as an immortal being, and death came only as a judgment of God upon sin. "Wherefore, as by one man, sin entered into the world, and death by sin; and so death passed upon all men, for that all have sinned" (Rom. 5:12).

Now a remarkable fact brought to light by modern gerontology (the study of aging processes) is that probably no one actually dies simply of old age. Rather, aging so increases susceptibility to disease and so decreases the operational efficiency of bodily organs and functions that, finally, there is a complete breakdown of some particular aspect of the body's mechanism, and this causes death. This may happen earlier or later in various individuals, but eventually it happens to all.

The fundamental factor in longevity, therefore, is the rate of the aging process and the environmental influences which affect it. There are various theories of aging, but the one apparently supported by the best evidence is the somatic mutation theory. A somatic mutation is a sudden, random change in the structure of a cell of the body. Since almost all mutations are harmful, the gradual accumulation of mutations in the cells of various organs and tissues will inevitably lead to impaired bodily efficiency and eventually to complete breakdown of one or more bodily components.

Now various environmental factors may cause mutations, but probably the most important is radiation, both from the sun and from other radiational sources. Radiations also cause genetic mutations in the germ cells, although these are much better shielded than the somatic, or body, cells. Though much less frequent than somatic mutations for this reason, genetic mutations, which are also almost always harmful, are transmitted to the children and thus affect not only the individual, but also all his descendants.

It seems reasonable to suggest, therefore, that somatic mutations lead to the aging and death of the individual, and genetic mutations to the aging and death of the species, with both primarily attributable to radiations in the environment. Other factors also are involved, of course, but this seems to be the most universally prevalent cause.

Before the Flood, the "waters above the firmament" (Gen. 1:7) probably were in the form of a vast blanket of invisible water vapor in the upper atmosphere. Not only would this have produced a wonderful "greenhouse effect," maintaining a mild and calm climate over all the world, but also it would have provided a highly efficient filter for the lethal radiations bombarding the earth from outer space.

Thus the "background radiation" of the environment before the Flood was much less than it is at present, and this could certainly have contributed significantly to the long ages of men before the Flood. These upper waters later condensed and fell to the earth as one of the causes of the great Flood, and so are no longer available for this function in full. However, even the 1½″ of water vapor remaining in the present atmosphere maintains enough of a greenhouse effect and radiation filter to sustain life at least in its present less efficient and durable form on the earth. The drastically changed climate and denuded earth after the Flood, together with the inbreeding necessitated for the very few survivors of the cataclysm, undoubtedly also contributed to the general decline in longevity and viability. In any case, there is no good reason to doubt the reasonableness of the Biblical record of the antediluvian patriarchs and their great ages.

4. Question: "Was the Biblical Flood worldwide or only a local flood?"

Answer: The Bible writers undoubtedly describe the Flood as universal in extent and effect. Most geologists reject the historicity of such a flood, and this has therefore become one of the chief points of conflict between Biblical Christianity and the modern evolutionary philosophy. Some Christian writers have tried to promote the compromise view that the Flood was only a great river overflow on the Euphrates or some other river in the Middle East.

However, the Biblical case for a global deluge is quite convincing. The following are just a few of the many reasons for this position.

(1) More than thirty statements of the universal character of the Flood and its effects occur in Genesis 6 through 9.

(2) The purpose of the Flood was to destroy not only all mankind, but also all animal life on the dry land as well (Gen. 6:7; 6:17; 7:22).

(3) The Flood was even sent to "destroy the earth" (Gen. 6:13).

(4) The Flood covered all the mountains (Gen. 7:19, 20).

(5) The Flood lasted over a year (Gen. 7:11; 8:13).

(6) The ark had a volumetric capacity of more than 500 standard stock cars, far more than adequate to hold two of every known species, past or present, of dry land animals.

(7) The ark was ridiculously unnecessary for Noah, the animals, and especially the birds, to escape from a mere local flood.

(8) God's promise (Gen. 8:21; 9:11, 15) never again to send such a flood has been broken repeatedly if it were only a local flood.

(9) All men in the world today are said to have descended from Noah's three sons (Gen. 9:1, 19).

(10) Many later Biblical writers accepted the historicity of the worldwide Flood (note Job 12:15; 22:16; Ps. 29:10; 104:6-9; Isa. 54:9; I Peter 3:20; II Peter 2:5; 3:5, 6; Heb. 11:7).

(11) The Lord Jesus Christ believed in the universal Flood and took it as the type of the coming destruction of the world when He returns (Matt. 24:37-39; Luke 17:26, 27).

The above and other Biblical proofs that could be added, if necessary, prove that not only the author of the book of Genesis but the other Biblical authors as well, and even Jesus Christ Himself, accepted the Flood as of worldwide extent and effect. To this evidence could be added the well-known fact that practically all nations and tribes in the world have retained some kind of tradition of the Flood at the dawn of their history.

The fact that most modern geologists reject these evidences stems from the philosophy of uniformitarianism and evolutionism that has formed the backbone of geological interpretations for the past century. The uniformity principle, popularized originally by Hutton and Lyell (a medical man and a lawyer, respectively) claims that all of earth's past history should be explained in terms of ordinary natural processes as they occur today. The evolutionary philosophy popularized by Charles Darwin (an apostate divinity student turned naturalist) says that the origin of all the forms of life and of life itself must likewise be explained in terms of present natural processes. These two philosophies are at the foundation of the evolutionary interpretation of the earth's supposed geological ages, and they obviously preclude the Biblical record of special creation and the Flood.

Thus the fossils of former living plants and animals, as found in the sedimentary rocks of the earth's crust, are used to "date" the rocks and to determine the particular geologic age of the formation containing them. This is done primarily on the assumption that rocks containing "simple" fossils must be older and those containing "complex" fossils must be younger, since all things have developed by a process of evolution over the ages.

But then these geological ages and their fossil record supposedly provide the best (indeed the only) historical proof of the "fact" of evolution over the ages! This is a notorious case of the flagrant circular reasoning that is frequently used for evidence in modern scientific philosophy.

It is significant that, before the time of Lyell and Darwin, and their followers and popularizers (Marx, Spencer, Huxley, Nietzsche, et al.) the dominant theory of geology for the preceding century, that of the great awakening in science, had been the Flood theory, which understood the sedimentary rocks and their fossil contents as having been originally deposited as sediments during the awful year of the Great Flood and the century or so following.

This explanation of the geologic strata was never disproved. It was simply rejected as inconsistent with the philosophies of progress and humanism and evolutionary socialism that came into vogue in the nineteenth century.

Actually, there is much evidence that most of the strata must have been deposited rapidly, not gradually (otherwise, for example, how could their fossil contents have been preserved?). Furthermore, instead of a universal principle of evolutionary progress in the world, the Second Law of Thermodynamics combines with all actual human experience to indicate rather that there prevails a universal law of decay and deterioration in the world.

Although creationism and catastrophism, as opposed to evolutionary uniformitarianism, does represent a minority view in science today, it is an increasingly recognized view. For example, the Creation Research Society, organized in 1963, has over 350 scientist members (M.S. degrees at least) in its membership, all committed to belief in special creation and the worldwide Flood. This organization[3] publishes a quarterly journal of scientific articles refuting evolutionism and supporting the Biblical record of creation and the Flood. There is thus not only overwhelming Biblical testimony, but also adequate supporting scientific data, to warrant acceptance of the universality of the Noahic Flood.

5. Question: *"How could Noah get two of each of the millions of animal species into the ark?"*

Answer: This is a standard objection that critics frequently lodge against the Biblical record of the Great Flood. They like to ridicule the thought of Noah setting off on trapping expeditions to Alaska and Australia, and they especially seem to relish the thought of the insuperable difficulties encountered by Noah's family in feeding and cleaning up after the animals during their year in the ark! The fact that conservative Christian scholars have answered these objections many times in the past is not known to religious "liberals," of course, since they almost never read books written by "conservatives."

Genesis 6:15 gives the dimensions of the ark as 300 cubits by 50 cubits by 30 cubits, and the cubit was at least 17½ inches long. On

---

[3] For information or application forms, write Creation Research Society, c/o Prof. W. H. Rusch, 2717 Cranbrook Road, Ann Arbor, Michigan 48104.

this basis, the volumetric carrying capacity of the ark can be calculated as at least the equivalent of that of 522 standard railroad stock cars. A standard stock car can transport 240 sheep, so that the ark could have carried at least 125,000 sheep. The average dry-land animal undoubtedly is considerably smaller than a sheep, as there are only a few large animals.

The ark had to transport only land animals, of course, so that the mammals, birds, and reptiles were essentially all that needed accommodations. The ark was constructed in three stories, and each was fitted with "rooms" or "nests" (Gen. 6:14)—evidently tiers of cages or stalls—to store the different kinds of animals.

The Genesis "kind" is undoubtedly a more flexible term than our biological "species." However, even assuming they are the same, there are not very many species of mammals, birds, amphibians, and reptiles. The leading systematic biologist, Ernst Mayr, gives the number as 17,600. Allowing for two of each species on the ark, plus seven of the few so-called "clean" kinds of animals, plus a reasonable increment for known extinct species, it is obvious that not more than about, say, 50,000 animals were on the ark. This is obviously much less than the 125,000 that could easily have been carried. There was also ample room for food storage and for living quarters for Noah and his family.

In fact, the ark was so commodious that the whole story makes sense only if the Flood were a universal flood. The ark was far too large for a mere regional fauna. For that matter, if the Flood were only local, no ark would have been needed at all! The problem of preserving human and animal life could have been solved far more easily by merely moving out of the endangered flood plains.

As far as the problem of obtaining the animals is concerned, the Lord solved this merely by sending them to Noah (note Gen. 6:20), so that he didn't have to go searching for them at all. Animals can and do migrate long distances, especially when impelled to do so by imminent weather changes. These still-mysterious "instincts" were implanted somehow within those animals the Lord wanted preserved, and He thus caused them to "come unto" Noah and the place of safety from the gathering storm.

Once they were safely on board, lodged in their stalls, and properly fed, most of them very likely settled down for a long period of dormancy, or hibernation. The sudden darkness and chill in the air, when "the sluiceways of heaven were opened," quite probably set in action those remarkable physiologic powers, which seem to be shared in some degree by all orders of the animal kingdom.

The animal world seems to have, in fact, these two remarkable mechanisms for coping with unfavorable climatic conditions—namely, migration and hibernation. Modern biologists, despite much study, have still been unable to provide a satisfactory explanation for the origin and operation of these fantastic capabilities. The known facts fit the hypothesis that God imparted these abilities, perhaps by new "information" conveyed to the "genetic code" at this time, to those animals selected by Him to go to the ark. Their new migratory instincts enabled them to travel to the ark, and their new hibernation mechanisms enabled them to pass the awful year of the deluge in relative quiet and comfort. The descendants of those animals that "went forth from the ark" have all inherited these capacities in greater or lesser degrees, still enabling them, as necessary, to escape unfavorable environmental conditions by one or both mechanisms.

Before the Flood, it is likely that there was a worldwide warm, pleasant climate. This is indicated both by the fact that such a climate is implied in the fossils and sediments from practically all the so-called geologic "ages" prior to the Pleistocene ice age, and also by the fact that the Bible record of the "waters above the firmament" points to a great antediluvian canopy of invisible water vapor in the upper atmosphere which would have produced just such a "greenhouse effect" all over the world.

Thus, before the Flood, animals had no need for migration and hibernation, and probably all kinds of animals were dispersed more or less uniformly all over the world. When the thermal vapor blanket condensed and precipitated at the time of the Flood, there was a rapid change of climate, which led finally to the ice age and then eventually to the present climatologic regime of the world.

Evidence and documentation for all the above and many other aspects of the great Flood are given in the writer's book, *The Genesis Flood*, now in its 14th printing. It is recognized that this is a minority view in science (as a matter of fact, Biblical Christians represent a minority in any field), but there are hundreds of qualified scientists who do agree with it in all essentials. In any case, the actual observed facts agree with it, so far as known at present. The decision to accept or reject any part of the Biblical record (confirmed as fully historical and factual, even in its stories of creation and the Flood by Christ and His apostles in the New Testament) is therefore not a scientific decision at all but a spiritual decision!

107

6. Question: *"Where do the fossils of dinosaurs and other extinct animals fit into the Bible record?"*

Answer: Most of the earth's land surfaces today are underlain by sedimentary rocks, which are sediments that have been gradually turned into stone through pressure and chemical reactions. Most sedimentary rocks were originally unconsolidated sands and gravels, silts and clays, which were eroded by water, transported by water, and finally deposited under water.

Such sedimentary rocks often contain fossils, which are the remains of former living things, in the form of bones, casts, petrifactions, tracks, or other marks of the organism which formed them. In fact, fossils are very abundant in sedimentary rocks, so much so that they are almost universally used as the chief means of identifying the geologic "age" of a particular rock. The study of fossils and their supposed evolutionary history is called paleontology. Although there are actually only a relatively small number of professional paleontologists in the world, this field of study has become of critical importance in the standard evolutionary interpretation of earth history.

This is so because the fossil record is by far the most important evidence for the theory of evolution. All other supposed evidences for evolution are strictly circumstantial in nature, consisting merely of various types of similarities between organisms and various types of small biologic changes which may occur in different species. Such evidences as these can, of course, be understood as well or better in terms of an original creation of all the basic "kinds" of organisms, with degrees of similarity between organisms in proportion to the similarities of function and purpose intended for them by their Creator, and with provision in their respective genetic systems for a fairly wide range of variation (though always within definite limits) in response to environmental changes in time and space.

The fossil record in the sedimentary rocks, however, is supposed to demonstrate the actual evolutionary development of life into more and more complex and specialized forms over the vast span of geologic time. Thus the true nature of this fossil record and its proper interpretation are critical to the evolution question.

Fossil assemblages (especially certain marine "index fossils") indeed provide the chief mechanism for dating rocks in the "geologic column." The geologic time scale has in fact been developed over the past 150 years primarily on this basis. Other factors, such as lithologic characteristics, radioactive mineral ages, vertical superposition of strata, etc., are also used, but the fossils are always of determinative importance whenever conflicting data (and this is quite often) are discovered.

Obviously an important question is: "How do we know which fossils belong to which age, so that we can use them with such assurance to determine age?" The answer is that they are required to conform to the evolutionary history of life! Since simple marine organisms such as trilobites must have evolved early, rocks containing only such fossils are assumed to be quite old. Since man supposedly evolved most recently, rocks containing human fossils must be very recent. And so on. The detailed order of the fossils, and therefore the geologic column which is built up from it, is based directly on the assumption of the slow, gradual evolution of life over vast stretches of cosmic time.

This might be reasonable if we somehow knew (by divine revelation, perhaps) that evolution were really true. But, as a matter of fact, the only real evidence for evolution is this same fossil record! And this is where we came in!

The zeal with which this evolutionary circle of reasoning is guarded is seen clearly in the approach taken with respect to its problems and contradictions. When radioactive mineral age determinations conflict with the paleontologic dating (as they frequently do) they are abandoned as having been somehow altered since deposition. When, in a given location, a formation of a certain age rests conformably and naturally on a formation of a much earlier age, with all the intervening ages omitted (and this kind of thing is found almost everywhere), then it is assumed that these missing ages were ages of uplift and erosion rather than deposition, even if no evidence of this exists. When fossils from different "ages" are found together in the same formation (as does happen with some frequency), then it is assumed that earlier deposits have been "re-worked" and mixed together. And when (as very often is the case) formations with "ancient" fossils are found lying conformably on top of formations with "recent" fossils, then great earth movements and "overthrusts" must be invoked to get the column out of its proper evolutionary order, even though in many cases there is no evidence of such movements and even though there is no adequate physical mechanism which could produce them!

There thus appear to be sound reasons for questioning the orthodox evolutionary interpretation of the fossil record and its uniformitarian framework of earth history. Furthermore, there does exist a legitimate alternative explanation.

It is significant that fossils, especially of large animals such as the dinosaur, must be buried quickly or they will not be preserved at all. Furthermore, the sediments entrapping them must harden into stone fairly quickly, inhibiting the action of air, bacteria, etc., or else they will soon be decomposed and disappear. The very nature of fossilization thus seems to *require* catastrophism. Most certainly must this be true of the great dinosaur beds, the massive fish-bearing shales, the tremendous deposits of elephants and other animals in the arctic regions, and the great numbers of other "fossil graveyards" with which the geologic column abounds.

According to the Bible, death did not even "enter the world" until after Adam's sin (Rom. 5:12). And the fossil record, more than anything else, is a record of death—in fact, of sudden death—and on a worldwide scale!

At the end of the creation period (Gen. 1:31), God pronounced everything in the whole universe "very good." Thus the struggling, groaning creation (Rom. 8:22) everywhere evident in the fossil record must be dated Biblically as occurring after man's sin and God's curse on man's dominion (Gen. 3:15). And this can only mean that most of the sedimentary rocks of the earth's crust, with their fossils. were laid down during the awful year of the great Flood, when "every living substance was destroyed which was upon the face of the ground" (Gen. 7:23).

This must have included the dinosaurs and all other terrestrial animals, except those preserved in Noah's ark. Evidence is available (in the form of human and dinosaur footprints in the same formation, of dinosaur pictographs left by primitive tribes in Africa and North America, and of the universally prevalent traditions of dragons among ancient peoples) that dinosaurs lived contemporaneously with early man. The geologic column, rightly interpreted, therefore does not tell of a long, gradual evolution of life over the geologic ages, but rather its polar opposite—the rapid extinction of life as a result of God's judgment on the antediluvians when "the world that then was, being overflowed with water,.perished" (II Peter 3:6).

7. Question: "Where did all the different nations come from?"

Answer: One of the greatest hindrances to the attainment of peace in the world is the existence of so many different nations in the world, each with its own particular national characteristics and selfish interests. Attempts to weld all the nations into a one-world community have been made many times in man's history, but all have soon disintegrated. Various great nations have attempted unsuccessfully to impose a unification of their own on all of mankind. World leaders have tried a League of Nations, and, currently, a United Nations Organization, among others, but such schemes inevitably collapse. The International Communist cancer will also certainly destroy itself before it has attained the universal rule toward which it continually maneuvers.

The origin of so many different and competing national interests and characteristics, perpetually thwarting every attempt to impose a world brotherhood on mankind, is indeed one of the great problems of history. Evolutionists face a quandary here, as they are confronted with only two possible evolutionary explanations, neither of which is comfortable to them.

If evolution is true, then the present races and nations must have come either from a single common ancestral pre-human population, diverging into the separate tribes and nations after the completion of the basic evolutionary process leading to man (the mono-phyletic theory), or they must all have arisen by parallel evolution from a number of different groups of pre-human primates (the poly-phyletic theory).

The actual historical evidence, seen in evolutionary perspective, seems to favor the poly-phyletic theory, and many evolutionists have advocated it. As far back as written historical records go, there have been highly civilized nations in various places. Whether in Babylonia, China, India, Egypt, Yucatan, England, Peru, Persia, or wherever, the earliest records indicate a complex civilization, with highly individualistic and competing nations.

By the poly-phyletic theory, these national and racial distinctives are very ancient, reflecting parallel evolution from different origins. Inevitably this leads to racism and the conviction that one race or nation is better than another because of a longer or more efficient evolutionary sequence in the one case than in the other.

Of course, racism is not much in vogue today among Western "liberals." In the recent past, however, it has been an integral part of the speculations of such eminent evolutionists as Darwin, Marx, Nietzsche, Arthur Keith, Adolph Hitler, Cecil Rhodes, and many others. In any case, it is important to remember that true racism has its roots in the theory of evolution. The Bible does not once recognize the existence of different races or even the very concept of "race"—the latter is strictly a category of modern evolutionary biology!

Most evolutionary anthropologists today, because of sociological considerations, tend to support the mono-phyletic theory, believing that all present races have diverged from a common ancestor in recent geologic time. Beyond this agreement, however, there is then a great divergence of opinion among them as to which line led up to this first man and as to the mechanisms and directions of the supposed subsequent diversification into the different "races."

How, for example, assuming a common inter-breeding ancestral population, could such a wide variety of characteristics—skin color, stature, physiognomy, posture, etc.—have developed in the different groups, so much so that each nation and tribe is distinct and highly specialized in its own culture right at the beginning of its known history? Genetic theory does not yet have an answer to this question.

And, of course, the main distinctive of the different national and tribal groups is that of language! There are almost 3,000 distinct human languages extant in the world, in addition to a considerable number of dead languages. All of these are very complex systems, as far removed genetically from the chattering of a chimpanzee as a Shakespearean play is from the paper on which it was written. The evolutionist has no explanation whatever for the origin of human languages.

One turns with relief to the simple and powerful history of the nations as recorded in the Bible. "God hath made of one blood all nations of men for to dwell on all the face of the earth, and hath determined the times before appointed, and the bounds of their habitation; That they should seek the Lord, if haply they might feel after him, and find him, though he be not far from every one of us" (Acts 17:26, 27). "When the Most High divided to the nations their inheritance, when he separated the sons of Adam, he set the bounds of the people" (Deut. 32:8).

The division and separation of the nations took place at Babel, when "the Lord did there confound the language of all the earth: and from thence did the Lord scatter them abroad upon the face of all the earth" (Gen. 11:9). This judgment followed man's first attempt after the great Flood to build a "United Nations," established for the purpose of exalting man's will against that of God.

The amazingly accurate tenth chapter of Genesis names the earth's seventy original national units, resulting from this dispersion. Archaeology and ethnology have confirmed the existence and migrations of most of these primeval nations in a remarkable way, and the chapter deserves much more study and application than it has yet received.

112

It concludes with the statement: "These are the families of the sons of Noah, after their generations, in their nations: and by these were the nations divided in the earth after the flood" (Gen. 10:32).

This is the true beginning of the original nations. As they were separated and forced to survive by inbreeding for a time, the distinctive national traits quickly surfaced through genetic variation, mutation, selection, and segregation processes, in addition to the supernatural physiologic changes established by God when He changed their languages. Other nations have emerged later through recombination, migration, inter-marriage, and other processes.

There are no known facts of human history which contradict this Biblical outline, and many which confirm it. Finally, although there is no possibility of establishing a truly united world before Christ returns, it is true today that eternal salvation, through faith in Jesus Christ, is freely available, and men "of all nations and kindreds, and peoples, and tongues" (Rev. 7:9) are responding to the gospel message.

Chapter IX

SOUND DOCTRINE

1. *Question: "Don't we need a new gospel for today's world?"*

Answer: There is really only one gospel. The Greek word in the New Testament which is translated "gospel" means, literally, "good news." It is not, therefore, "good advice" about what to do or not to do to build a better world or a better personal life. It is, rather, God's own "good news" to men of all times and places, informing them that God has provided salvation for lost sinners, available as a free gift to all who will receive it.

The word is used many times in the New Testament, always with this precise meaning. It is explicitly defined in I Corinthians 15:1-4, as follows: "Moreover, brethren, I declare unto you the gospel, which I preached unto you, which ye have received, and wherein ye stand; By which also ye are saved, . . . For I delivered unto you first of all that which I also received, how that Christ died for our sins according to the scriptures; and that he was buried, and that he rose again the third day according to the scriptures."

Thus the gospel is simply the good news that the Lord Jesus Christ, the Son of God, has also become man, that He might die in atonement for the sins of man, and then, after His body was buried for three days, rise again from the grave, forever settling man's sin-debt before a holy God.

Note clearly, from the quoted passage, that the gospel is simply to be "received" (evidently by faith, as a free gift), that it is the gospel "by which ye are saved" (that is, from the just and otherwise certain punishment for your sins), and that it is the gospel "wherein ye stand" (thus continuing to rest solely on the merits of Christ alone for your salvation).

Men today are sinners just as were their forefathers, and thus are equally in need of God's forgiveness and cleansing. The death of Christ was the "propitiation for our sins, and not for ours only, but also for the sins of the whole world" (I John 2:2). The Lord Jesus gave the promise 1,900 years ago, "Him that cometh to me I will

114

in no wise cast out" (John 6:37), and men today are still finding His promise true and powerful.

The gospel does seem contrary to natural human reasoning. The natural man tends to think either in terms of materialism (that is, that the present life is all there is and therefore no one is really "saved"), or universalism (that is, that all people will somehow eventually be saved), or moral relativism (that is, that those who are saved are saved by their good works, and those who are not saved are lost for lack of good works).

To people who reason as above, the gospel of Christ does seem unreasonable, "But the natural man receiveth not the things of the Spirit of God, for they are foolishness unto him" (I Cor. 2:14).

Nevertheless, the false gospels proposed by men are utterly inadequate. Materialism denies that God is a God of love and wisdom, and in effect says that nothing has real meaning or purpose. Universalism ignores the holiness and justice of God, supposing that He will not punish sin and ultimately settle all accounts. Moral relativism assumes there is no objective moral standard in the universe, against which all decisions and actions must be measured and thus that any divine decision as to a person's destiny is merely capricious. None of these human philosophies are really satisfying, either intellectually or spiritually. Therefore none of them will offer a man a confident hope for eternity.

The gospel of Christ, on the other hand, when received by faith, does meet every need of human life. "For the preaching of the cross is to them that perish foolishness; but unto us which are saved it is the power of God" (I Cor. 1:18).

Since it provides a full forgiveness of all sins, it delivers one from the sufferings of a guilt-burdened conscience, as well as fear of death and hell. We may now "draw near with a true heart in full assurance of faith, having our hearts sprinkled from an evil conscience" (Heb. 10:22). Since Christ has paid the full price for all our sins, He can "deliver them who through fear of death were all their lifetime subject to bondage" (Heb. 2:15).

The gospel also provides the only conceivable means by which God's love and holiness can both be satisfied. His infinite holiness demands that all sin be punished, yet His perfect love desires that all men be saved. Since all men are sinners, no man can save himself. But "He hath made him to be sin for us, who knew no sin; that we might be made the righteousness of God in him" (II Cor. 5:21). This infinitely gracious act of God is not forced upon man, of course, but

115

it is offered as a free gift, to be received by faith with thanksgiving, "that he might be just, and the justifier of him which believeth in Jesus" (Rom. 3:26).

Man was, in fact, created for the very purpose of fellowship with God. He can never be truly happy or live a truly satisfying life, either now or in eternity, if he is separated from God's presence. He desperately needs to respond to God's love for him with genuine love in his own heart for God, and the gospel of Christ is the perfect answer. It perfectly reveals God's love to man and thus most powerfully draws out man's love to God. "In this was manifested the love of God toward us, because that God sent his only begotten Son into the world, that we might live through him. . . . We love him, because he first loved us" (I John 4:9, 19).

No, there is no modern substitute for the gospel. Men may talk about a "social gospel," a "full gospel," a "new gospel," or some other gospel, but there is only one gospel, and that is the "everlasting gospel" (Rev. 14:6). No wonder Paul said: "But though we, or an angel from heaven, preach any other gospel unto you than that which we have preached unto you, let him be accursed" (Gal. 1:9).

The gospel is still the good news, and there will never be another.

2. Question: "Will all men eventually be saved?"

Answer: Most everyone has a vague hope and trust that things will eventually turn out all right and that he will sooner or later get to heaven. Few and far between are the funeral services at which the preacher dares to suggest that the deceased may have departed in the other direction!

Nevertheless, men need to be aware that the Lord Jesus Christ clearly warned that it is easy to end up in hell. "Enter ye in at the strait gate," He said, "for wide is the gate, and broad is the way, that leadeth to destruction, and many there be which go in thereat: because strait is the gate, and narrow is the way which leadeth unto life, and few there be that find it" (Matt. 7:13, 14).

This same Lord Jesus, who spoke so often and so fervently of God's love, and who Himself perfectly manifested the love of God, was at the same time the one who spoke more often of hell than did anyone else in the Bible. He warned, for example, that the time would come when He would have to say to many people: "Depart from me, ye cursed, into everlasting fire, prepared for the devil and his angels" (Matt. 25:41).

The doctrine of the "remnant" is found through all Scripture. In

116

every age there has been only a small number of people who were approved of God. In the days before the great Flood, Noah was a "preacher of righteousness" for many years, but won no converts except his own family. The Bible says that "few, that is eight souls, were saved" (I Peter 3:20) and that, for the others, "God spared not the old world, . . . bringing in the flood upon the world of the ungodly" (II Peter 2:5). Jesus Christ said: "The flood came and destroyed them all" (Luke 17:27).

The days of the early patriarchs were similar. "These all died in faith, not having received the promises, but having seen them afar off, and were persuaded of them, and embraced them, and confessed that they were strangers and pilgrims on the earth" (Heb. 11:13).

The Jews, alone among the nations, were then called and prepared as God's chosen people. To them, God said: "The Lord thy God hath chosen thee to be a special people unto himself, above all people that are upon the face of the earth. The Lord did not set his love upon you, nor choose you because ye were more in number than any people; for ye were the fewest of all people" (Deut. 7:6, 7).

But even among the Jews there were only a few who really cared for God. "Then they that feared the Lord spake often to one another: and the Lord hearkened, and heard it, and a book of remembrance was written before him for them that feared the Lord, and that thought upon his name" (Mal. 3:16).

This condition was not significantly changed by the coming of Christ. As far as the Jews were concerned, some, of course, believed on Him as Messiah and Saviour, but the nation as a whole rejected Him. The Jewish "remnant" was to be recognized thereafter by their acceptance of Jesus as their long-awaited Redeemer. Paul said: "God hath not cast away his people which he foreknew. . . . Even so then at this present time there is a remnant according to the election of grace" (Rom. 11:2, 5).

Beginning from Jerusalem, the gospel of Christ was commanded by Him to be preached to all nations. But there was never a promise that all who heard the good news would believe it and turn to Christ. To the contrary, Paul warned in his final letter that "all who will live godly in Christ Jesus shall suffer persecution" (II Tim. 3:12).

The very meaning of the word "church" (Greek *ekklesia*, meaning "those who are called out"), indicates that the true Christian church would always be composed of a relatively small group of believers called out of the masses of men to be "separated unto God." Emphasizing this, the Lord Jesus promised: "Fear not, little flock;

for it is your Father's good pleasure to give you the kingdom" (Luke 12:32).

Therefore, when Christian preachers and evangelists preach that most men are lost and warn them to "flee from the wrath to come," it is not because they are unloving and self-righteous, but rather because they could not be truly Christian and do otherwise. They simply believe the words of Christ and try to obey His command.

Once, indeed, someone asked Jesus the direct question: "Lord, are there few that be saved?" (Luke 13:23). He answered simply: "Strive to enter in at the strait gate: for many, I say unto you, will seek to enter in, and not be able."

Now the remarkable thing about all this is that, although most men will die without ever being saved, any person can be saved simply by believing on Christ as his Lord and Saviour! The "narrow way" which leads to eternal life is Christ Himself. Jesus said: "I am the way, the truth, and the life; no man cometh unto the Father, but by me" (John 14:6).

Christ died on the cross to atone for all our sins, and rose again to assure our full forgiveness and justification before God. Now, anyone who really desires to be saved can receive this great salvation merely by trusting in the Lord Jesus as his personal Saviour. He says: "And whosoever will, let him take the water of life freely" (Rev. 22:17). But to the great numbers of men who will die in their sins, he says: "Ye will not come to me that ye might have life" (John 5:40).

3. Question: "Is not the doctrine of Christ the only doctrine that should be preached today?"

Answer: There is a widespread feeling among professing Christians today, especially among the young people, that Bible doctrines are confusing and divisive and that we should therefore simply "preach Christ." However, many such people really do not understand the full scope and implications of the "doctrine of Christ" as the Scriptures present it. And it must be remembered, of course, that it is in the Bible, and the Bible alone, that we have any real information about Christ or His teachings.

The phrase itself occurs only once in the Bible, in II John 9, 10. "Whosoever transgresseth, and abideth not in the doctrine of Christ, hath not God. He that abideth in the doctrine of Christ, he hath both the Father and the Son. If there come any unto you and bring not this doctrine, receive him not into your house, neither bid him God speed." The vital importance of the doctrine of Christ is strikingly evident in this passage. The "house" spoken of is probably the "church," so it is stressed here that no one should be invited as a speaker, or admited as a member, or in any way encouraged in his activities, if he rejects this doctrine.

It is most important therefore that we understand what the doctrine of Christ entails. The Greek word for "doctrine" means simply "teaching" and is often so translated. Thus the doctrine of Christ is simply the "teaching of Christ." Furthermore, the Greek construction here means, not the "teaching about Christ," but rather the "teaching by Christ."

Thus the doctrine of Christ means nothing less than the body of truth included in the teachings of the Lord Jesus Christ, and is therefore a whole system of doctrine. Everything taught by Christ concerning Himself, the world, and all things is incorporated therein.

These teachings can all be conveniently grouped in three categories: (1) the person of Christ; (2) the work of Christ; and (3) the lordship of Christ. Or, in other words, who He is, what He does, and what this means to us. The correct "doctrine" concerning each of these is absolutely essential to genuine Christianity and to the true knowledge of Christ.

Thus, with respect first to the doctrine of the person of Christ, He said: "I am the way, the truth and the life; no man cometh unto the Father, but by me" (John 14:6). He also said: "He that believeth on him is not condemned: but he that believeth not is condemned already, because he hath not believed in the name of the only begotten Son of God" (John 3:18).

Not only must we believe in His deity as the unique Son of God, but also in His perfect humanity, as the Son of man. "Hereby know ye the Spirit of God: Every spirit that confesseth that Jesus Christ is come in the flesh is of God: And every spirit that confesseth not that Jesus Christ is come in the flesh is not of God" (I John 4:2, 3). He must also be accepted as the Christ— that is, as the promised Messiah, the anointed Saviour. "Who is a liar but he that denieth that Jesus is the Christ? He is antichrist, that denieth the Father and the Son" (I John 2:22).

Thus the eternal God has become flesh in Jesus Christ. He is not part God and part man, but rather wholly God and wholly man—the God-man. He was not a sinner, however, but was man as God had originally intended man to be. He is the "last Adam" (I Cor. 15:45), but did not fall as did the first Adam. In order to be free from inherent sin, He came into the world by miraculous conception and virgin birth, and, as God, He likewise remained free from actual sin. All of this—His eternal pre-existence as the living Word, His incarnation through the Virgin Birth, His perfect and sinless humanity united forever in full identity with His absolute deity, His anointing as the eternal Prophet, great High Priest, and King of Kings, is included in the doctrine of the person of Christ.

Secondly, with respect to the work of Christ, He said: "Thus it is written, and thus it behoved Christ to suffer, and to rise from the dead the third day: And that repentance and remission of sins should be preached in his name among all nations" (Luke 24:46, 47). The atoning death of the Lord Jesus on the cross, followed by His wonderful resurrection from the grave, is the central and climactic event of history. The "gospel" of Jesus Christ is the "glad tidings" concerning what He has done for us.

His work includes the work of creation, the work of conservation (that is, of "salvation") and the work of consummation. "By him were all things created" (Col. 1:16), and "by him all things consist [or 'hold together']" (Col. 1:17). Furthermore, "having made peace through the blood of his cross, by him to reconcile all things unto himself" (Col. 1:20), God will ultimately "gather together in one all things in Christ, both which are in heaven and which are on earth, even in him" (Eph. 1:10). "For of him, and through him, and to him are all things: to whom be glory forever" (Rom. 11:36).

The doctrine of the work of Christ therefore includes the doctrine of creation, all the doctrines of salvation, and all the doctrines associated with His second coming and the consummation of all things. And all of this is included in the "gospel"—the "good news" which we are to "preach to every creature" (Mark 16:15). It is significant that the word for "gospel" occurs 105 times in the New Testament. The first occurrence, Matthew 4:23, stresses the ultimate consummation, and the last occurrence, Revelation 14:6, looks back to the original creation. The central (53rd) occurrence is in the definitive passage on the gospel, I Corinthians 15:1, 2, where the Apostle Paul says: "I declare unto you the gospel which I preached unto you, which also ye received [literally 'received once for all'], and wherein ye stand [literally 'continue to stand']; by which also ye are saved [literally 'being saved']." He then proceeds to define the gospel as follows: ". . . that Christ died for our sins according to the scriptures; and that he was buried, and that he rose again the third day according to the scriptures" (I Cor. 15:3, 4).

The pre-eminent importance of believing and preaching this gospel, and no other, is indicated by Paul in Galatians 1:8, 12: "But though we, or an angel from heaven, preach any other gospel unto you than that which we have preached unto you, let him be accursed. . . . For I neither received it of man, neither was I taught it, but by the revelation of Jesus Christ."

The doctrine of the lordship of Christ is the third and final part of the "doctrine of Christ," and this includes all His other teachings. When one truly accepts Christ as his Saviour, he also accepts Him as Lord of his life (Rom. 10:9). He will therefore gladly believe all His teachings and seek, as God enables, to obey His commandments. If he deliberately rejects or disobeys His word, there is room for serious doubt as to the genuineness of his acceptance of Christ, and therefore of his salvation. This great doctrine of the lordship of Christ has already been discussed in Section V - 4, to which it would be well for the reader to refer again at this point.

4. Question: "How can God hold man responsible for his actions if He has foreordained all things?"

Answer: The old theological conflict between "predestination" and "free will," usually associated respectively with the names Calvinism and Arminianism, can probably never be settled completely, since it is impossible for finite human minds to comprehend adequately the infinite wisdom of God. Everyone of sound mind is conscious continually of facing and making decisions of many kinds. Yet, when he makes such a decision, he must recognize that there have been many factors beyond his control which affected his decision. In fact, it could even be argued that if all such factors could be analyzed, it would turn out that it was actually inevitable that he would make the particular decision he did. His decision was really his own decision, and therefore he is responsible for it, and yet at the same time it was a foreordained certainty that he would make that decision!

This seems on the face of it contradictory, and yet it is somehow intrinsic in the nature of things. The problem itself is independent of whether a person believes in God or not. It has an exact counterpart in the scientific realm, in the conflict between determinism and indeterminacy. Many scientists believe that, if all the characteristics of all particles could be determined at any one instant, it would be theoretically possible to calculate all subsequent positions of the particles and, therefore, that all events were fundamentally predetermined by the initial conditions when the universe began. On the other hand, the famous principle of uncertainty says in effect that, since it must always be theoretically impossible to measure both the location and position of any given particle at any instant, one can never predict its future behavior. In that sense, therefore, every such particle is "free." This paradox is also reflected in the well-known problem of the dual nature of light, which behaves both as a wave motion and as a particle motion, even though these seem superficially to be mutually exclusive.

In the psychological realm, the term "behaviorism" is often applied to the system teaching that the actions of each person are directly caused by genetic and environmental factors over which he has no control and for which he therefore has no responsibility. This, of course, must be somehow balanced against the psychological awareness by each rational person that he does to some extent at least have freedom to make decisions and to control his own behavior.

The only really satisfying resolution of these basic paradoxes is to recognize that both sides of the coin are real, even though we can view only one side at a time. It is like the two parallel lines which finally come together at a distance of infinity.

It is not contradictory therefore, but rather complementary, to hold that man determines his own decisions and actions and yet also to recognize that God in some inscrutable way has foreordained those very things. Although admitting we cannot really understand this paradox, we can accept both aspects of it by faith and then act accordingly, trusting God to make it all clear in eternity.

The most important decision of all, of course, is the decision to accept or reject God's offer of eternal salvation through the Lord Jesus Christ. All other decisions and their corresponding actions are either contributory to, or derivative from, this decision. The relation between predestination and free will is most clearly brought to focus on this question.

One thing seems quite certain—the Scriptures teach that both God's sovereignty and man's free responsibility are components of this supremely important decision. The Bible emphasizes the universal fact of sin and guilt on man's part. "As it is written, There is none righteous, no not one. . . . that all the world may become guilty before God" (Rom. 3:10, 19).

It also stresses that the death and resurrection of the Lord Jesus Christ were of adequate universality and efficacy to atone for the sin and guilt of all men everywhere. "He is the propitiation for our sins; and not for ours only, but also for the sins of the whole world"

(I John 2:2). ". . . that he by the grace of God should taste death for every man" (Heb. 2:9).

God, in His Word, offers this great salvation freely to anyone who will simply believe and receive it as an unmerited gift. "For the wages of sin is death; but the gift of God is eternal life through Jesus Christ, our Lord" (Rom. 6:23). "Whosoever will, let him take the water of life freely" (Rev. 22:17).

Also, each man is held responsible for the consequences of making a wrong decision. "He that believeth not the Son shall not see life but the wrath of God abideth on him" (John 3:36). "The Lord Jesus shall be revealed from heaven with his mighty angels, In flaming fire taking vengeance on them that know not God, and that obey not the gospel of our Lord Jesus Christ" (II Thess. 1:7, 8).

It is clear, therefore, that every person, without exception, can be saved if he wants to be, by coming in simple faith to accept Jesus Christ as his personal Lord and Saviour. And yet, we also read that Jesus said, "No man can come to me, except the Father which hath sent me draw him" (John 6:44). He also said, "Ye have not chosen me, but I have chosen you" (John 15:16). When the gospel was preached, it was said that "As many as were ordained to eternal life, believed" (Acts 13:48).

A person who has accepted Christ and been born again through faith in Him knows that he has done so voluntarily. Yet, when he reflects more carefully, he sees that many different circumstances—his family background, his friends, his personal difficulties, the messages and testimonies he has heard, the Scriptures he has read—have all contributed to that decision.

Then he begins to see that God was working in his life long before he came to the actual point of decision. It's as though he had come to a single great doorway in an endless wall, over which was inscribed the words: "By me, if any man enter in, he shall be saved" (John 10:9). And so, he voluntarily accepts the invitation and enters the door.

To his astonished gratitude, he finds himself in a magnificent paradise stretching as far as he can see. Glancing back at the gateway through which he had entered, he is amazed that there is no gate to be seen at all. Instead, on the wall are emblazoned the words: "Chosen in him before the foundation of the world" (Eph. 1:4).

Although we cannot, in our present finite understanding, completely resolve the mystery surrounding God's "determinate counsel and foreknowledge" (Acts 2:23), we may nevertheless derive great joy

123

and strength from His assurance that we who have acknowledged His Son as Saviour and Lord have been "predestinated according to the purpose of him who worketh all things after the counsel of his own will" (Eph. 1:11).

For those who are not yet believing Christians, on the other hand, the issue remains one of human responsibility—either to live a life of absolute holiness and sinless perfection from birth to death (as did Jesus Christ), or else to come in repentant faith to that One who died for man's sin and was raised for his justification. For it is written that "whosoever believeth in him should not perish, but have eternal life" (John 3:15).

5. "Question: Can a person who has been saved ever lose his salvation?"

Answer: The Scriptures contain many sharp warnings against spiritual complacency. It is easily possible for a person who is a professing Christian to fall into gross sin, or even to become an apostate from the faith. "For if after they have escaped the pollutions of the world through the knowledge of the Lord and Saviour Jesus Christ, they are again entangled therein, and overcome, the latter end is worse with them than the beginning. For it had been better for them not to have known the way of righteousness, than, after they have known it, to turn from the holy commandment delivered unto them" (II Peter 2:20, 21).

Such warnings as the above, and there are many in the Bible, clearly indicate the real danger in a superficial "decision" or "acceptance" of Christ. In fact, one who falls away from the faith, after he has really understood the truth of the gospel in its fulness, can never be brought back again! "For it is impossible for those who were once enlightened, and have tasted of the heavenly gift, and were made partakers of the Holy Ghost, And have tasted the good word of God, and the powers of the world to come, If they shall fall away, to renew them again to repentance; seeing they crucify to themselves the Son of God afresh, and put him to an open shame" (Heb. 6:4-6).

From these passages and many others, it seems quite certain that if a "saved" person ever comes to the point of repudiating his faith in the Holy Scriptures and the Lord Jesus Christ, he becomes irrevocably condemned and lost. He, knowing that Christ is God and that He died and rose again for his redemption, has knowingly and wilfully rejected Him, and there is nothing else God can do for such a man. "There remaineth no more sacrifice for sins, but a certain

124

fearful looking for of judgment and fiery indignation" (Heb. 10: 26, 27).

But there does remain the legitimate question as to whether such a person was ever really saved. The Bible, in fact, seems to indicate otherwise. John, speaking of such people, says, "They went out from us, but they were not of us; for if they had been of us, they would no doubt have continued with us" (I John 2:19).

The classic example is Judas Iscariot. He was one of the twelve original apostles, apparently a believer and a close follower of the Lord Jesus for over three years. Yet all along he was actually unsaved! Early in His ministry, Jesus said, in fact, "Have not I chosen you twelve, and one of you is a devil [or, literally, an 'adversary']?" (John 6:70). When he finally betrayed Jesus and fell from his position, it was so that "he might go to his own place" (Acts 1:25).

It would, in fact, be a contradiction in language if a person could really be "saved" and then become unsaved again. He has been "saved" from the penalty of sin (Rom. 5:9), from condemnation (Rom. 8:1), and from hell (Jude 23). If, then, he finally ends up condemned to hell, he obviously was not "saved" from these things.

A similar anachronism would be the gift of "eternal life" if it were not really eternal! And yet the Scripture says, "He that believeth on the Son hath [not 'hopes to have,' but 'has' right now!] everlasting life" (John 3:36). If one ever could lose such a life, it obviously would not have been everlasting.

One of the clearest emphases of the gospel is that salvation is a free gift (Eph. 2:8, 9; Rom. 6:23, etc.), attained not by works of any kind. Again, it is semantically inconsistent to suggest that, although a man is not saved by good works, he must maintain good works to keep his salvation. For if he must keep salvation by his works, it is obvious that he cannot really attain it without these works. If salvation is really the gift of God's grace, on the other hand, as the Bible teaches, then how can there be a price one has to pay to earn it?

On top of all this, we have the positive assurance of Christ Himself: "My sheep hear my voice, and I know them, and they follow me: And I give unto them eternal life; and they shall never perish, neither shall any one pluck them out of my hand" (John 10:27, 28). Thus we don't hang on to Him—rather He holds us! In the upper room, He prayed, "Holy Father, keep through thine own name those whom thou hast given me. . . . I pray . . . that thou shouldst keep them from the evil one" (John 17:11, 15). There can of course be no doubt that the Father will answer the prayer of His beloved Son.

125

The Scriptures seem plainly to teach, therefore, that one who is really saved, "in Christ Jesus before the world began" (II Tim. 1:9), is eternally saved and secure in Christ.

On the other hand, these marvelous assurances must be balanced by the many Biblical warnings against falling away from the faith. These two apparently paradoxical lines of truth do not contradict, but rather complement and reinforce each other. There is firm ground for assurance of salvation, but there is no ground for presumption.

A person who has really and certainly been "born of the Spirit" (John 3:6) has been made "partaker of the divine nature" (II Peter 1:4), and "he cannot [practice] sin because he is born of God" (I John 3:9). He has been given the spirit of a "sound mind" (II Tim. 1:7) and has been "transformed by the renewing of his mind" (Rom. 12:2), so that he no longer is a doubter and critic of God's Word, but rather seeks to understand and believe all of it. Such a person indeed "shall never fall" (II Peter 1:10), for "he that is begotten of God keepeth himself, and that wicked one toucheth him not" (I John 5:18). He may stumble on occasion, and must continually seek God's forgiveness and restoration to joy and peace (I John 1:7-9), but henceforth the "love of Christ constrains him," so that he will seek no longer to "live unto himself, but unto him who died for him and rose again" (II Cor. 5:14, 15).

The essential thing, therefore, is for each man to make absolutely sure that he is really saved. He must not base his hope of salvation on his good works, his church, a religious experience, or anything else, except the Lord Jesus Christ and His substitutionary death and resurrection, as revealed in the Scriptures. "Examine yourselves, whether ye be in the faith; prove your own selves" (II Cor. 13:5).

And if he is really saved, having come to Christ in true repentance and faith, he has been "born again" (I Peter 1:23), and the Holy Spirit has come "that he may abide with you forever" (John 14:16).

6. Question: *"Since all religions are basically the same, why do Christians insist that one must believe in Christ to be saved?"*

Answer: All religions are *not* the same—Biblical Christianity is absolutely unique among all the religions and philosophies of mankind. Its claim to be necessary for salvation is based squarely on the uniquely powerful evidences for its truth and finality. Actually, true

Christianity is not a religion, but a person, Jesus Christ. "By him, and for him, were all things created" (note Col. 1:16, 17).

Thus Christianity is unique in the following fundamental respects, among many others:

(1) Only in the Bible is God revealed as the one eternal, personal Creator, who brought the entire universe into existence by His own Word. All other religions accept matter as eternal in some form, with their gods thus confined and limited in greater or lesser degree. The God of the Bible has all power and is Himself therefore the One who establishes the basis for human salvation.

(2) Christianity alone is centered in the historical events associated with a Person—the birth, death, resurrection, and imminent, glorious return of Jesus Christ. Other religions are invariably based on the teachings, rather than the acts, of their founders.

(3) Jesus Christ alone, of all men in history, has conquered man's greatest enemy—death. The founders of other religions are all dead and their tombs venerated. The tomb of Christ is empty, and His bodily resurrection from the grave is the best-proved fact of all history! The fact that He alone could overcome death demonstrates that He alone has all power. He Himself said, "I am the way, the truth, and the life: no man cometh unto the Father but by me" (John 14:6).

(4) All other religions of the world are fundamentally just one religion—one of salvation by works. Each religion sets up a particular set of religious rites, of commands and restrictions, and of ethical principles to follow, and then teaches that if a man does these things he will be saved. The human origin of each of these systems is indicated by the fact that each is humanly attainable. The Bible, however, sets its moral and ethical standard as the very holiness and perfection of God Himself, and demands nothing less than this for salvation. Obviously, no man would invent a standard which was utterly impossible for any man to keep.

(5) The man Christ Jesus, alone of all men who ever lived, maintained in every respect a life of perfect holiness and full obedience to the Father, thus demonstrating that He was the God-Man. He then died for the sins of all men and thus can offer full pardon and His own nature of perfect holiness to anyone who receives Him by personal faith. While other religions claim to offer salvation by supposed good works, Christ alone offers salvation by grace alone, to be received only through faith in Him. To the one who truly believes on

127

Him, He then gives through the Holy Spirit a new nature, enabling that one to live a life pleasing to God.

There is no mere "religion" in all the world like this. Jesus Christ is the world's Creator, and its only true Redeemer. "Neither is there salvation in any other; for there is none other name under heaven, given among men, whereby we must be saved" (Acts 4:12).

7. Question: "What is the gift of tongues?"

Answer: The practice of "speaking in tongues" has been common among people of the various "Pentecostal" denominations for about sixty years, and has been picked up by groups in many other denominations, both Catholic and Protestant, during the past fifteen years or so. These utterances are attributed by those who advocate the practice to a supernatural manifestation of the Holy Spirit in the body of the believer, often accompanied by visions and thrilling physical sensations. Some claim the experience is a necessary evidence of salvation; others view it as a special enduement of power for effective Christian life and witness.

Christian opponents of the practice, however, have believed it to be either a psychological phenomenon with a purely natural basis or else, in some cases, to be caused by demonic forces. While not doubting the sincerity or Christian character of those who speak in tongues, they insist that the phenomenon is neither a necessary nor a sufficient evidence of the operation of the Holy Spirit in one's life. That is, many of those who have experienced these "glossolalia" have later fallen into serious sins and even rank unbelief (therefore it is not sufficient in itself). On the other hand, there are great numbers of godly and evangelistically fruitful Christians who have never spoken in tongues (therefore it is not really necessary).

There seems often also to be a form of spiritual pride generated in people who have the experience, along with a tendency to consider others as second-rate Christians, who must be diligently persuaded to seek the experience for themselves.

It is significant that the phenomenon of speaking in ecstatic tongues is not unique to Christian sects. The practice is known to be present among pagan tribes, spiritists, certain Islamic cults, and various others who do not consider it in any way as one of the Christian gifts of the Holy Spirit. Furthermore, since there are some people at least who can work themselves up into a session of tongue-speaking more or less at will, using definite physiological techniques, the phenomenon

128

may at least sometimes have a purely naturalistic and physiological explanation.

The definitive answer, however, must always be the Biblical answer, not the variable and uncertain criteria of personal experience. Speaking in tongues is mentioned in only three books of the New Testament, indicating thereby that it is probably not one of the major doctrines or practices of the church.

The first reference is in Mark 16:17-20, where it is listed along with casting out demons, freedom from harm by snakebite and poison, and healing the sick, as signs that would confirm the word preached by the Lord's apostles. These signs were actually fulfilled on various occasions during the ministry of the apostles, but there is no statement in this passage alone as to the duration or frequency of such miracles.

The definitive passage on the subject is in Acts 2:1-12, when the believers for the first time were all "filled with the Holy Ghost and began to speak with other tongues, as the Spirit gave them utterance." The context makes it plain that these tongues were actual languages, and enabled the Christians to communicate in the diverse languages of the crowd in Jerusalem on the day of Pentecost, "the wonderful works of God." The miraculous nature of this sign so impressed the listeners that a great multitude of the assembled Jews accepted Christ when Peter preached the gospel to them.

The same sign of miraculous language ability was given when the Samaritans (a mixture of Jew and Gentile) first turned to Christ (Acts 8:14-17), again when Gentiles first accepted Christ (Acts 10:44-48), and finally when a special group at Ephesus who were apparently secondhand followers of John the Baptist first heard the true gospel (Acts 19:1-7). There are no other references to tongues in the book of Acts.

It is important to note from the foregoing that this gift was a "sign" to confirm the spoken word of the gospel, and also that it consisted of a miraculous ability to speak that gospel in a real human language hitherto unfamiliar to the speaker. It is important also to recognize that every use of the word in the New Testament can be understood in this way. There is no need at all, Scripturally, to think of a "tongue" as ecstatic gibberish. The word itself always means either a "language" or else the actual physical organ of speech.

The only epistle in which tongues are mentioned is I Corinthians, chapters 12, 13, and 14. The practice evidently was not in use, or at least was not a problem, in the other churches of the New Testament. It is listed as one of the "gifts of the Holy Spirit" to the Corinthian church (I Cor. 12:10), though it is plain that only certain ones in the church had that particular gift (I Cor. 12:28-30).

Because of its somewhat spectacular nature, those who had the gift of tongues were tending to display it unnecessarily and uselessly, since the congregation generally could not understand what they were saying (I Cor. 14:2, 5, 9, etc.). Paul commanded therefore that no one speak in tongues unless either he or someone else in the church could interpret (that is, "translate") the language in which he was speaking (I Cor. 14:13, 28). He reminded them again that this gift of tongues was intended as a "sign" to unbelievers (I Cor. 14:22), not as a thrill or a display to believers.

The contrast of Paul's descriptions and instructions regarding tongues in these chapters with the present-day phenomenon as usually practiced is quite sharp. One can hardly avoid the conclusion that the Biblical gift of tongues is not the same thing at all as its modern namesake.

This fact lends special significance to Paul's statement that "tongues shall cease" (I Cor. 13:8). As a gift of the Spirit for the purpose of "confirming the Word," it would be withdrawn when its use had been served. In the apostolic period, when there was no written Word to support the words preached, such a gift was of real value, especially when the gospel was first going to a new language group or into a new region. But once the New Testament Scriptures had been given, little or no need existed for this or other miraculous gifts, and they were gradually removed. This is quite likely what Paul meant when he said, "When that which is perfect is come, then that which is in part shall be done away" (I Cor. 13:10).

With the complete written Word of God as we now have it, there is no need or value any longer in special "signs." The Holy Scriptures can meet every need that anyone can ever have, if he will only believe and obey them.

130

Chapter X

THE CHURCH

1. Question: "Which is the true church?"

Answer: The doctrine of the church was introduced for the first time in the New Testament, at least by that name, when the Lord Jesus said: "I will build my church, and the gates of hell shall not prevail against it" (Matt. 16:18). Since that time there has been no little controversy as to which church is really His church. Many sects and denominations have claimed to trace their lineage directly back to the New Testament church. Many others have thought that the original church disappeared and that their particular denomination or group constituted a restoration of the apostolic church.

On the other hand, many Christians have reacted against the confusion of so many different kinds of churches, each with its own distinctive claims and characteristics, by insisting that Christ's church is not a visible church at all, but rather an "invisible church," with no buildings or meetings, composed merely of all true believers in Christ. This concept is also called the "universal church," or simply "the true church."

The question as to which of these claims is correct can be resolved only by careful study of the usage of the word "church" in the New Testament. The Greek word is *ekklesia*, which means literally "the called-out ones," and it occurs 115 times. In three of these occurrences it is translated "assembly" and refers to a meeting of the inhabitants of a city, who were "called out" of their homes and businesses to participate in a town meeting. Once it refers to the congregation of Israel, as the people assembled together in the wilderness prior to entering the promised land.

In the vast majority of its other occurrences, at least 86 and more likely 96 times, it clearly refers to an actual congregation of Christian believers in a particular community or, if in the plural, to several such congregations. For example, the final occurrence of the word, in Revelation 22:16, is with this meaning: "I Jesus have sent mine angel to testify unto you these things in the churches."

In the remaining occurrences (15, or possibly 25, times) the word seems to have a broader meaning than that of a particular local church. An example is Ephesians 5:25: "Christ loved the church and gave himself for it." Matthew 16:18, quoted earlier, is another example.

The fact that in the great majority of occurrences of the word a particular local church or group of such churches is meant (approximately 5 to 1) would seem to indicate that this must be the primary, definitive meaning of the word. Therefore any other meaning must be a derivative meaning tied in some clear way to the basic meaning. The idea of an actual physical assembly of people is thus implicit, as is evident also from the four times it is used for a non-Christian congregation.

The relatively few cases where the word is used in the broader sense can be harmonized with the basic meaning by recognizing two derivative meanings, both retaining the basic concept of a real assembly of Christian believers.

One is the "generic" usage, in which the concept of the local church, rather than a particular local church, is in view. An illustration is Philippians 3:6, where Paul, speaking of his pre-Christian experiences, mentioned as evidence of his former religion: "Concerning zeal, persecuting the church. . . ." In actuality, he was at that time persecuting many local churches.

The other is the "prophetic" usage, anticipating the time when a great future assembly of all who have believed in Christ since He first founded the church will be called in heaven. This is the emphasis of Hebrews 12:22, 23: "Ye are come unto mount Sion, and unto the city of the living God, the heavenly Jerusalem, and to an innumerable company of angels. To the general assembly and church of the firstborn, which are written in heaven, and to God the Judge of all, and to the spirits of just men made perfect." Similarly, in Ephesians 3:21: "Unto him be glory in the church by Christ Jesus throughout all ages, world without end." This heavenly and eternal church will ultimately be composed of all who have received Christ as their Saviour and Lord, but it has not yet actually come into being as a church, or assembly.

In the present world, therefore, New Testament usage compels us to recognize that the true church is a local group of Christian believers, not an "invisible" or "universal" entity of some kind with no physical substance, no meetings, no church officers, no ordinances, and no organized work of evangelism or worship or training.

Furthermore, a true local church is composed of both men and women, young and old, educated and uneducated, new believers and mature Christian leaders, people of all types of backgrounds, occupations, and abilities. This is especially emphasized in one of the key chapters on the church, I Corinthians 12, where the church is described as a "body," with all kinds of "members," each one serving its own unique function in the working of the whole body. "From [Christ] the whole body fitly joined together and compacted by that which every joint supplieth, according to the effectual working in the measure of every part, maketh increase of the body unto the edifying of itself in love" (Eph. 4:16).

Thus, a men's fellowship or a student evangelization society or a mission to alcoholics or any similar specialized fellowship or ministry is not a church, no matter how effective and worthwhile it may be, and regardless whether it functions on a local or national or international level. Neither is an organized denominational group of churches a "church."

The exact organizational form and methods of a local church are somewhat flexible, as is evident from the differences between, say, the first church at Jerusalem, the churches addressed in Paul's epistles, and the churches addressed by John in Revelation 2 and 3. The New Testament church obviously developed through different stages in the apostolic period, and there is likewise room today for differences in details of organization and emphasis, depending on the local situation. One should remember that there can be no such thing as a true *New Testament church* today, for the obvious reason that the church of the New Testament period did not yet have the New Testament to guide it, as we do!

Regardless of local and temporal differences, however, the true church in the Biblical context will be any local church which acknowledges the Lord Jesus Christ as its one Head, accepts the Holy Scriptures as the divinely inspired and fully authoritative basis of its doctrine and practice, and seeks to obey Christ's Great Commission, as given in Matthew 28:18-20, of winning men to Christ, baptizing them, and then training them in all phases of Christian truth and life.

2. Question: *"With so many cults and denominations, how can I decide which are true and which are false?"*

Answer: It is certainly understandable that even a very earnest and sincere seeker after truth would be confused over the religious situation today, with hundreds of denominations, sects, and cults in Christendom alone, as well as hundreds more in other countries and cultures, and with new religious movements arising almost every day. Nevertheless, God has provided adequate instruction for us to enable us to "know the spirit of truth and the spirit of error" (I John 4:6) if we really want to do so.

There are three criteria which are especially helpful in evaluating a particular cult or movement. These are the teachings of its leaders concerning the Bible, concerning Christ, and concerning the way of salvation, respectively.

1. *Attitude Toward the Bible.*—The Bible claims, many hundreds of times, to be the written Word of God. The Old Testament Scriptures were accepted by Christ and the Apostles as divinely inspired and completely infallible. Jesus said: "The scriptures cannot be broken" (John 10:35). With respect to the New Testament, He promised His apostles that "the Holy Ghost shall teach you all things, and bring all things to your remembrance, whatsoever I have said unto you" (John 14:26), and that "the Spirit of truth will guide you into all truth" (John 16:13).

Therefore, during the first century, the apostles who had been with Christ, had witnessed His resurrection, and had received these promises, gradually wrote down the Gospels and Epistles which now comprise the New Testament. These were readily received and recognized by the early Christians as inspired Scriptures. The apostles claimed, of course, that these writings were divinely inspired and authoritative, and true Christians have always accepted them as such.

Finally, the last of the apostles, John the Beloved, near the end of the first century, was enabled to look prophetically into the future ages and to write down the last of the true Scriptures, the book of Revelation. This completed God's written Word. To emphasize this, John closed the book with these awesome words, "For I testify unto every man that heareth the words of the prophecy of this book, If any man shall add unto these things, God shall add unto him the plagues that are written in this book: And if any man shall take away from the words of the book of this prophecy, God shall take away his part out of the book of life" (Rev. 22:18, 19).

These last words of Christ's apostles give us a most important rule. The Scriptures are fully inspired, even to the very words, and those who would add to them or take away from them are, to the extent they do so, false teachers.

In general, *cultists* have been guilty of "adding to" the Scriptures, claiming either that the writings of their own founders were divinely

134

inspired or that the interpretations of their leaders were uniquely necessary and authoritative. *Modernists* and *liberals*, on the other hand, have been guilty of the even more serious error of "taking away from" Scripture, culling out or allegorizing those portions which they decide are unscientific or unreasonable to modern man. The true teacher, however, will accept *all* of the Scriptures, and *only* the Scriptures, as the infallible Word of God.

2. *Attitude Toward Christ.*—A true Christian teacher will gladly accept and proclaim Jesus Christ as He is, true God and true man. "Who is a liar but he that denieth that Jesus is the Christ? He is antichrist, that denieth the Father and the Son" (I John 2:22). "For many deceivers are entered into the world, who confess not that Jesus Christ is come in the flesh. This is a deceiver and an antichrist" (II John 7). "There shall be false teachers among you, who privily shall bring in damnable heresies, even denying the Lord that bought [that is, 'redeemed'] them" (II Peter 2:1).

Error concerning the person of Christ can take either the form of the ancient Gnostic heresy, which denied His true humanity, or that of the modern Agnostic heresy, which denies His true deity. The latter considers Him to be a great man and great religious teacher and leader, but rejects His virgin birth, His sinless life, His substitutionary atonement, and His bodily resurrection and ascension. Any cult or denomination or religious movement which does not clearly and forcefully proclaim the Lord Jesus Christ both as the perfect Son of man and the only begotten Son of God, "the Lord, which is, and which was, and which is to come, the Almighty" (Rev. 1:8) is false, and should be rejected.

3. *Attitude Toward Salvation.*—The gospel of Christ is "the power of God unto salvation, to everyone that believeth" (Rom. 1:16). The word "gospel" means "good news," not "good advice." It does not tell us what we must do and not do in order to earn salvation, but rather what Christ has done to provide salvation as a free gift. "For by grace are ye saved through faith; and that not of yourselves; it is the gift of God; Not of works, lest any man should boast" (Eph. 2:8, 9).

Every other religion under the sun, whether pseudo-Christian or non-Christian, panders to man's pride by teaching him there is something he can do to earn, or to help in earning, his own salvation. Only true Biblical Christianity recognizes man as he really is, utterly lost in sin, destined for eternal separation from God. The gospel, "by which ye are saved," is the glorious news that "Christ died for our sins" (I Cor. 15:1, 3), and that we can be saved by grace, through personal faith in Christ, plus nothing else whatever! Any religion which teaches otherwise is, to that extent, false. Paul said, "If any man preach any other gospel unto you than that ye have received, let him be accursed" (Gal. 1:9). One who is truly saved by God's grace in Christ will, of course, then seek to follow Christ and His Word in all things, not to earn salvation, but in love and gratitude for His glorious gift of cleansing and everlasting life.

3. Question: *"Which is better—being an active member of a particular church, or being available to serve as needed in different churches and inter-church organizations?"*

Answer: Jesus Christ established only one organization for the propagation of His gospel, and He promised that it would survive until the very end of the age. That institution is the church. He said: "I will build my church and the gates of hell shall not prevail against it" (Matt. 16:18). The Great Commission was given to the church when He said: "Go ye therefore and teach [i.e., 'make disciples from'] all nations, baptizing them in the name of the Father, and of the Son, and of the Holy Ghost: Teaching [i.e., 'indoctrinating'] them to observe all things whatsoever I have commanded you: And lo, I am with you alway, even unto the end of the world. Amen" (Matt. 28:19, 20).

The ministry of the church, therefore, is first to win people to Christ, then to baptize them, and finally to teach and train them in the Christian faith and life. This ministry was first given to the twelve apostles, who established the first church in Jerusalem, and was to continue unchanged until Christ returns.

It is important, therefore, for Christians to understand the New Testament doctrine of the church and its ministry. The word "church" occurs 115 times in the New Testament. In the great majority of these occurrences, it refers clearly and specifically to a particular local church or group of local churches. Each local church (the Greek word translated "church" means basically "those who have been called out") consisted of the local believers—all ages, all classes, both sexes—organized together for the purpose of carrying out Christ's commission in their own locality. Each person was a "member" of the "body," with Christ Himself the "head" (I Cor. 12:12, 27; Col. 1:18; Eph. 4:11-16; Rom. 12:4, 5), with his own particular gift and function to fulfill in the ministry of the church.

Unfortunately, with the passing of time, disagreements arose within the churches as to particular aspects of the content and implications of Christ's commission, and eventually there developed the numerous different kinds of churches we have today. This in turn has led to a wide variety of inter-denominational councils and fellowships, all concerned with the re-establishment of some aspect of the original unity of the churches, especially in their evangelistic ministry.

In this admittedly confusing situation, we must not forget Christ's original promise of the perpetuity of the church and that this applies especially to the institution of the local church. There have thus always been, and always will be, local churches which carry out His Great Commission. They do this imperfectly, and they may make mistakes both in doctrine and in practice. Nevertheless, the Lord uses them and blesses their ministry, so long as they continue to adhere to the Scriptures as the infallible Word of God, believe in Christ as the eternal Son of God, preach Him as the only Saviour from sin, baptize those who accept Him by faith, and seek as best they understand it to teach His Word and keep His commandments.

By all means, therefore, a true Christian should be an active member of a local church in the community where he lives. This is the New Testament pattern, and this will not be rescinded before Christ returns. It is true nowadays that he must make a choice which the early Christians did not have to face, namely, which local church he should join. The choice should, of course, be made primarily on the basis of the degree of adherence of the church to the entire teaching of the Word of God, in so far as he understands it.

Many Christians today drift from one church to another for purely personal, rather than doctrinal, reasons and therefore are never really satisfied with their church relation. Sometimes they become active in one of the inter-denominational associations and allow this to become a substitute for the church.

This is not to say that there is not an important place today for such inter-denominational fellowships or associations of churches. But these should recognize the Scriptural priority of the local church as the basic institution for the accomplishment of Christ's commission, and should integrate their particular ministries into that framework. A good example is the Gideons, an association of Christian business and professional men whose purpose is to win people to Christ through personal evangelism and through placing Bibles in public places and giving New Testaments to boys and girls, servicemen, and others. Each member of the Gideons must first of all be a faithful member of a local church, recommended by his pastor. Financial support for the Scripture distribution comes primarily from the churches. The evangelistic thrust of the Gideons is thus as an arm of the church, and the association carefully avoids infringing on the teaching or other ministries of the church.

Scripturally, therefore, each Christian should first of all be a faithful member of a local church in his own community and then, as time and abilities permit, cooperate with other churches and interdenominational groups that are faithful to the Word of God.

4. Question: "What are the gifts of the Holy Spirit?"

Answer: It is unfortunate that the important doctrine of spiritual gifts has come to be identified today almost exclusively with "speaking in tongues" and "faith-healing." Because of the excessive emphasis which some have placed on these particular gifts, most Christians have over-reacted and tend to ignore all the Spirit's gifts. Nevertheless, the truth of the gifts of the Holy Spirit is basic in the proper functioning both of a local church and also of the universal fellowship of believing Christians everywhere.

There are three passages in the New Testament listing these spiritual gifts: I Corinthians 12:7-11, 27-28; Romans 12:4-8; and Ephesians 4:7-11. Each of the three gives a different list, though with some overlapping. Altogether, 17 such gifts are listed, with only the gift of "prophecy" and the gift of "teaching" included in all three lists. The gift of "apostleship," the gift of "helps" (or "ministry"), and the gift of "governments" (or "ruling") are mentioned in two of the lists. These listed only once are the gifts of evangelism, exhortation, mercy, generosity, wisdom, knowledge, faith, healing, tongues, interpretation of tongues, discerning of spirits, and working of miracles.

Two important conclusions may be drawn from the above data. First, the lists are not meant to be complete, since each is different. Therefore, there may be other gifts of the Spirit besides those listed, and the particular gifts manifested may vary with time and place. The second conclusion follows from the first, namely, that specified gifts may be withdrawn from a particular church or region when no longer needed and, indeed, may be withdrawn from the world altogether when their specific ministry has been accomplished. Conversely, other new gifts may be added from time to time as needed.

Thus the "apostles" (one prerequisite to the gift of apostleship was that the one so gifted must have personally seen Christ after His resurrection, as shown in I Cor. 9:1; 15:7-9) ceased to exist in the church after the "Apostolic Era" of the first century. Similarly, the gift of "prophecy" was to cease (I Cor. 13:8), as well as "tongues" and supernatural "knowledge." The church was to be "built upon the foundation of the apostles and prophets" (Eph. 2:20), and once the foundation was laid there was no need for continually re-laying it.

Next to that of the apostleship (I Cor. 12:28), prophecy was the most important of the gifts in the early church (note especially I Cor. 14:1-5). This was the gift by which God transmitted divine revelations to His people (note II Peter 1:21). Before the New Testament Scriptures had been written, it was essential that both the witnessing and worship activities of the church be validated and directed by the Holy Spirit, through the means of His gifts to individuals in the fellowship (see Heb. 2:3, 4).

But once the Scriptures were completed by the "apostles and prophets" who transcribed them, there was no further need for either of these gifts. "That which was perfect [that is, 'complete'] had come, so that which was only partial could be done away" (I Cor. 13:10). In fact, a grave warning against any further pretended "prophecy" was given in the closing words of John, the last of the apostles (Rev. 22:18, 19).

Except perhaps on rare occasions to meet very unusual needs, therefore, most or all of the supernatural gifts of the Holy Spirit were no longer needed or appropriate after the Scriptures were completed. The gift of "pastor-teacher," with the permanent function of leading and training the flock in the understanding and application of the Scriptures, thenceforth replaced that of "prophecy" as the key gift of the Spirit. This is supported by all the other gifts (including new ones from time to time) appropriate for the extension and building-up of the body, as distinct from the earlier ministry of laying the foundation. The gifts of evangelism, helps, governments, etc., are all, of course, essential in the carrying-out of Christ's Great Commission, until He comes again.

It is very important for Christians to understand that the Holy Spirit gives one or more such gifts "to every man to profit withal" (I Cor. 12:7). All true Christians have been endowed with some gift, therefore, and should recognize it as such. No matter how insignificant such a gift may seem, it is neverthelesss quite necessary (I Cor. 12:22) for the proper accomplishment of God's work. The church janitor is as essential as the pastor, and the baby-sitter in the nursery as necessary as the teacher, if the church is to function effectively.

On the other hand, no matter how much attention and praise may be given to one exercising a particular gift (such as the pastor, or evangelist, or musician), he should remember that "all these worketh that one and the selfsame Spirit, dividing to every man severally as He will" (I Cor. 12:11). He is therefore warned "not to think of himself more highly than he ought to think; but to think soberly, according as God hath dealt to every man the measure of faith" (Rom. 12:3).

The above admonition also cautions against one's attempting to exercise a gift which he does not have, or which he has not properly cultivated. For example, there are many who are teaching Bible classes and preaching in pulpits today who really ought not to be! James warns: "My brethren, be not many teachers, knowing that we shall receive the greater condemnation" (James 3:1).

The analogy of the body and its many members, even the least of which is important, is employed in all three of the main passages dealing with the Spirit and His gifts (Rom. 12:5; I Cor. 12:27; Eph. 4:16). This truth of the "body of Christ," and the importance of the ministry of each member in that body, has application both to each local church and also to the eternal and universal church "which is his body, the fulness of him who filleth all in all" (Eph. 1:23).

It is vital, therefore, that each believer carefully determine those gifts that the Holy Spirit has entrusted to him and the means by which he can most effectively contribute to the ministry of his own local church and also to the work of Christ everywhere. He should "stir up the gift of God that is in thee" (II Tim. 1:6), cultivating, training, and using it in the best way possible (I Cor. 14:12). It is legitimate also for him, through prayer and study, to seek also "the best gifts" (I Cor. 12:31; 14:1). And, finally, "as every man hath received the gift, even so minister the same one to another, as good stewards of the manifold grace of God" (I Peter 4:10).

5. Question: "How important is baptism?"

Answer: There is no doubt that the doctrine of baptism is one of the most divisive elements among the various sects and denominations in Christendom and, in fact, one of the chief factors in the establishment of the different denominations in the first place. For example, Baptists and many similar groups believe baptism consists solely of the full immersion of one who has already been saved through personal faith in Christ. A number of other denominations, such as the various groups that developed from the ministry of Alexander

Campbell and others in the early nineteenth century, believe that such immersion is itself a prerequisite to salvation.

Many denominations, including the Roman Catholics and most of the larger Protestant denominations, practice either pouring or sprinkling instead of immersion. In some of these, baptism is considered necessary for salvation, and thus infants are sprinkled, as well as adult converts. Infant baptism, however, is also practiced by various denominations who regard it more as an act of dedication than of salvation.

There are some, including the Greek Orthodox and various Brethren groups, who require "trine immersion," once in the name of each member of the Trinity. Some sects baptize only in the name of Jesus, although most use the Trinitarian formula of Matthew 28:19. A few groups, such as the Quakers and the so-called "ultra-dispensationalists," do not practice water baptism at all.

This is only a sampling of the wide variety of beliefs and practices regarding baptism. In nearly every case, baptism is specified as a prerequisite to membership in the church, and so it is obviously a divisive issue between churches and has been a significant barrier to church union movements.

Each denomination is, of course, able to present a logical defense of its own position on baptism, based on Scripture or tradition or both. In the current generation, however, there has developed a strong reaction against both Scripture and tradition, as well as against the church itself, so it is not surprising that the doctrine of baptism is no longer advocated very strenuously by many professing Christians. This attitude has affected even conservative and fundamentalist groups, so that even in these circles numerous inter-denominational fellowships have sprung up which stress evangelism and Bible study, but which tend to avoid the subjects of baptism and church membership.

Though such a reaction against the divided state of Christendom is understandable, no problem is ever solved by avoiding it. Christianity without baptism is, in fact, not Biblical Christianity at all, as even a superficial reading of the New Testament will show.

The Christian era was introduced in the first place by John the Baptist, who baptized in the Jordan those who desired to prepare themselves for the coming of Christ. The first public act of Christ Himself as He began His ministry was to be baptized by John, thus, as He said, "fulfilling all righteousness" (Matt. 3:15), and serving, in this as in all other aspects of His life, as the perfect Example for those who "follow his steps" (I Peter 2:21). All of Christ's twelve disciples were prepared for Him "beginning from the baptism of John" (Acts 1:22). During His own public ministry, He also, through His disciples, continued the practice of baptizing His converts in water (John 3:22).

After His death and resurrection, and just before His ascension into heaven, the Lord Jesus gave the Great Commission to His church, which was thenceforth to be its basic concern and the focus of all its activities until His return at the end of the age. The Commission consists of three parts, in the following order (see Matt. 28:18-20): (1) "Making disciples from all nations"; (2) baptizing them in the name of the Father, and of the Son, and of the Holy Ghost," and then (3) "teaching them to observe all things whatsoever I have commanded you" (see also Mark 16:15, 16).

Thus, baptism is an integral part of the Christian's Commission from His Lord, and is therefore of highest importance. That the early Christians so regarded it is evident from the fact that wherever it is mentioned in the book of Acts, the above order was always observed. That is, immediately after a man or woman was truly converted to Christ, he was forthwith baptized and thereby identified with the local church, where he was thereafter instructed in the full scope of Christian faith and life. Baptism was not considered as a part of the gospel, by which men are saved (I Cor. 15:1-4), as Paul made clear when he said: "Christ sent me not to baptize, but to preach the gospel" (I Cor. 1:17), but it is an essential part of the Great Commission.

Thus baptism followed immediately upon conversion in the case of the thousands saved on the day of Pentecost (Acts 2:41), the Samaritan believers (Acts 8:12), the Ethiopian eunuch (Acts 8:36), Paul (Acts 9:18), Cornelius (Acts 10:47), Lydia (Acts 16:14, 15), the Philippian jailer (Acts 16:30-33), the Corinthians (Acts 18:8), and others. No exception to this rule is ever mentioned. It seems simply to have been an accepted fact that, as soon as a person trusted in Christ, he would publicly identify himself with the Lord and with His church in his own community by following the Lord in baptism.

In fact, this identification with the Lord is the testimony of the act of baptism itself. "For we are buried with him by baptism into death; that like as Christ was raised up from the dead by the glory of the Father, even so we also should walk in newness of life" (Rom. 6:4).

This brief study has not attempted to discuss or evaluate the particular interpretations of baptism held by specific churches or denominations. In view of the present widespread indifference to the doctrine of baptism itself, it seems necessary first of all to stress the fact of its basic importance. A Christianity which is not rooted in the local church and which does not insist upon baptism as the initial step in the Christian life, no matter how "relevant" it may try to be to the modern world, is simply not Biblical Christianity. Once the believer sees the primary importance of baptism, he should then, of course, search the Scriptures for himself to ascertain their instructions concerning all other aspects thereof.

6. Question: *Why do Christian churches send missionaries to other lands, when they already have their own religions and when there are so many people who still need to be reached here in this country?"*

Answer: There are three main reasons why we should support foreign missions.

The first is simply that Christ commanded it. The Great Commission, which He gave to His disciples, explicitly commands: "Go ye into all the world, and preach the gospel to every creature" (Mark 16:15). He also said: "Ye shall be witnesses unto me both in Jerusalem, and in all Judaea, and in Samaria, and unto the uttermost parts of the earth" (Acts 1:8).

Whether we understand fully the reason for the Commission or not, or even whether we agree with it or not, is therefore beside the point. Since the Lord Jesus commanded it, true Christians must and will try to follow it, either by going themselves or by supporting those who do go. "If a man love me, he will keep my words," Jesus said (John 14:23).

The second reason for foreign missions is that all men desperately need to know the way of salvation. The Bible is exceedingly clear in its emphasis that all men are sinful and rebellious against God and therefore are lost and need to be saved. "There is none that understandeth, there is none that seeketh after God. . . . Now we know that what things soever the law saith, it saith to them who are under the law; that every mouth may be stopped, and all the world may become guilty before God" (Rom. 3:11, 19).

It is true that there are many who do not have the Bible and many who know very little about the true God and His will; in fact, there are no two individuals anywhere who are exactly "equal" in terms of their opportunities to know God. Nevertheless, all men have at least some "light" (in nature, in history, in their own consciences) which points them to God, but they have all rejected or ignored it. "Because that which may be known of God is manifest in them: for

God hath shewed it unto them . . . so that they are without excuse" (Rom. 1:19, 20).

Therefore all men urgently need to learn how to be saved. "For whosoever shall call upon the name of the Lord shall be saved. How then shall they call on him in whom they have not believed? and how shall they believe in him of whom they have not heard? and how shall they hear without a preacher? and how shall they preach, except they be sent?" (Rom. 10:13-15).

The third reason for foreign missions is that only Jesus Christ can meet the need that each man has for salvation. "He is the propitiation for our sins; and not for ours only, but also for the sins of the whole world" (I John 2:2). Jesus said: "I am the way, the truth and the life; no man cometh unto the Father but by me" (John 14:6).

Jesus Christ is uniquely the eternal Son of the only true and living God. His atoning death on the cross paid the price of redemption for all who will come to Him in faith. "Neither is there salvation in any other; for there is none other name under heaven given among men, whereby we must be saved" (Acts 4:12).

Since there is no other God, no other Saviour, and no other way of salvation, it is imperative that Christians do all they can to confront all men everywhere with the offer of free forgiveness and eternal life to all who will receive Christ as personal Saviour. There have been multitudes of individuals, "of all nations, and kindreds, and people, and tongues" (Rev. 7:9), who have responded to this invitation and who gladly testify that Christ has indeed met their need for both present confidence in living and assurance of eternal salvation. Christ alone is sufficient, for people of all ages, nations, and classes, and men from all types of cultural and religious backgrounds do respond to Him.

People in our own country have exactly the same great need of salvation as those in other lands, and Christians should earnestly try to lead their friends and acquaintances to Christ. At the same time, it is obvious that they have already had many opportunities to hear the gospel. Bibles are easily available in this country, gospel-preaching churches are available, radio broadcasts, Christian literature, Christian friends, etc. Surely no one in this country has even the semblance of an excuse for not being a Christian, though admittedly relatively few have really accepted Christ. If anything, therefore, there is much greater need and urgency for foreign missions than even for home missions and evangelism, though both are essential activities of all true Christian churches.

144

Chapter XI

THE LIFE IN CHRIST

1. Question: *"How can I know the will of God for my life?"*

Answer: One of the most wonderful discoveries that a person can make is that he has a very definite purpose in life. God sent each one of us into the world for a particular mission, and the only way we can enjoy a truly meaningful and happy life is to find and accomplish that mission. The great tragedy of our own generation is that most people have lost sight of God and His purpose and are drifting more or less aimlessly through life, interested only in satisfying their own personal desires and ambitions. Even much that passes for altruism and religion is basically motivated by self-interest and characterized by futility.

"It is more blessed to give than to receive," Jesus said (Acts 20: 35). The word "blessed" means "happy," and it is wonderfully true that real happiness is found in giving—giving of one's time and money, of course, but even more in giving oneself—and not in getting. Above all, we need to give our own selves to the Lord (II Cor. 8:5), to do His will, and not our own.

First, of course, if we wish to do His will, we must trust in Jesus Christ as our personal Saviour and Lord. For He is "not willing that any should perish, but that all should come to repentance" (II Peter 3:9).

Second, before we can expect to know His will for us personally, we must be willing to do it. We cannot bargain with God, expecting to decide whether to follow His will after He tells us what it is. We must come to the place in life where we realize that He is absolutely pre-eminent and that being in His will is more important than even life itself. "I beseech you therefore, brethren, by the mercies of God, that ye present your bodies a living sacrifice, holy, acceptable to God, which is your reasonable service. And be not conformed to this world, but be transformed by the renewing of your mind, that ye may prove [i.e., 'know experimentally'] what is that good and acceptable and perfect will of God" (Rom. 12:1, 2).

Once we have come to this point, where we are completely yielded to the Lord and His will, whatever it may be, then we can expect Him to reveal it. This He does through His Word, through providential circumstances, and by the witness of the Holy Spirit—all in response to continued prayer and trust.

The more we study and absorb the great teachings of Scripture, the more clearly will come into focus the type of life and ministry He has ordained for us. Obviously, it is never going to be His will for us to do anything that is contrary to His Word, for He cannot contradict Himself. Many possible choices will thus be eliminated by the Word itself, thus bringing more clearly into focus the true course of His will for our lives.

Then, as we pray for guidance and continue in obedience to His Word, He will direct our paths by the various circumstances of life. The natural abilities and talents He has given us, the opportunities for service He opens before us, the doors that open and the doors that close—these and other like circumstances will point the way. "In all thy ways, acknowledge Him, and He shall direct thy paths" (Prov. 3:6).

Finally the Holy Spirit, who dwells within the bodies of all true Christians (I Cor. 6:19, 20), will guide us. Jesus said: "Howbeit when he, the Spirit of truth, is come, he will guide you into all truth" (John 16:13). This He does, not through an audible voice or a supernatural vision, but through a quiet, yet firm, witness within our hearts.

When the testimony of God's Word, the direction of circumstances, and the witness of a Spirit-illumined conscience all unite in their testimony, then we can be sure we have found the will of God for our lives. "For this cause we also, since the day we heard it, do not cease to pray for you and to desire that ye might be filled with the knowledge of His will in all wisdom and spiritual understanding" (Col. 1:9).

2. Question: "How can one know when God has called him?"

Answer: There is a very wonderful promise in the New Testament to everyone who has been "called" by God. The Scripture says, "All things work together for good to them that love God, to them who are the called according to his purpose" (Rom. 8:28). This comprehensive assurance has through the centuries been a source of great strength and comfort to believers who were undergoing times of testing and difficulty. Note that the promise is to those who "love

God" and also to "the called," which evidently therefore are synono-
mous terms.

The word "called" (Greek *kletos*) occurs eleven times in the New
Testament, and the word "calling" (Greek *klesis*) also occurs eleven
times. They are always used in a distinct technical sense, to describe those who have received a definite "call" from God, to follow
a certain divine "calling." However, such a call is by no means limited
to some kind of full-time Christian work, as, say, that of a pastor
or missionary. When combined with the preposition "out," it becomes the word for "church" (Greek *ekklesia*), which occurs 115
times in the New Testament and means simply the "called-out ones."

A true church, therefore, is composed of individuals who have
been called by God out of the world unto Himself. Their beliefs,
their activities, their entire lives, are thus not to be "conformed to
this world" (Rom. 12:2), but rather they are to "walk worthy of the
calling" wherewith they were called (Eph. 4:1).

Indeed, this calling for some may be to full-time Christian service
in the highest sense. Paul said he was "called to be an apostle, separated unto the gospel of God" (Rom. 1:1). But, at the same time,
those to whom he wrote these words, the ordinary members in the
local church at Rome, he said, were "also the called of Jesus Christ"
(Rom. 1:6). Some of these people were actually slaves, and thus
could not choose their own occupations. To these he gave assurance
that even this could constitute God's calling for them and that they
could serve in this way to God's glory. To the Christian slaves in
Corinth, he said, "He that is called in the Lord, being a servant, is
the Lord's freeman: likewise also he that is called, being free, is
Christ's servant" (I Cor. 7:22).

God's call is not based therefore on the standards that men have
devised to select employees or to choose leaders. "For ye see your
calling, brethren, how that not many wise men after the flesh, not
many mighty, not many noble, are called. But God hath chosen the
foolish things of the world to confound the wise, and God hath chosen
the weak things of the world to confound the things which are
mighty" (I Cor. 1:26, 27).

Neither is God's call based on a man's good works. "God hath
saved us and called us, not according to our works, but according to
his own purpose and grace, which was given us in Christ Jesus before
the world began" (II Tim. 1:9).

This calling, therefore, derives simply from God's own divine purpose and His grace. It is made effectual through the gospel, the good

news of salvation and forgiveness in Jesus Christ. "God hath from the beginning chosen you to salvation through sanctification of the Spirit and belief of the truth: Whereunto he called you by our gospel, to the obtaining of the glory of our Lord Jesus Christ" (II Thess. 2:13, 14).

Furthermore, the calling is permanent, whether or not the person appropriates and follows it. "For the gifts and calling of God are without repentance" (Rom. 11:29).

All of the above can be summarized by saying that every genuine believer in the Lord Jesus Christ, one who truly "loves God," has been "called according to his purpose." God has a purpose for each one He saves, and He desires both to make His will known and to enable the individual to accomplish it. This purpose may, and usually does, consist of many phases and components, to be revealed and implemented as one "grows in grace and in the knowledge of our Lord and Saviour Jesus Christ" (II Peter 3:18).

At the same time, God does not compel anyone to accept His call and follow His will, any more than He forces an unsaved man to accept His call to come to Christ and be saved. In both the matter of salvation and the matter of doing God's will, it is sadly true that "many are called, but few are chosen" (Matt. 22:14).

Nevertheless, the life of greatest joy and blessing, especially as measured in the light of the eternal ages, which are certainly stretching out ahead of us, is a life lived in obedience to God's will and in fulfillment of His calling.

First of all, the apostle exhorts each professing Christian to "give diligence to make your calling and election sure" (II Peter 1:10). That is, "be sure you have obeyed God's call to come to Jesus Christ in repentance and faith, receiving Him as Lord and Saviour and, furthermore, that you are not knowingly resisting His Word and His will for your life in any way."

Then that Christian is in position to pray, with Paul, "That the God and Father of our Lord Jesus Christ, the Father of glory, may give unto you the spirit of wisdom and revelation in the knowledge of him: The eyes of your understanding being enlightened; that ye may know what is the hope of his calling" (Eph. 1:17, 18). In answer to sincere prayer and willingness to do His will, the Lord will in good time make clear the specific nature of His calling for each person who seeks it, doing this first through the Scriptures, then through providential circumstances, and finally through inward conviction and assurance.

And having finally ascertained with full confidence the nature of the calling, then it becomes the great joy and privilege of the believer to serve the Lord with his whole heart in that capacity. As the Apostle Paul says, "Brethren, I count not myself to have apprehended: but this one thing I do, forgetting those things which are behind, and reaching forth unto those things which are before, I press toward the mark for the prize of the high calling of God in Christ Jesus" (Phil. 3:13, 14).

3. Question: "How can one be filled with the Holy Spirit?"

Answer: It is not only possible for a Christian to be "filled with the Holy Spirit," he is, in fact, commanded to do so! "And be not drunk with wine, wherein is excess; but be filled with the Spirit" (Eph. 5:18).

However, this is a teaching on which there is a great deal of confusion today. Many Christians believe it describes an experience which God gives only to a select group, enabling them perhaps to preach with outstanding power or even to work miracles. A Spirit-filled person, others tend to think, is someone who is fanatically religious, or possibly someone who constantly lives a very pious life, devoid of all problems and temptations.

However, in the definitive passage cited above, it is evident that the key thought is one of "control." In contrast to one whose actions and words are under the control of wine, as a drunken man, the Christian should be a person completely guided and controlled by the indwelling Spirit of God (I Cor. 6:19, 20).

It is instructive to study the fifteen times in which this filling of the Holy Spirit is mentioned in the New Testament. It is significant that the first mention is in connection with John the Baptist, whom Jesus said (Matt. 11:11) was the greatest man who ever lived. Before his birth, the angel prophesied, "For he shall be great in the sight of the Lord, and shall drink neither wine nor strong drink; and he shall be filled with the Holy Ghost, even from his mother's womb" (Luke 1:15). Here again the Spirit's filling is associated with the absence of any such other controlling agent as wine or strong drink. It is also of real interest to note that John, even though continually filled with the Holy Spirit, "did no miracle" (John 10:41). It is certain, therefore, that supernatural manifestations are not at all necessary evidences of the Spirit's fullness.

On at least one occasion each, both of John's parents were filled with the Spirit (Luke 1:41, 67). Also, Jesus Himself was of course

149

"full of the Holy Ghost" (Luke 4:1). In His case, it is most important to note, that in the very same-verse, it is said that the Spirit led Him into the wilderness to be tempted of the devil. Therefore, being controlled by the Holy Spirit does not mean being free from temptations and sufferings, but it does assure victory over such circumstances! (I Cor. 10:13).

The early disciples, including all or most of the members of the first local church, in Jerusalem, were filled with the Holy Spirit on at least two different occasions (Acts 2:4; 4:31). This proves that the filling is not a once-for-all experience, but may be repeated, and furthermore it may be for different purposes and produce different specific results. In the first of the above instances the disciples were miraculously enabled to preach God's Word in different languages; in the second, it says merely that "they spake the Word of God with boldness." Whatever the specific manifestation, it is clear that when the Holy Spirit really controls a man's tongue, that man will speak words which are uncompromisingly true to God's Word!

Certain disciples are also mentioned as being filled with the Holy Ghost on special occasions requiring unusual courage or wisdom, e.g., Stephen (Acts 7:55), Peter (Acts 4:8), and Paul (Acts 13:9). The filling of the Spirit is mentioned as being also accompanied by fullness of wisdom (Acts 6:3), fullness of faith (Acts 6:5; 11:24), and fullness of joy (Acts 13:52).

Now, although the above passages make it clear that the Holy Spirit's filling comes on repeated occasions and often for special and immediate needs, it is also true that a Christian's entire life can and should be characterized by this fullness of the Holy Spirit. The Apostle Paul became so filled almost as soon as he became a Christian (Acts 9:17), and both Stephen (Acts 6:5) and Barnabas (Acts 11:24) were commonly recognized as being men "full of the Holy Ghost." In fact, one of the specific requirements laid down for the first deacons to be chosen by the early church was that they should be "full of the Holy Ghost and wisdom" (Acts 6:3).

The apparent contradiction between the teaching of repeated fillings of the Holy Spirit for particular needs, and a life consistently characterized by the fullness of the Spirit, is easily resolved by noting again the key concept of "control." If a person allows his actions to be controlled in any degree by wine—or by drugs, or by money, or by pride, or by anything else, then of course they are not controlled by the Holy Spirit, and he is therefore not filled with the Spirit. On certain occasions of great need, or great conviction, however, a

150

Christian may for a time truly become filled (that is, controlled in his words and deeds) by the Holy Spirit. Too often, however, he soon lapses back into his old ways and, even though he may be a sincere and generally good Christian, really allows other things to rule his life most of the time. But how much better if he habitually and regularly looks for direction for his life in all circumstances to God the Holy Spirit, and carefully and conscientiously follows His leading and enabling in meeting every need. He then is a man of whom it can properly be said that he is "full of the Holy Spirit."

The definitive passage, which summarizes all the rest, is the one cited at the beginning of this study, Ephesians 5:18. A very literal translation of this passage would be: "And do not even begin to be drunk with wine, wherein is debauchery, but rather be continually being filled with the Spirit."

The context of this verse is very important. Leading up to it, evidently because these are prerequisites to a truly Spirit-controlled life, are admonitions to "walk circumspectly" (Eph. 5:15), to "redeem the time" (Eph. 5:16), and to "understand what the will of the Lord is" (Eph. 5:17). That is, one can hardly expect to have a Spirit-controlled life unless he is really concerned to order all his behavior and to use all his time in a way that conforms to God's will. He must allow nothing else (of which "wine" is the typical example) to gain any control over his life.

And then, following the verse, are given the results and manifestations of a Spirit-filled life. It will be a life filled with true joy and "melody in your heart," and a tongue used to speak and to sing God's Word (Eph. 5:19). It will be a life characterized not by complaining and envying, but rather of continual thankfulness "for all things" (Eph. 5:20), always "in the name of our Lord Jesus Christ."

Furthermore, the Spirit-filled life is one in which the spirit of pride and self-seeking which so typically characterizes the natural man is displaced by a spirit of submission and unselfishness (Eph. 5:21). In short, a Christian life filled and controlled by God the Holy Spirit is the life of greatest joy and victory which a person can have, since it is the life which God Himself desires His children to experience.

4. Question: "What is the 'deeper life'?"

Answer: A variety of terms have been used at different times in recent Christian history to describe a supposedly advanced stage of Christian experience which relatively few believers enjoy. One reads or hears, for example, of the "deeper life," the "higher life," the "over-coming life," the "sanctified life," the "crucified life," and numerous others. Even the phrase, "the normal Christian life" has been used with a similar connotation.

Various initiatory experiences or acts on the part of the individual Christian are presented by various authorities as methods by which one may enter upon such a "victorious life." Some speak of an act of "surrender" or of "consecration." Others understand the baptism of the Holy Spirit to be a spiritual experience subsequent to, and separate from, the initial work of the Holy Spirit in regeneration, which is evidenced by "speaking in tongues" or some other spectacular manifestation. Some think of kneeling at the altar, of "praying through," or other means, as leading to a "second blessing," a "second work of grace" which results in complete "eradication" of one's sinful nature and desires. Still others speak merely of a conscious appropriation by faith, through an act of the will, of the blessings of the "fuller life."

Those who presumably are experiencing this "abiding life" speak often in such terms as "practicing the presence," of "constantly abiding," of the "love principle" as the rule of life, and other ostensibly spiritual sentiments. They also are usually quite insistent in pressing the claims of a "deeper experience" upon those Christians who have not yet entered therein.

There is undoubtedly a certain measure of Biblical truth in all of this, and many proponents of these experiences are sincere and spiritually minded Christians. However, certain cautions are in order.

It is significant that none of the various terms and phrases as quoted in the foregoing are actually found in the Bible. In fact, the only adjective attached to the word "life" in the New Testament is the word "everlasting" or "eternal," and of course everlasting life is God's gift (Rom. 6:23) to everyone who accepts the Lord Jesus Christ as his Saviour, not to only a select group of spiritual Christians.

Furthermore, there is no clear exposition in the Scriptures of this supposed deeper life, nor is there any indication that there are two categories of Christians, distinguished by their having experienced or not experienced the initiation phenomenon which hopefully gains entrance thereto.

Judged by many advocates of the deeper-life experience, there do seem to be two specific dangers in the movement. The first danger is that it tends to produce an unhealthy introspection and self-centeredness on the part of the Christian who is seeking such an experience. At the same time, the one who believes he has reached these spiritual heights can hardly avoid an attitude of pride over his attainment, and this is perilous. "Let him that thinketh he standeth take heed lest he fall" (I Cor. 10:12).

The second danger is that the Christian will become so enamored of his experience in living what he thinks is an "abundant life" that he will begin to neglect and perhaps even to deny many of the vital truths of Bible doctrine. He tends to rely on his emotions and impressions, considering these to indicate the direct leading of the Holy Spirit. He may even get to the point where he receives what he believes are direct revelations from God Himself, so that he no longer has need for personal Bible study. Such "revelations" are nearly always either innocuous and trivial or else actually contrary to Scripture. Most new cults have in fact been started in just such a fashion.

It should be obvious, on the other hand, that the Holy Spirit will never lead anyone to do or to believe anything which is contrary to the Scriptures, which He caused His holy prophets and apostles to record "for our admonition" (Rom. 15:4). Before the New Testament was written, there was need for the churches to receive special guidance through direct revelation to men gifted by God as prophets, but "when that which is perfect [i.e., 'complete'] is come" and the canon of Scripture established forever, then such "prophecies" would be "done away" (I Cor. 13:10; Rev. 22:18).

The real secret of an abundant, victorious, fruitful Christian life is no secret at all! Just as one begins his physical life as a babe and then grows to maturity and usefulness through proper sustenance and training, so it is with his spiritual life. One must simply "grow in grace, and in the knowledge of our Lord and Saviour, Jesus Christ" (II Peter 3:18).

The sustenance for spiritual growth is the Word of God. There is absolutely no short-cut and no substitute for systematic, life-long study of the Holy Scriptures. "As newborn babes, desire the sincere milk of the word, that ye may grow thereby" (I Peter 2:2). Of course, one must not only study the Bible, but also believe and obey it, or else he will remain a spiritual babe. "Be ye doers of the word, and not hearers only, deceiving your own selves" (James 1:22).

Through prayerful, obedient study of God's Word, not only do we grow in the "knowledge" of Christ (and it is only there, of course, that such knowledge is found), but the Holy Spirit also is able to fill our lives increasingly with His grace.

5. *Question: "Is prayer mainly of psychological benefit, or does God really hear and answer?"*

Answer: The psychological and therapeutic values of prayer are very real and important. The Bible itself teaches this. "In everything by prayer and supplication, with thanksgiving, let your requests be made known unto God; and the peace of God, which passes all understanding, shall keep your hearts and minds through Christ Jesus" (Phil. 4:6, 7).

But there is much more to prayer than its psychological uplift. We are, in fact, commanded to pray. Jesus said: "Men ought always to pray" (Luke 18:1). The Apostle Paul said: "I exhort, therefore, that first of all, prayers, intercessions, and giving of thanks, be made for all men" (I Tim. 2:1)

Furthermore, God has promised to answer prayer, not only in terms of our general well-being, but also in granting specific requests. "And whatsoever we ask, we receive of Him, because we keep His commandments, and do those things that are pleasing in His sight" (I John 3:22). Jesus said: "Ask, and it shall be given you; seek and ye shall find; knock, and it shall be opened unto you" (Matt. 7:7). These promises have been confirmed, over and over again, in the lives and experiences of all true Christians down through the years.

There are, however, certain conditions to be met before we can rightly expect God to answer our prayers. The first is that there be no unconfessed sin in our lives. If we are deliberately living in disobedience to God's Word, then obviously we cannot expect Him to grant our requests. "If I regard iniquity in my heart, the Lord will not hear me" (Ps. 66:18). "For the eyes of the Lord are over the righteous, and His ears are open unto their prayers: but the face of the Lord is against them that do evil" (I Peter 3:12).

The greatest sin of all, of course, is for a person to reject, or even to fail to accept, the Lord Jesus Christ as his own personal Saviour and Master. "He that believeth on Him is not condemned; but he that believeth not is condemned already, because he hath not believed in the name of the only begotten Son of God" (John 3:18). No one has a right to pray to God for personal needs if he has ignored God's Son and the tremendous sacrifice He made for us on the cross, in paying the price of our redemption from sin and death, and hell. Jesus said: "I am the way, the truth and the life: no man cometh unto the Father but by me" (John 14:6).

Thus, both for salvation and for answered prayer, we can approach

God only through Christ. He said: "And whatsoever ye shall ask in my name, that will I do, that the Father may be glorified in the Son" (John 14:13).

In addition to a right relationship with Christ, trusting Him as our Saviour, and obeying His Word as our Lord, we must also be in right relationship with the members of our own family. "Likewise, ye husbands, dwell with them according to knowledge, giving honour unto the wife, as unto the weaker vessel, and as being heirs together of the grace of life; that your prayers be not hindered" (I Peter 3:7). Husbands must be the spiritual leaders in their homes, loving and providing for their wives and children; wives must honor and submit to their husbands' authority; children must obey their parents; and parents must train and discipline and love their children—or else their prayers will be futile.

Another condition for answered prayer is faith that God will keep His Word. "And all things, whatsoever ye shall ask in prayer, believing, ye shall receive" (Matt. 21:22). "Let him ask in faith, nothing wavering. For he that wavereth is like a wave of the sea driven with the wind and tossed. For let not that man think that he shall receive anything of the Lord" (James 1:6, 7).

Finally, one's purpose in prayer is important. Selfish, covetous prayers obviously are not pleasing to God. "Ye ask, and receive not, because ye ask amiss, that ye may consume it upon your lusts" (James 4:3).

Here the Lord Jesus Himself is the perfect example. Even facing the cross, He could pray: "Nevertheless not my will, but thine, be done" (Luke 22:42). The highest aim of our prayers, as well as of every phase of the Christian life, ought to be the will of God.

As we grow in grace and in the knowledge of Christ, we can more readily discern His will and pray accordingly. "And this is the confidence we have in him, that, if we ask anything according to his will, he heareth us; and if we know that he hear us, whatsoever we ask, we know that we have the petitions we desired of him" (I John 5:14, 15).

Furthermore, we have the promise that, even when we do not know His will, if we pray with a willingness to follow His will, then the Holy Spirit, who indwells the Christian believer, will undertake the prayer burden Himself: "Likewise the Spirit also helpeth our infirmities; for we know not what we should pray for as we ought. . . . He maketh intercession for the saints according to the will of God" (Rom. 8:26, 27).

With such promises as this, and upon meeting the conditions, whether our prayers are answered in the way we wanted or in a better way of God's own choosing, we can rest in the tremendous assurance of Romans 8:28: "And we know that all things work together for good to them that love God, to them who are the called according to his purpose."

Chapter XII

PRACTICAL CHRISTIAN LIVING

1. *Question: "How can a person determine what is right and what is wrong?"*

Answer: One of the most disturbing trends of the twentieth century has been the rapid growth of belief in moral relativism—that is, the belief that there are no fixed standards of right and wrong and that, consequently, every man may "do that which is right in his own eyes" (Judges 21:25). In our day this philosophy has been called "situational ethics," according to which the morality of any particular action depends on the situation, and is to be determined by the individual himself on the basis of his own judgment. Thus, under certain circumstances, it is supposed to be perfectly right to commit adultery, to steal, or even to murder, provided one does it in a "loving" way, or as a means to supposedly worthwhile ends.

But it is obvious that this mis-named "new morality" is really "no morality." If each man is free to determine his own standard, then in effect each man becomes his own god, and this is the ultimate and worst form of idol-worship.

At the same time, it is significant that, even though such individual standards of right and wrong may vary widely with time and place, people of all times and places somehow possess the intuitive knowledge that there is a difference between right and wrong and that they "ought" to do right. That is, all men have a basic moral consciousness, or "conscience." This is not an attribute of even the highest animals, and is thus a clear evidence that, in the beginning, "God created man in his own image" (Gen. 1:27).

Therefore, it should be evident that the true standard of man's belief and behavior is to be established by God the Creator, not by man the creature. And that standard is the very "image of God" in which he was created! Anything which falls "short of the glory of God" is explicitly defined as "sin" (Rom. 3:23). The Christian is specifically commanded: "Whether therefore ye eat, or drink, or whatsoever ye do, do all to the glory of God" (I Cor. 10:31). The

157

true standard of morality, therefore, is simply to act in accordance with the will of God and to do that which brings honor to His name.

The question still remains, however, as to the way by which we can determine which actions truly glorify God and obey His will. Obviously, since God is our Creator, the only way we can really know what is true and what is right is for Him to tell us. And that is exactly what He has done, through the Holy Scriptures! God's revelation, His communication, His law, His Word, is the standard, and there is no other.

Therefore the most basic of all sins—the root of all other sins—is rebellion against God's Word. The establishment of any other criterion of truth or morality in preference to, or even equal to, the revealed Word of God is sin in its most fundamental and deadly form, because all other sins are based upon resistance to God's Word.

This was the sin of Satan himself, in his primordial rebellion against God in heaven. God had told him there had been a "day that thou wast created," as the "anointed cherub . . . upon the holy mountain of God" (Ezek. 28:13, 14). But he refused to believe that he was actually of a different and lower order than God, "created" rather than eternal, and so said, "I will be like the most High" (Isa. 14:14).

This sin of unbelief and self-idolatry was also the sin with which he tempted Eve. "Yea, hath God said . . . ?" was his approach, followed by his blatant denial of God's Word. "Ye shall not surely die: . . . ye shall be as gods . . ."! (Gen. 3:1, 4, 5).

In like manner, sin in its essence is still simply unbelief in, and therefore disobedience to, the Word of God" (Rom. 10:17). "For whatsoever is not of faith is sin" (Rom. 14:23).

Specifically, God's will was written down as "the Law"—the ten commandments, supplemented by all the other teachings and instructions of the Bible. Of course, in interpreting and applying the law, one must be careful to consider the whole context and not isolated texts only, carefully recognizing the intended scope and duration of each instruction. But the most important point to recognize is that God's written Word, and not one's subjective feelings, must provide the basic framework within which specific decisions are to be made.

For those people who have not possessed the written Word, God has provided an unwritten law, engraved in their own consciences. "For when the Gentiles, which have not the law, do by nature the things contained in the law, these, having not the law, are a law unto themselves: Which shew the work of the law written in their hearts, their conscience also bearing witness, and their thoughts the meanwhile accusing or else excusing one another" (Rom. 2:14, 15).

Note, however, that this law of conscience, if exercised properly, must always yield answers consistent with the Scriptures, since both have the same Author. Furthermore, it can never take priority over the Scriptures, nor can it give the detailed and precise understanding of God's will that is obtained from systematic Bible study.

Finally, the pre-eminent role of God's Word as the absolute standard of right and wrong is demonstrated by its role in the future judgment. With respect to the written law as recorded by Moses, Jesus said, "There is one that accuseth you, even Moses, . . . For had ye believed Moses, ye would have believed me" (John 5:45, 46). The Scripture also says, "By the law is the knowledge of sin" (Rom. 3:20), and "For whosoever shall keep the whole law, and yet offend in one point, he is guilty of all" (James 2:10), and "Cursed is every one that continueth not in all things which are written in the book of the law to do them" (Gal. 3:10).

With respect to His own teachings, Jesus said, "He that rejecteth me, and receiveth not my words, hath one that judgeth him: the word that I have spoken, the same shall judge him in the last day" (John 12:48).

At the final judgment, it is written, ". . . and the books were opened, . . . and the dead were judged out of those things which were written in the books, according to their works" (Rev. 20:12). In every case, of course, a man's "works" will fall short of the standard recorded in "the books," since "all have sinned and come short of the glory of God" (Rom. 3:23). He must therefore be condemned and sent into hell, unless he has been "redeemed from the curse of the law" (Gal. 3:13) through personal trust in the Redeemer, Jesus Christ. "The wages of sin is death, but the gift of God is eternal life, through Jesus Christ our Lord" (Rom. 6:23).

And here is the supreme way in which the Word of God is the standard. Jesus Christ Himself is the living "Word of God" (Rev. 19:13), just as the Bible is the written Word, each in perfect unity and consistency with the other. He has perfectly revealed God's will and perfectly obeyed God's will. His substitutionary death for our sins, received by Him, provides a perfect salvation, both from the penalty of sin in the judgment and the practice of sin in the present.

2. Question: "How can I decide whether a particular activity—such as smoking, gambling, etc.—is right or wrong?"

Answer: In the first place, Christianity is not a list of taboos. "For by grace are ye saved through faith; and that not of yourselves: it is the gift of God; Not of works, lest any man should boast" (Eph. 2:8, 9). Remember that the Lord Jesus Christ has already suffered and died for all our sins in order that we might be freely forgiven and saved, through an obedient trust in Him.

In the second place, it is not our right to pass judgment on someone else and his activities. As the Bible says: "Let us not therefore judge one another any more; but judge this rather, that no man put a stumblingblock or an occasion to fall in his brother's way" (Rom. 14:13). Most of us are quick to criticize others, but it is far more important to be sure our own conduct is pleasing to the Lord. "For if we would judge ourselves, we should not be judged" (I Cor. 11:31).

Of course, it is very important for a real Christian, one who has been saved through personal faith in the Lord Jesus Christ, to live a life that is honoring to his Saviour and that is helpful to his fellow Christians and to those he should try to lead to Christ. In order to evaluate particular activities and problems, God has established a number of general principles in His Word for our guidance. Some of these are as follows:

(1) If there is a specific warning or commandment in Scripture dealing with a particular matter, then there is no question. Thus, murder, adultery, fornication, drunkenness, theft, etc., are always wrong; such sins as these are clearly and definitely condemned in numerous Scriptures.

(2) When there is no specific Scriptural reference, it is good to ask, not whether a certain thing is wrong, but rather if it is definitely good. The Bible says, for example, to "redeem the time" (Col. 4:5). Our few days here on earth are so short and precious, in relation to eternity, that we ought never to waste time on selfish trivia, but to use it only on that "which is good, to the use of edifying" (Eph. 4:29).

(3) A good test is to determine whether we can honestly, in good conscience, ask God to bless and use the particular activity for His own good purposes. "Whether therefore ye eat, or drink, or whatsoever ye do, do all to the glory of God" (I Cor. 10:31). If there is room for doubt as to whether it pleases God, then it is best to give it up. "For whatsoever is not of faith is sin" (Rom. 14:23).

(4) We need to remember that our bodies, as well as our souls, have been redeemed and belong to God. "What? know ye not that your body is the temple of the Holy Ghost which is in you, which ye have of God, and ye are not your own? For ye are bought with a price; therefore glorify God in your body, and in your spirit, which are God's" (I Cor. 6:19, 20). This great truth should have a real bearing on what we do and where we go with our bodies.

(5) We must evaluate our actions not only in relation to God but also in relation to their effect on our family, our friends, and other people in general. Even if a particular thing may not hurt us personally, if it harmfully influences or affects someone else, it is wrong. "It is good neither to eat flesh, nor to drink wine, nor any thing whereby thy brother stumbleth, or is offended, or is made weak. . . . We then that are strong ought to bear the infirmities of the weak, and not to please ourselves" (Rom. 14:21; 15:1).

(6) Remember, finally, that Jesus Christ is our Lord and Saviour, and nothing else can be allowed to take priority over our conformity to His will. No habit or recreation, or ambition can be allowed to have an undue control over our lives—only Christ has that authority. "All things are lawful for me, but I will not be brought under the power of any" (I Cor. 6:12). "Whatsoever ye do in word or deed, do all in the name of the Lord Jesus" (Col. 3:17).

3. Question: "When Christ turned the water into wine, did He thereby approve intoxicating beverages?"

Answer: This question presupposes that the wine created by Christ at the wedding feast in Cana (John 2:1-11) was fermented, and thus intoxicating wine. This is probably not the case, as a careful examination of the circumstances will indicate.

Wine has been manufactured from earliest times and is first mentioned in the Bible in connection with the drunkenness of Noah (Gen. 9:21), which in turn led to the sin of his son, Ham. The vineyard provided one of man's first sources of both the sugar so necessary for his health and the alcohol so harmful to his health.

The "pure blood of the grape" (Deut. 32:14) is, in itself, not only harmless but sweet and healthful. It is only after the grape sugar, through the fermentation process caused by the yeast bacteria that collect on the grape skins, is broken down into alcohol and carbon dioxide, that the wine becomes harmful. Fermentation is essentially a decay process, in which the complex sugar molecules are caused to break down into the simpler molecules of alcohol. At body temperature, sugar taken into the system is inhibited from this type of decay and instead is a prime source of energy for the body's activities. Alcohol, on the other hand, is itself a cause of bodily decay, entering the blood stream undigested and thence attacking the nervous system and the entire bodily structure, causing damage everywhere it goes and, eventually, if enough is ingested, death.

In the Old Testament two Hebrew words ("tirosh" and "yayin") are both translated "wine," the former meaning the fresh juice of the grape and the latter the fermented or decayed juice. However, in the Greek language the same word, *oinos*, was used for both. That is, the term "wine," in the New Testament, can mean either the fresh "fruit of the vine" or its decay product, as the context may require. A parallel usage in modern English would be our use of the word "cider" to refer either to sweet cider or to hard cider, as the context may indicate. There is an abundance of both ancient Hebrew and Greek secular literature available to verify that both fermented and unfermented "wines" were in common use by the people of that day.

It is significant that nowhere does the Bible actually endorse the drinking of wine or other intoxicating drinks. On the contrary, there are numerous warnings against it. For example: "Be not drunk with wine, wherein is excess; but be filled with the Spirit" (Eph. 5:18). A more precise translation of the first clause is: "Do not even begin to be drunk with wine, wherein is debauchery!" The word *methusko*, which is used here, means "begin to be drunk," rather than simply "be drunk," and thus the verse is clearly a command to abstain from alcohol.

Similarly, Proverbs 23:31 commands: "Look not thou upon the wine when it is red, when it giveth his colour in the cup, when it moveth itself aright." There are many other warnings against intoxicating drinks and especially against drunkenness. And of course, even small amounts of alcohol produce at least a small measure of drunkenness—that is, a decay of inhibitions, of alertness, of judgment, etc. The fact that Paul permitted a medicinal use of wine to Timothy (I Tim. 5:23) probably indicates fresh grape juice but in any case cannot contradict the Bible's repeated warnings against it.

It is significant that, in establishing the Lord's Supper, Jesus was always careful to use the phrase "fruit of the vine," instead of "wine," lest He be misunderstood. Alcohol, the product of putrefaction and decay and thus the perfect symbol of death, could certainly not repre-

162

sent the life-giving quality of the blood of the Lord Jesus symbolized in the cup at His table. Furthermore, He frequently warned against drunkenness (note Luke 21:34; 12:45, etc.).

Thus it is extremely unlikely that He would create a substance at a wedding feast which would cause drunkenness! The guests had already exhausted the copious supplies of intoxicating wine on hand and were in fact already drunk (as the phrase John 2:10—"have well drunk" should have been literally translated). He transformed approximately 150 gallons of water into that many gallons of "good wine" (John 2:6, 10), and if this was intoxicating wine, it would certainly have turned the wedding celebration, with the guests already inebriated and demanding more wine, into a drunken brawl! No wonder He rebuked His mother, who made the request of Him, by saying, "Woman, what have I to do with thee?" or, more literally, "What is there in common between you and me?" (John 2:4).

The wine which He made was, in fact, new wine, freshly created! It was not old, decayed wine, as it would have to be if it were intoxicating. There was no time for the fermentation process to break down the structure of its energy-giving sugars into disintegrative alcohols. It thus was a fitting representation of His glory and was appropriate to serve as the very first of His great miracles (John 2:11).

4. Question: "If we are saved by grace, is a Christian therefore free to live as he pleases?"

Answer: The New Testament, of course, is very clear in its teaching that we are justified by grace through faith, not by works. "For by grace are ye saved through faith; and that not of yourselves: it is the gift of God: Not of works, lest any man should boast" (Eph. 2:8, 9). "Not by works of righteousness which we have done, but according to his mercy he saved us, by the washing of regeneration, and renewing of the Holy Ghost; Which he shed on us abundantly through Jesus Christ our Saviour" (Titus 3:5, 6).

This does not mean that our salvation is one of "cheap grace." Although we receive it as a free gift, if we receive it at all, it is infinitely costly. "Ye were not redeemed with corruptible things, as silver and gold, . . . But with the precious blood of Christ" (I Peter 1:18, 19). "Herein is love, not that we loved God, but that he loved us, and sent his Son to be the propitiation for our sins" (I John 4:10). The Lord Jesus Christ, the very Son of God, suffered

163

all the desolation of hell itself when He died on the cross, taking the punishment which each man deserves to receive for his own sins, thus bearing "our sins in his own body on the tree" (I Peter 2:24).

Since He has paid the price of our redemption, we may obtain full forgiveness and eternal salvation simply by receiving Him through personal repentance and faith. When an individual thus opens his heart to Christ, the Holy Spirit enters his life and he is "born again" to a new life. "If any man be in Christ, he is a new creature; old things are passed away; behold, all things are become new" (II Cor. 5:17).

His entire attitude and motivation are changed. He desires to live in a way that will honor the Lord Jesus and draw others to Him, in thankfulness for Christ's love and sacrifice for him. "The love of Christ constraineth us; because we thus judge, that if . . . he died for all, that they which live should not henceforth live unto themselves, but unto him which died for them, and rose again" (II Cor. 5:14, 15).

The true Christian is thus indeed free to live as he pleases, but he will please to live for Christ! Although he may at times fail the Lord in various ways, the real motivation of his life will be, not to please himself, but to please the Lord. This must be so, because he has been regenerated by the Spirit of God. "I am crucified with Christ; nevertheless I live; yet not I, but Christ liveth in me" (Gal. 2:20). If his motivation is still basically self-centered, there is no real evidence that he has been truly converted. Such persons should sincerely "examine yourselves, whether ye be in the faith; prove your own selves" (II Cor. 13:5).

The genuine Christian seeks to live a life pleasing to God, not in order to be saved, or in order to keep saved, but because he is saved! His life is therefore a life of true thanksgiving to his Saviour.

5. Question: "To what extent should a Christian insist on freedom of speech?"

Answer: There is, of course, a great difference between a Christian's responsibility as a citizen of his country and his responsibility as a "citizen of heaven" (Phil. 3:20). Whenever there is conflict, the former must give priority to the latter. This is especially evident in the area of communication and conversation—both his written speech and his oral speech. Although he may have a legal right, for example, to use profanity in his speech, he does not have the moral right to do so. "The Lord will not hold him guiltless, that taketh his name in vain" (Ex. 20:7).

When a person becomes a true Christian, through personal faith in Jesus Christ as Lord and Saviour, he is "born again" (I Peter 1:23). Although he has been "delivered from the law" (Rom. 7:6), he has been "bought with a price" and is "not his own" (I Cor. 6: 19, 20). He is to "present his body as a living sacrifice" (Rom. 12:1) to his Lord and Saviour, Jesus Christ.

The tongue is the most important member of that body, and the most difficult to yield to Christ's control. "If any man offend not in word, the same is a perfect man, and able also to bridle the whole body" (James 3:2). Because of its critically strategic role in one's entire Christian testimony, it is supremely important, therefore, that the tongue be subjected to the restraints and constraints of God's Word.

A Christian's speech, for example, should not be idle and uncontrolled. "If any man among you seemeth to be religious, and bridleth not his tongue, that man's religion is vain" (James 1:26). "Every idle word that men shall speak, they shall give account thereof in the day of judgment" (Matt. 12:36). "Study to be quiet and to do your own business" (I Thess. 4:11).

Certainly a Christian should never indulge in cursing or vulgarity! "Out of the same mouth proceedeth blessing and cursing. My brethren, these things ought not so to be" (James 3:10). "Put off all these; anger, wrath, malice, blasphemy, filthy communication out of your mouth" (Col. 3:8). "Neither filthiness, nor foolish talking, nor jesting, which are not convenient: but rather giving of thanks" (Eph. 5:4.)

Neither should his speech be complaining or grumbling. "Do all things without murmurings and disputings" (Phil. 2:14). "Let all bitterness, and wrath, and anger, and clamor, and evil speaking, be put away from you, with all malice" (Eph. 4:31).

A Christian should definitely not be a gossip. "And withal they learn to be idle, wandering about from house to house: and not only idle, but tattlers also and busybodies, speaking things which they ought not" (I Tim. 5:13). He must be especially careful to see that his conversation is not deceptive or misleading. "Wherefore putting away lying, speak every man truth with his neighbor" (Eph. 4:25).

All of the foregoing admonitions are essentially negative—that is, things which a Christian should seek to avoid in his speech. However, this is only a small part of the picture. The Christian's speech should not only be characterized by freedom from these things (verbosity, vulgarity, profanity, bitterness, gossiping, lying, grumbling, and such like) but should have certain very positive characteristics instead.

For example, it should not be bland and pointless! "Let your speech be always with grace, seasoned with salt, that ye may know how ye ought to answer every man" (Col. 4:6). Not merely an absence of harmful contents, but a positive presence of useful and meaningful words, should be its essence. "Let no corrupt communication proceed out of your mouth, but that which is good to the use of edifying, that it may minister grace unto the hearers" (Eph. 4:29).

The Christian's speech should be, in so far as possible, gentle and kind. "The servant of the Lord must not strive; but be gentle unto all men, apt to teach, patient, In meekness instructing those that oppose themselves" (II Tim. 2:24, 25). He must even be willing to endure personal criticism and insult without retaliation. "For even hereunto were ye called: because Christ also suffered for us, leaving us an example, that ye should follow his steps: Who did no sin, neither was guile found in his mouth: Who, when he was reviled, reviled not again; when he suffered, he threatened not; but committed himself to him that judgeth righteously" (I Peter 2:21-23).

At the same time, the Christian, though he is not to be self-defensive, must be bold in his witness and in defense of God's truth. He should pray, as did the apostles: "And now, Lord, behold their threatenings: and grant unto thy servants, that with all boldness they may speak thy word" (Acts 4:29). "Be not thou therefore ashamed of the testimony of our Lord" (II Tim. 1:8). "Preach the word; be instant in season, out of season; reprove, rebuke, exhort with all longsuffering and doctrine" (II Tim. 4:2). "Ye should earnestly contend for the faith which was once for all delivered unto the saints" (Jude 3).

Thus, the Christian's speech should be, in the ultimate sense, a continual testimony to God's grace and truth. It should be gentle, yet courageous and uncompromising. It should be characterized, not by man's banalities and vanities, but by the positive assurance of God's Word. "If any man speak, let him speak as the oracles of God" (I Peter 4:11). "Whatsoever ye do, in word or deed, do all in the name of the Lord Jesus" (Col. 3:17).

All these admonitions concerning the Christian's use of his tongue must also apply with even greater urgency to the use of his pen.

Spoken words may quickly vanish, but written words endure much longer and travel farther.

Finally, as with all the Lord's commands, these are much easier to hear than to obey! Every believer (the present writer included) fails to control his spoken and written words the way he should. The Lord, in His grace, continues to forgive in response to sincere confession. And even though "the tongue can no man tame" (James 3:8), even this member of the body can be brought under control by God if we "yield our members, as instruments of righteousness, unto God" (Rom. 6:13).

6. Question: "Does God require tithing in this Christian age?"

Answer: One should, of course, recognize that all of his income stems from God and that he, therefore, is merely a steward, and not the absolute owner, of his possessions. We cannot actually "give" anything to God. Everything we have is His, and He is able to take it away if we are not faithful in our stewardship. "Moreover it is required in stewards that a man be found faithful" (I Cor. 4:2).

This is doubly true for the Christian. Not only do he and his property belong to God by creation, but also by right of redemption. "Ye are not your own . . . ye are bought with a price: . . ." (I Cor. 6:19, 20). He "hath delivered us from the power of darkness, and hath translated us into the kingdom of his dear Son: In whom we have redemption through his blood, even the forgiveness of sins" (Col. 1:13, 14).

The true Christian consequently will recognize the tremendous value of "so great salvation" (Heb. 2:3), and in love and gratitude to Christ seek to use all his possessions (time and talents, as well as money) in ways that will honor God and draw others to Him. "Whether therefore ye eat, or drink, or whatsoever ye do, do all to the glory of God" (I Cor. 10:31).

God has promised to "supply all our needs" (Phil. 4:19), provided we give first priority to "the kingdom of God and his righteousness" (Matt. 6:33). We can rightly regard our food, clothing, shelter, transportation, and life's other necessities, and the means by which these are obtained (our health, education, talents, job, family, etc.) as God's faithful provision for His children.

As a matter of fact, He normally supplies even more than we really need, in order that we might have the greater joy and blessing of sharing with others (and thus perhaps being the Lord's channel for supplying their needs!) and of enabling the work of preaching the gospel to progress more effectively.

In Old Testament days, God actually required the Jewish people to return a "tithe" (i.e., a "tenth") of their income to the Levites for these purposes. In fact, there is some indication in Scripture that as many as three tithes were required for various purposes, as well as sundry other "offerings." God's material and spiritual blessings often had to be withheld from His people because of their failures in these stewardship responsibilities. "Bring ye all the tithes into the storehouse," said the Lord, and "I will pour you out a blessing, that there shall not be room enough to receive it" (Mal. 3:10).

The Christian now has far more blessings and thus far greater responsibilities than did his Old Testament Jewish counterpart. It is extremely shallow theology that would excuse a Christian from these responsibilities because he is "not under law, but under grace." We are actually under a higher law, and because we more fully know the grace of God, we are under the greater compulsion to show and share that grace. "He which soweth sparingly shall reap also sparingly; and he which soweth bountifully shall reap also bountifully. Every man according as he purposeth in his heart, so let him give; not grudgingly, or of necessity; for God loveth a cheerful giver. And God is able to make all grace abound toward you; that ye, always having all sufficiency in all things, may abound in every good work" (II Cor. 9:6-8).

Although tithing, as such, is not specifically required of the Christian in the New Testament, the greater blessings which are his would certainly imply that he would wish to go far beyond merely tithing in the use of his possessions and income for the Lord's service. He does this, not as a matter of legalistic compulsion, but as a "cheerful giver," and out of a heart of love and gratitude for what the Lord Jesus means to him.

Each person must, of course, decide this for himself. "According as he purposeth in his heart, so let him give." His love for Christ is measured, not by how large a proportion he gives, but how much he uses on himself. The Christian ought to devote all he can to the Lord and the needs of others; his own tastes and personal requirements should be relatively simple and inexpensive.

Finally, in the discharge of his stewardship responsibilities, he must be prayerful and judicious even in his giving. Certainly he should not channel money into those institutions (charities, schools, foundations, even some churches) whose teachings or activities are subversive of the Word of God and the true gospel. In general, the most effective (because most Scriptural) agency for the receipt and utilization of the tithes and offerings of a Christian is a Bible-believing, missionary-minded local church.

7. Question: "When a person believes the Bible, doesn't he have to close his mind and simply exercise faith?"

Answer: It is quite true that one can know God and receive salvation through faith only. "Without faith it is impossible to please God; for he that cometh to God must believe that he is, and that he is a rewarder of them that diligently seek him" (Heb. 11:6).

However, this faith is a reasonable faith, not a blind faith. Rather than closing a person's mind, it really opens and enlarges it, so that he can now think in terms of the true nature of things—spiritual as well as physical. "We know that the Son of God is come, and has given us an understanding, that we may know him that is true" (I John 5:20).

No matter how brilliant a man may be intellectually, in his natural condition he is not able to understand the gospel or other aspects of divinely revealed truth (such as special creation, the trinity, the divine-human nature of Christ, justification by grace, the spirit-filled life, and many others). "The natural man receiveth not the things of the Spirit of God, for they are foolishness unto him; neither can he know them, for they are spiritually discerned" (I Cor. 2:14).

The Bible says, in fact, that the minds of unsaved men are actually blind. "The god of this world [that is, the devil] hath blinded the minds of them that believe not" (II Cor. 4:4). They have "corrupt minds, reprobate concerning the faith" (II Tim. 3:8). They have "the understanding darkened, being alienated from the life of God through the ignorance that is in them, because of the blindness of their heart" (Eph. 4:18).

Therefore a person can never be won to the Christian faith by mere intellectual reasonings and arguments. But this by no means suggests that the Christian faith is unreasonable or anti-intellectual. On the contrary, once a man has been "transformed, by the renewing of his mind" (Rom. 12:2), he is then able for the first time to understand things as they really are. Because he is still in the flesh, he still understands the reasoning of the world and the natural man, but now he is able also to see the hidden presuppositions and fallacies of this reasoning, and gradually to comprehend in all its fullness "even

169

the hidden wisdom, which God ordained before the world unto our glory" (I Cor. 2:7).

It is possible, however, for him to continue in his old ways of thinking and reasoning if he doesn't diligently feed on the Word of God. Like that of the unbeliever, his mind can be "corrupted" (II Cor. 11:3) by the naturalistic reasonings of the world. The pressure of the "contradiction of sinners" against God's revelation can cause him to be "soon shaken in mind" (Heb. 12:3; II Thess. 2:2). It is sadly true that a great number of "decisions for Christ" are made in response to over-simplified and emotional appeals by evangelists or Christian workers, when the person has only the vaguest understanding of what he is being urged to accept. Too often such an individual is one who "heareth the word, and anon with joy receiveth it; Yet hath he not root in himself, but dureth for a while: for when tribulation or persecution ariseth because of the word, by and by he is offended" (Matt. 13:20, 21).

It is critically important that a Christian come to Christ in complete submission to His will and His Word, and that he study the Scriptures intelligently and faithfully. If he does this, there is no limit to the potential development and use of his own mind. In Christ, the Scripture says, "are hidden all the treasures of wisdom and knowledge" (Col. 2:3). "For who hath known the mind of the Lord, that he may instruct him? But we have the mind of Christ" (I Cor. 2:16).

Many of the greatest scientists of the past, men whose writings and discoveries have been of the greatest benefit to mankind, were men who believed the Bible and who sincerely sought to honor the Lord and His Word in all their studies. In this category are men like Newton, Kepler, Pascal, Kelvin, Faraday, Pasteur, Linnaeus, Mendel, and countless others. Even in today's cynical and agnostic world, and despite propaganda to the contrary, there are literally thousands of scholars who still accept the Scriptures as God's infallible Word.

The Christian by no means is justified in mental inertia. He is exhorted to "stir up" his mind (II Peter 3:1), to "gird up" his mind (I Peter 1:13), and to no longer think "as a child" (I Cor. 13:11), but to, rather, "in understanding be men" (I Cor. 14:20).

On the other hand, and even more importantly, he should be "casting down imaginations, and every high thing that exalteth itself against the knowledge of God, bringing into captivity every thought to the obedience of Christ" (II Cor. 10:5). He will "put on therefore, as the elect of God, . . . humbleness of mind" (Col. 3:12), no longer "vainly puffed up in his fleshly mind" (Col. 2:18). And surely, he will try, as God enables him, to keep the first and greatest commandment, which includes the exhortation to "love the Lord thy God . . . with all thy mind" (Matt. 22:37).

It is not true reason, therefore, that conflicts with faith in Christ and His Word, but rather the "oppositions of science falsely so called" (I Tim. 6:20), the "foolish wisdom of this world" (I Cor. 1:20). A person makes a fatal mistake if he allows those who "profess themselves to be wise" and who do "not like to retain God in their knowledge" (Rom. 1:22, 28) to dissuade him from believing the Word of God. "For the preaching of the cross is to them that perish foolishness; but unto us which are saved it is the power of God" (I Cor. 1:18).

The mind is thus never at odds with true faith. Rather it is really only "through faith we understand" (Heb. 11:3).

Chapter XIII

THE CHRISTIAN AND SOCIAL PROBLEMS

1. Question: "Why doesn't the Bible tell us how to build a world of peace and security?"

Answer: The Bible does give us the formula for world peace, but the problem is that men will not believe and obey it. As someone said: "It is not that Christianity has been tried and found wanting; rather it has been found difficult and not tried."

The key to world peace is the same as the key to neighborhood peace and to individual peace—namely, the Prince of Peace! The angels sang, when He first came into the world: "Glory to God in the highest, and on earth peace, good will toward men" (Luke 2:14). When Christ comes the second time, the Scriptures promise that "Of the increase of his government and peace there shall be no end" (Isa. 9:7).

In the meantime, unhappily, it is futile to hope that man will ever be able to secure a peaceful world by his own efforts. "From whence come wars and fightings among you? come they not hence, even of your lusts that war in your members?" (James 4:1). As long as individual men are covetous, selfish, proud, vengeful [and who isn't, in his natural state?], there are going to be wars and fightings, says the Apostle James. National and international wars are the normal and inevitable extension of man's own nature. "As it is written, There is none righteous, no, not one: ... Their feet are swift to shed blood: Destruction and misery are in their ways: And the way of peace have they not known" (Rom. 3:10, 15-17).

It is doubtful if there has ever been a year in which war did not break out somewhere in the world. Even in our "enlightened" modern world, we have seen wars or revolutions or serious fighting erupt in recent years in Viet Nam, Israel, Biafra, China, India, San Salvador, Tibet, Libya, Czechoslovakia, and numerous other countries—not to mention the streets and campuses of our own country. There have already been two World Wars in this century, and Red China continually boasts that she soon will plunge us into another one, in which

172

Mao-tse-Tung says that probably one third of the world's population will be destroyed as the necessary preparation for world communism. No wonder the angel Gabriel told Daniel, 2,500 years ago, that "unto the end wars and desolations are determined" (Dan. 9:26).

The fundamental reason why men can't get along with each other is that they are alienated from God. They must first make peace with God before they can be at peace with one another, or even with themselves. But the wonderful thing is, that God has already made full and perfect provision for man's reconciliation to Himself, and therefore for perfect peace, through Jesus Christ. "For he is our peace" (Eph. 2:14).

The first mention of "peace" in the Bible is in Genesis 14:18, 19, where it speaks of "Melchizedek, king of Salem" (that is, "of peace"), who blessed Abram in the name of God the Creator. This ancient priest-king, as we are taught in Hebrews 7:1-22, was a type of Christ. He was the "King of Peace" in his time, as Christ is the "Prince of Peace" for all time.

The first mention of "peace" in the New Testament is in Matthew 5:9, where Christ promised: "Blessed are the peacemakers" (not "pacifists," incidentally, but "peacemakers"). On the other hand, it should be noted that He also said: "Think not that I am come to send peace on earth: I came not to send peace, but a sword" (Matt. 10:34).

As a matter of fact, one of the signs of the last days is an intense, but futile, preoccupation with the attainment of peace and security. "The day of the Lord so cometh as a thief in the night. For when they shall say, Peace and safety; then sudden destruction cometh upon them, . . . But ye, brethren, are not in darkness, that that day should overtake you as a thief" (I Thess. 5:2-4).

What, then, does it mean to be a "peacemaker," and how can we actually find peace in such a world as this? The true peacemaker is Jesus Christ, who has "made peace through the blood of his cross, by him to reconcile all things unto himself" (Col. 1:20). By dying for our sins, He has made it possible for us to be brought into right relation with our Creator, and then into right relation with all others who have been redeemed by His blood. "For he is our peace, who hath made both one and hath broken down the middle wall of partition between us; . . . for to make in himself of twain one new man, so making peace" (Eph. 2:14, 15).

The man who comes in faith to the Lord Jesus Christ, acknowledging Him as Lord and Saviour, thus receives forgiveness of all his sins and is restored to fellowship with his heavenly Father. "Therefore being justified by faith, we have peace with God through our Lord Jesus Christ" (Rom. 5:1).

It is significant that all the New Testament epistles of Paul and Peter open with some such salutation as "Grace to you and peace from God our Father, and the Lord Jesus Christ" (Rom. 1:7). To the Christian, God is pre-eminently the "God of peace" (Rom. 15:33; 16:20; Phil. 4:9; Heb. 13:20; etc.), and therefore he experiences in a very real and wonderful way the "peace of God" (Col. 3:15; Phil. 4:7).

The Christian therefore is exhorted by Paul: "If it be possible, as much as lieth in you, live peaceably with all men" (Rom. 12:18). The Lord Jesus promised: "Peace I leave with you, my peace I give unto you: . . . Let not your heart be troubled, neither let it be afraid" (John 14:27). He also said: "These things I have spoken unto you, that in me ye might have peace. In the world ye shall have tribulation: but be of good cheer: I have overcome the world" (John 16:33).

Until Christ returns, the world can never find real peace, though it is undoubtedly well to work and pray for at least a measure of peace in our time. But the individual can, right now, find perfect peace of heart and mind by submitting to Jesus Christ as his Lord and Saviour. "Now the God of hope fill you with all joy and peace in believing, that ye may abound in hope, through the power of the Holy Ghost" (Rom. 15:13).

2. Question: "Is there a Biblical answer to the problem of environmental pollution?"

Answer: The first commandment given by God to man after He had created him was: "Be fruitful and multiply, and fill the earth, and subdue it" (Gen. 1:28). Even before man's creation, God had said man was to "have dominion . . . over the earth" (Gen. 1:26).

It was therefore in accord with God's divine purpose for man to increase his population on the earth. Likewise it was proper for man to study and understand the earth and its processes and then to control and utilize them. Science and technology, therefore, are implied and justified in this primeval commandment of the Creator.

In the beginning, of course, man had a perfect environment over which to exercise his dominion. "God saw everything that he had made and, behold, it was very good" (Gen. 1:31). All of nature was in perfect balance and harmony, reflecting the power and wisdom of its Maker. Man's dominion, of course, was that of a steward, not a despot. He was "under God" and was to utilize his authority in such a way as best to serve God's purposes for the world and mankind.

But the tragic fact of history is that man rebelled against God and therefore brought upon himself and his entire dominion the great Curse of decay and death (Gen. 3:17-20). The definitive New Testament passage on this subject is Romans 8:20-22: "For the creation was made subject to vanity [or better, 'futility], not willingly, but by reason of him who hath subjected the same in hope. Because the creation itself also shall be delivered from the bondage of corruption into the glorious liberty of the children of God. For we know that the whole creation groaneth and travaileth in pain together until now."

This universal condition of "corruption" extends throughout the physical, biological, and mental realms. The Bible speaks of "corruptible things, as silver and gold" (I Peter 1:18), of "corruptible seed . . . as the flower of grass (I Peter 1:23, 24), and of corruptible man (Rom. 1:23), making it plain in each case that the corruption is universal and continually increasing. The word "corruption" itself means simply "decay," or an "inescapable tendency toward disintegration and death." This bondage of decay, under which the whole creation is groaning, corresponds exactly to what scientists have recognized as the Second Law of Thermodynamics, which states that everything in the universe, so far as can be observed, is tending toward an ultimate state of randomness and death.

Man, however, is still in the "image of God," even though that image has been corrupted by his rebellion. Therefore he is still responsible to God, not only in how he exercises his now uncertain "dominion" over the earth, but even more in how he responds to God's work of redeeming and delivering the creation from its bondage of corruption. Therefore the first prerequisite to the solution of the problem of pollution is for individual men to turn in repentance and faith to Jesus Christ. It is "by him" that "all things were created" (Col. 1:16), "by him" that "all things consist" (Col. 1:17), and "by him" that "all things have been reconciled," "through the blood of his cross" (Col. 1:20). The shedding of the blood of the Son of God is the redemption price (I Peter 1:19) for the deliverance both of individual souls who trust Him, and ultimately of the whole creation.

As long as men continue to reject Christ and the Scriptures, there is no real solution to the problem of pollution or corruption, until Christ returns. In fact, Biblical prophecy indicates it will grow much worse.

For example, "the fourth part of the earth" will be killed "with sword and with hunger, and with pestilence, and with the beasts of the earth" (Rev. 6:8). Further, the "third part of trees . . . and all green grass" will be "burnt up" (Rev. 8:7). "And many men died of the waters, because they were made bitter" (Rev. 8:11). "And there arose a smoke out of the pit, as the smoke of a great furnace; and the sun and the air were darkened by reason of the smoke of the pit" (Rev. 9:2). "And there fell a noisome and grievous sore upon the men which had the mark of the beast — and the sea became as the blood of a dead man — and men were scorched with great heat — and they gnawed their tongues for pain" (Rev. 16:2, 3, 9, 10).

Finally, the great "Babylon" will be utterly destroyed, "and the merchants of the earth shall weep and mourn over her; for no man buyeth their merchandise any more" (Rev. 18:11).

It is significant also that the fulfillment of these prophecies, and many others of like kind, will take place at a time when there is a large population in the earth. Of those who are saved and in heaven it says there is "a great multitude, which no man could number" who came "out of the great tribulation" (Rev. 7:9, 14), and undoubtedly the number of the unsaved experiencing this "great tribulation" (Matt. 24:21) is even greater. Revelation 9:16 describes an army of 200 million "horsemen" who were to slay the "third part of men."

God has shown us the terror of these future events in the Holy Scriptures in order to warn us to "flee from the wrath to come" (Luke 3:7) by turning to Christ as our Redeemer and Lord. For those who believe on Him, "God hath not appointed us to wrath, but to obtain salvation by our Lord Jesus Christ" (I Thess. 5:9).

Eventually the earth will be made new, with the total environment radically transformed and revived. "For behold, I create new heavens and a new earth: . . . They shall not hurt nor destroy in all my holy mountain, saith the Lord" (Isa. 65:17, 25). The Lord Jesus promised: "Behold, I make all things new. . . . And there shall be no more curse" (Rev. 21:5; 22:3).

In the present earth, however, the effects of man's sinfulness and selfishness will inevitably continue to deteriorate his environment. The judgments that are coming are in part to "destroy them which destroy the earth" (Rev. 11:18). The only possible respite from an accelerated deterioration would be a widespread return to faith in the true God and His Son through the Holy Scriptures.

The genuine Christian has been made "a new creation in Christ Jesus" (II Cor. 5:17). He is one who loves and respects his chil-

176

dren and seeks to "bring them up in the nurture and admonition of the Lord" (Eph. 6:4). A large family of this kind will thus never be an over-population problem, but rather a blessing to society (note Ps. 127:1-5).

Similarly, the Christian, like his heavenly Father, has compassion even for the animal kingdom (note Matt. 6:26; 10:29; Ps. 147:7-9, etc.) and will oppose its exploitation and destruction. His standard of living is (or at least should be) relatively simple and frugal (see, for example, I Tim. 6:6-10), and therefore his demands on the earth's environment and its resources also fairly simple. He will be considerate of others and should never knowingly satisfy his own material desires at the cost of injuring or hindering someone else, and he will do what he can to encourage his government and his company and his other associates to do the same.

The real answer to pollution, therefore—just as the real answer to sin, which is its basic cause—is to be found only in Jesus Christ, first as one's personal Saviour and then ultimately as the world's coming King.

3. Question: "Why does God allow innocent people to suffer?"

Answer: This is one of the most difficult questions for Christians to answer.

The "problem of pain," as the well-known Christian scholar, C. S. Lewis, once called it, is atheism's most potent weapon against the Christian faith.

All true science and history, if rightly understood, support the fact of God. This evidence is so strong that, as the Bible says: "The fool hath said in his heart, There is no God" (Ps. 14:1).

Most atheists, therefore, without any objective evidence on which to base their faith in "no God," must resort finally to philosophical objections. And this problem of suffering is the greatest of these. That is, they say, how can a God of love permit such things in His world as war, sickness, pain, and death, especially when their effects often are felt most keenly by those who are apparently innocent? Either He is not a God of love and is indifferent to human suffering, or else He is not a God of power and is therefore helpless to do anything about it. In either case, the Biblical God who is supposedly one of both absolute power and perfect love becomes an impossible anachronism. Or so they claim!

This is a real difficulty, but atheism is certainly not the answer, and neither is agnosticism. While there is much evil in the world,

177

there is even more that is good. This is proved by the mere fact that people normally try to hang on to life as long as they can. Furthermore, everyone instinctively recognizes that "good" is a higher order of truth than "bad." People continue to believe in their deepest hearts that somehow, ultimately, "right" will prevail over "wrong." These innate beliefs are in themselves evidence that there is a God who is a moral being, and who has implanted these hopes in the human soul.

That being so, we need also to recognize that our very minds were created by God. We can only use these minds to the extent that He allows, and it is therefore utterly presumptuous for us to use them to question Him and His motives. "Shall not the Judge of all the earth do right?" (Gen. 18:25). "Shall the thing formed say to him that formed it, why hast thou made me thus?" (Rom. 9:20). We ourselves do not establish the standards of what is right. Only the Creator of all reality can do that. We need to settle it, in our minds and hearts, whether we understand it or not, that whatever God does is, by definition, right.

Having settled this by faith, we are then free to seek for ways in which we can profit spiritually from the sufferings in life as well as the blessings. As we consider such matters, it is helpful to keep the following great truths continually in our minds.

(1) There is really no such thing as the "innocent" suffering. Since "all have sinned and come short of the glory of God" (Rom. 3:23), there is no one who has the right to freedom from God's wrath on the basis of his own innocence. As far as babies are concerned, and others who may be incompetent mentally to distinguish right and wrong, it is clear from both Scripture and universal experience that they are sinners by nature and thus will inevitably become sinners by choice as soon as they are able to do so.

(2) The world is now under God's Curse (Gen. 3:17) because of man's rebellion against God's Word. This "bondage of corruption," with the "whole world groaning and travailing together in pain" (Rom. 8:21, 22) is universal, affecting all men everywhere. God did not create the world this way, and one day will set all things right again. In that day, "God shall wipe away all tears from their eyes; and there shall be no more death, neither sorrow, nor crying, neither shall there be any more pain" (Rev. 21:4).

(3) The Lord Jesus Christ, who was the only truly "innocent" and "righteous" man in all history, nevertheless has suffered more than anyone else who ever lived. And this He did for us! "Christ died for

our sins" (I Cor. 15:3). He suffered and died, in order that ultimately He might deliver the world from the Curse, and that, even now, He can deliver from sin and its bondage anyone who will receive Him in faith as his personal Lord and Saviour. This great deliverance from the penalty of inherent sin, as well as of overt sins, very possibly also assures the salvation of those who have died before reaching an age of conscious choice of wrong over right.

(4) With our full faith in God's goodness and in Christ's redemption, we can recognize that our present sufferings can be turned to His glory and our good. The sufferings of unsaved men are often used by the Holy Spirit to cause them to realize their need of salvation and to turn to Christ in repentance and faith. The sufferings of Christians should always be the means of developing a stronger dependence on God and a more Christ-like character, if they are properly "exercised thereby" (Heb. 12:11).

Thus, God is loving and merciful even when, "for the present," He allows trials and sufferings to come in our lives. "For we know that all things work together for good to them that love God, to them who are the called according to his purpose" (Rom. 8:28).

4. Question: "Why do so few educated people believe the Bible?"

Answer: It does seem strange at first that relatively few educated men, especially those with advanced degrees, will accept the inspiration and authority of the Bible. After all, there are many strong and persuasive evidences of its divine origin—its fulfilled prophecies, its remarkable preservation, its unity in diversity, its own claims, its spiritual power, archaeological confirmations of its accuracy, and many others. Furthermore, Bible scholars have been able to answer and refute all the charges of its so-called contradictions and mistakes. One would think that educated men, supposedly experienced in examining and evaluating objective evidence, would be the ones most readily convinced of its divine inspiration.

As a matter of fact, there have been many great scientists and scholars who actually were Bible-believing Christians. Such men as Isaac Newton, Michael Faraday, Clark Maxwell, Lord Kelvin, Louis Pasteur, Blaise Pascal, and many other great scientists of the past fit this description. It would also be possible, if necessary, to give the names of thousands of men living today, each holding one or more advanced degrees in some scholarly field, who believe the Bible to be the inspired Word of God and who have received the

Lord Jesus Christ as their personal Saviour and as the God of creation. It is certainly a false claim that "no" educated men believe the Bible!

It is admittedly true, however, that such believing scientists and scholars are in the minority. As a matter of fact, this is true of most other professions and vocations as well. Jesus Himself said: "Strait is the gate, and narrow is the way, which leadeth unto life, and few there be that find it" (Matt. 7:14).

But unbelief does seem to be especially characteristic of modern intellectuals. They seem to be the ones who are most committed to the evolutionary theory of origins, to the proposition that the Bible is just one of many ancient and outdated religious books, to the concept of Jesus merely as a great human teacher, and to the false gospel of social, rather than individual, salvation.

The Bible indeed predicts exactly this state of affairs: "Not many wise men after the flesh, not many mighty, not many noble, are called" (I Cor. 1:26). "The Lord knoweth the thoughts of the wise, that they are vain" (I Cor. 3:20).

From the human point of view, this condition can be attributed primarily to the sin of pride. It was pride which caused the primeval sin of Satan (note Isa. 14:13; Ezek. 28:17; I Tim. 3:6) and which led to the fall of Eve (Gen. 3:6). As a matter of fact, unbelief is merely another name for pride. That which causes man to reject God's Word is simply pride in his own autonomous reason, by which he presumes the right to evaluate the truth or falsity of what God has said. It is pride in his own personal integrity which leads him to deny God's testimony of his sinfulness. It is pride in his ability to bring about his own salvation that makes him reject Christ as God's unique provision for salvation. Every other sin which a man commits will, if one probes deeply enough, be found to have its root in this twin sin of unbelieving pride.

Pride manifests itself in various ways—pride of person, pride of wealth, pride of power, pride of knowledge, pride of many other things. Each will, if unconquered, prevent one from coming in simple faith to the Lord Jesus Christ for salvation. To be saved, a man must recognize and confess himself to be an absolutely helpless and worthless sinner, completely lost and unable to save himself; then he must accept in gratitude and humility the free gift of eternal life purchased through the suffering and death of Jesus Christ for his sins. There is certainly no room for human pride or skepticism in such a transaction as this, and one who tries to come to Christ in any attitude except that of unconditional trust will never be saved. "Except ye be converted and become as little children, ye shall not enter into the kingdom of heaven," Jesus said (Matt. 18:3).

This cancer of pride and unbelief does seem to afflict the intellectual more deeply than most others. His entire training has been directed toward this. The "creation" of new knowledge through research, the attainment of recognition and prestige for his discoveries through publications, the desire to be considered progressive and scientific—all tend to glorify human reason and accomplishments. It is extremely difficult for him to acknowledge there is anything outside the reach of his scientific method, requiring faith for its comprehension. It is especially difficult for him to accept the Bible by faith, since it continually confronts him with the fact of his own helplessness and sinfulness, and the fact that his Creator will one day become his Judge. Therefore, he either consciously or subconsciously rejects it and attempts to rationalize his rejection by looking for mistakes and contradictions in it.

Thus it is that "the natural man receiveth not the things of the Spirit of God; for they are foolishness unto him" (I Cor. 2:14). That pride of wisdom which had its first beginning in Satan himself has enabled him who is now "the god of this world" to "blind the minds of them which believe not, lest the light of the glorious gospel of Christ, who is the image of God, should shine unto them" (II Cor. 4:4).

But as the Apostle Paul has said: "For what if some did not believe? Shall their unbelief make the faith of God without effect? God forbid; yea, let God be true, but every man a liar" (Rom. 3: 3, 4). The true wisdom is found only in God and in His Word, and it is utterly presumptuous for man, as God's creature, to imagine otherwise. "In Christ are hid all the treasures of wisdom and knowledge" (Col. 2:3).

5. Question: "How soon after conception does a baby have a soul?"

Answer: The one greatest difference between man and the animals is that man has an eternal spirit, "created in the image of God" (Gen. 1:27). He also has a body and a soul, and these are also marvelous creations of God. That there is a distinction between the soul and spirit is evident from I Thessalonians 5:23 and Hebrews 4:12, among other passages.

The soul is, in general, the "mind," possibly including also something of what we mean by "will" and "emotion." To some uncertain

181

extent, these qualities are possessed also by the higher animals, and it is significant that the same terms, "living creature" and "living soul" (both being translations of the same Hebrew word "nephesh"), were applied both to these higher animals (Gen. 1:21, 24) and to man (Gen. 2:7) at the time of their first creation. The soul, or mind, functions by means of the body, especially the brain and the nervous system, and each is quite dependent on the other. Both physical and mental characteristics, furthermore, are transmitted genetically from parents to child. The latter possesses his full complement of genes and chromosomes, with all their genetic "information" which will direct his future development, right from the very moment of conception. He is in every sense a "living soul" from that instant until he dies.

But what about his spirit? This is that component of man's being which can have spiritual fellowship with God and with other people, which discerns right and wrong, truth and falsehood, beauty and ugliness. This is man's religious nature, his ability to worship and to love either the true God or a false god. It is often difficult to discern between the soul and spirit in man, since their respective capacities are often intricately interrelated, and since both are included in the salvation received through faith in the Lord Jesus Christ, but there is definitely a difference. No animal has spiritual qualities, but each man does have an eternal spirit, which will exist somewhere forever.

When a man dies, his body decays back to the dust, there to await the resurrection at the second coming of Christ. The Bible says, however, that "the spirit shall return unto God who gave it" (Eccles. 12:7). The Scripture also says that God "formeth the spirit of man within him" (Zech. 12:1; see also Isa. 42:5; Ps. 139:14-16; etc.).

The Spirit which is thus "given" and "formed" by God within his soul and body must be initially in embryonic form, just as are his physical and mental attributes. All must grow as a personal unity, first in the mother's womb, later in her arms, and finally in an independent responsibility of his own.

But it should be obvious that the spirit must exist contemporaneously with the soul and body right from the beginning. Just as biological life as a distinct and complete genetic entity exists from the moment of conception, so must its associated spiritual life. Though there is much of mystery involved here, we are justified in believing that the omnipotent God creates an eternal spirit for each man which He infuses into his body at the instant of his conception. There is no time later than this at which such a miraculous fusion would be appropriate, nor is there any evidence that it takes place at any other time.

Thus, the sexual union of a man and woman is far more than an expression of marital love and pleasure, though these are quite real and important. It also involves the possible presence of God Himself, in the act of creating a new person, destined for eternity! No wonder, therefore, that the Bible always treats marriage and conception as sacred, and always strongly warns against adultery, fornication, and all other sexual distortions and perversions.

We know very little, of course, about the nature of an infant's personal consciousness, as none of us can recall his own birth or the events of the first year or so after birth. There is no doubt, however, that a baby does possess conscious awareness in some measure and that his experiences may have profound effect on his later life. Why, then, should not this also be true with his life during the months in his mother's womb?

There are at least hints in the Bible to this effect. Before the twins, Jacob and Esau, were born to Rebekah, "the children struggled together within her," because, as the Lord said, "Two nations are in thy womb . . . and the one people shall be stronger than the other people" (Gen. 25:22, 23).

Similarly, when the Virgin Mary, soon after she "was found with child of the Holy Ghost" (Matt. 1:18), visited her cousin Elizabeth, the child who had already spent six months in Elizabeth's womb and was destined to be John the Baptist, the forerunner of Christ, "leaped in her womb." Elizabeth, "filled with the Holy Ghost," said to Mary, "Lo, as soon as the voice of thy salutation sounded in mine ears, the babe leaped in my womb for joy" (Luke 1:41, 44).

In view of the divine authentication of both these important examples of pre-natal consciousness, one should be slow to dismiss them as mere figures of speech. "As thou knowest not what is the way of the spirit, nor how the bones do grow in the womb of her that is with child: even so thou knowest not the works of God who maketh all" (Eccles. 11:5).

There is every reason to believe, therefore, and no reason to doubt, that each individual becomes a whole person—body, soul, and spirit— at the very moment of his conception. Whether or not he survives through childhood, or even survives to birth, he has an eternal spirit which will live forever.

In view of these facts, the current sudden increase in legalized abortion practice is very disturbing. Regardless of what changes may be taking place in legal and medical practice, abortion is still murder in the sight of God. The parents, the abortionist, and all who participate in thus denying a helpless infant his right to see the world outside his mother's womb, will some day have to face him again at the throne of God.

6. Question: "Is government control the best remedy for the over-population problem?"

Answer: In spite of all the alarming propaganda of the past few years, there is really no serious population problem for the world as a whole. However, the supposed population explosion has been appropriated as one of the weapons in the arsenal of those doctrinaire liberals who are working hard to establish universal governmental controls.

God's very first command to Adam was to "be fruitful and multiply and fill the earth" (Gen. 1:28). After the great Flood had destroyed the antediluvian population, He told Noah once again, "Be fruitful and multiply, and fill the earth" (Gen. 9:1). It was therefore God's intent that man should fill the entire earth, at least to the extent of its optimum productivity. Since this has not yet been accomplished, it is overt disobedience to God's command to seek now to impose population controls to prevent it.

There are obviously vast areas in the world which could support many more people than are now living there. In the United States, especially, countless rural and semi-rural areas are in economic straits because of too few—not too many—people.

Furthermore, living standards may well go up—not down—as the population increases—that is, if people are productively employed and not supported in idleness by government doles. Thus Japan and Holland, two of the world's most densely populated nations, are also high in national productivity (despite very limited natural resources). Some of the most impoverished nations, on the other hand (e.g., Arabia, Afghanistan, Mongolia, etc.) are nations with very low population densities.

It is true, of course, that the present world population growth rate of two percent per year cannot be sustained indefinitely. But this does not mean that we should allow current hysteria to pressure us into supposed remedies that are worse than the disease. "De-populationists" today are seriously advocating not only widespread promotion of contraceptive measures and legalized abortion, but even increased homo-sexuality and enforced sterilization—all in the name of population control!

Furthermore, these measures are being proposed mainly for the United States and other countries with high living standards, rather than countries which really *do* have significant population and nutritional problems. Not only would births be seriously restricted if some were to have their way, but also the type of births would be controlled—that is, by application of new techniques of "genetic engineering" which supposedly will be available in the near future.

It is quite obvious that all of this can be accomplished only by a tremendous expansion of government control over the private lives of all citizens. Herein undoubtedly will be found, if one probes deeply enough, the fountainhead of all the population-scare propaganda. It is no accident that most of the leading advocates of these sundry population measures are found near the left end of the political spectrum, for whom a totally planned economy in a socialistic-totalitarian world society is a desirable goal.

Some have been quite vocal recently in attacking God's primeval commandment to man. They say His command to "multiply" is the cause of our population problem, and His command to "subdue the earth" is the cause of our supposed ecological crisis.

We can be confident, however, that God knew what He was doing when He gave these commands, and that genuine obedience will result in blessing, not destruction, for man's world. Whatever the world's "optimum" population may be, the same God who created the marvelous process of human procreation will also modify it as necessary, when the earth is actually "filled" to that optimum. In the animal world, in fact, much evidence exists that reproduction rates are inversely proportional in some way to population density, entirely aside from any so-called "struggle for existence" against predators. That is, there seem to be built-in genetic and social mechanisms which rather quickly stabilize a given population of an animal species at its optimum for the given ecological region.

There is another factor, too—that of eschatology! This present order of things is not destined to last forever. Long before the world population ever reaches a lethal density, the Lord Jesus Christ is coming again and the population of the earth will be drastically reduced by at least two great events.

In the first place, all living believers, redeemed by faith in Christ, will be suddenly taken out of the world to meet Him in the air (I Thess. 4:17). Secondly, those who remain will face the awful seven-

185

year judgment period on the earth known as the Great Tribulation. Of these, one fourth will be slain in one set of judgments (Rev. 6:8) and again a third part of the remainder by another set (Rev. 9:18). Other catastrophes likewise take their toll so that, finally, "the curse hath devoured the earth, and they that dwell therein are desolate: therefore the inhabitants of the earth are burned, and few men left" (Isa. 24:6). All of this is preparatory to the earth's promised millennial age.

In the meantime, for all those in this age who truly are trusting in God and His Word, "Marriage is honorable in all, and the bed undefiled" (Heb. 13:4). And for Christian parents, who will seek to bring their children up "in the nurture and admonition of the Lord" (Eph. 6:4), God's Word is still valid when He says: "Lo, children are an heritage of the Lord: and the fruit of the womb is His reward" (Ps. 127:3).

Chapter XIV

MISUNDERSTOOD BIBLE CHARACTERS

1. *Question: "How could Abraham really love Isaac and yet offer him as a sacrifice?"*

Answer: Probably no word in the English language has been so distorted and misused as the word "love." All kinds of self-seeking, heresy, immorality, and even violence are being justified today in the name of "love." The so-called "situational ethics" seeks to legalize this rejection of fixed and eternal standards of truth and rightness in deference to individually defined and conveniently applied criteria of "love."

The true meaning of love, however, can be understood only from Biblical revelation. The word is introduced for the first time in the Bible in the story of Abraham and Isaac, where God told Abraham to "take now thy son, thine only son, Isaac, whom thou lovest, and offer him up for a burnt-offering" (Gen. 22:2). The love of a father for his son is thus, as it were, set forth in Scripture as the first, and thus definitive, meaning of love.

At first this seems strange, even though Isaac was the miraculously born son of promise, and thus in a most peculiar way was the dearly beloved son of his father. But this unexpected definition becomes perfectly fitting when we see, from later Scriptures, that Abraham and Isaac form a beautiful type of God the Father and God the Son. Just as the first mention of "love" in the Old Testament is found in connection with the love of a human father for his son, so the first mention of "love" in the New Testament is the testimony of the heavenly Father concerning His love for His Son. "This is my beloved Son, in whom I am well pleased" (Matt. 3:17; Mark 1:11; Luke 3:22).

Just before He was to go to the cross, the Lord Jesus, the only begotten of the Father, prayed thus: "Father, I will that they also, whom thou has given me, be with me where I am; that they may behold my glory, which thou hast given me: for thou lovest me before the foundation of the world" (John 17:24). The first love that ever existed, and thus the root and ground of all other loves, was the love of the Father for His Son, in the fellowship of the Godhead before time began. The love of husband and wife, the love of a mother for her children, the love of children for parents, the love of friends for one another, love for country—all loves find their source in the eternal love of God the Father for God the Son, and the meaning of any kind of human love must be measured ultimately against this standard.

And now we can begin to see the significance of the fact that Abraham, in the very place where God acknowledged his deep love for Isaac, was commanded to slay his son and offer him as a burnt-sacrifice to God. The questioning agony of Abraham's heart must have been like a fire in his own soul, but all we are told is that "Abraham rose up early in the morning . . . took Isaac his son . . . and went unto the place of which God had told him" (Gen. 22:3).

God of course spared Isaac's life before he was slain, but Abraham passed the test of real love. "By faith Abraham, when he was tried, offered up Isaac: and he that had received the promises offered up his only begotten son. Of whom it was said, That in Isaac shall thy seed be called: Accounting that God was able to raise him up, even from the dead; from whence also he received him in a figure" (Heb. 11:17-19).

Abraham's faith in the Word of God was so strong that he knew that whatever God desired for Isaac would be that which was best for him. And though it mean the death of Isaac and the crushing of his own heart, the depth of his love for his son was so great that he must believe and obey the Word of God as it related to him, whether he could understand or not.

Because Isaac thus "died" and was raised from the dead "in a figure," God then was able to use him to bring great blessing to multitudes in all the years to come. Abraham's love was a sacrificial love, glorifying God and thus setting the pattern for the full revelation of God's own love.

God the Father loved His Son before the foundation of the world. As noted above, His love is first introduced in the three synoptic Gospels, Matthew, Mark, and Luke, by the voice from heaven, identifying Jesus as His beloved Son. But then, in the Gospel of John—the Gospel which most fully sets forth the doctrine of love—the first mention of the word is found in the most glorious words ever written: "For God so loved the world, that he gave his only begotten Son, that

188

whosoever believeth on him should not perish, but have everlasting life" (John 3:16).

Though God loved His Son with an everlasting love, He loved lost men and women so much that He gave Him as a sacrifice, dying for their sins, that they might be redeemed.

And, like Isaac, who knowingly and willingly permitted Abraham to bind him to the altar of sacrifice, so the Lord Jesus willingly suffered and died for us. "He loved me and gave himself for me" (Gal. 2:20).

This is what love really is. It is sacrificial love, love that makes a man obey the Word, and believe the promise of God, regardless of the cost to himself. His decisions and actions are governed, not by his own will, but by that which will most benefit the one he loves— the Lord first of all, then his Christian brother, and then his fellow man.

Real love is thus, above all, a self-less love. And yet, in God's wonderful plan, the more one loves in true self-sacrifice, the more is one rewarded in real happiness. It was even thus with Christ Himself, ". . . who for the joy that was set before him, endured the cross, despising the shame, and is set down at the right hand of the throne of God" (Heb. 12:2). The love of the Father permitted even the death of His Son, knowing of the greater joy through all eternity which He would share in fellowship with those He had redeemed and who would therefore love Him forever.

2. Question: "How could God bless a dishonest man like Jacob in preference to a good man like Esau?"

Answer: The widespread belief that Jacob, the father of the twelve tribes of Israel, was a shrewd crook, whose schemes robbed his brother Esau of his birthright and his uncle Laban of his flocks and herds, has undoubtedly been one of the chief popular myths supporting the repeated waves of anti-Semitism over the past three millenniums. Many people have been far too anxious to believe that the Jews, all of whom are descendants of Jacob, have inherited their father's character and as a result are dishonest manipulators, interested only in money and power.

Esau, on the other hand, is pictured as a noble, hard-working outdoor type of man, who in his trusting nature was cheated in a moment of weakness out of his rightful inheritance by his crafty brother Jacob. Esau was the father of the Edomites, now extinct as a nation, but whose descendants have mixed with other non-Israelite descendants of Abraham to produce the Arab peoples.

However, a closer look at the story of Jacob, as found in Genesis 25 through 35, will yield a much more favorable view of his true character. Esau and Jacob were twins, with Esau slightly the older. Before the boys were born, God had told his parents: "The elder shall serve the younger" (Gen. 25:23).

There was nothing wrong with this divinely ordered arrangement at all; no divine law had ever ordained that the firstborn son should receive the bulk of the inheritance or that, in the special case of the divine lineage extending from Adam to Christ, the oldest son should be the one to maintain this line (Seth, Shem, Isaac, Judah, David, and many others in this Messianic line were not firstborn sons).

Rather, God chose the one in each family whose heart was most closely attuned to God's will and plan for the world's redemption through the coming Saviour. Knowing the characters of Jacob and Esau before they were born, God chose Jacob, and made this plainly known to their parents. "Was not Esau Jacob's brother? saith the Lord: yet I loved Jacob, and I hated Esau" (Mal. 1:2, 3).

Esau's character, as it began to develop, was one given over to fleshly appetites, unconcerned with God's will at all. He was a "cunning hunter, a man of the field," indicating he spent most of his time perfecting his skill as a hunter, probably helping very little with the family duties and showing little interest in his family's great spiritual heritage. This was further proved when he married two Hittite women, from one of the Canaanite nations, rather than a wife from his own people, although this was clearly contrary to God's will (Gen. 26:34, 35).

Jacob, on the other hand, was a "plain man" (Gen. 25:27). It is significant that the word "plain" is the same Hebrew word as that usually rendered "perfect." Thus, Jacob was a righteous man, obedient to his parents, working hard at his family responsibilities, and, most important, deeply concerned about his spiritual birthright, as promised to him by God before he was born.

Despite all this, however, Isaac in his old age (he was over 100 at this time) had grown partial to Esau, evidently because of the latter's skill at obtaining and preparing tasty meat for him (note Gen. 25:28; 27:1-4). He resolved to pronounce the blessing on him which should have gone to Jacob (compare Gen. 27:29 with Gen. 12:3 and Gen. 25:23). This "blessing" entailed God's prophetic promise, originally given to Abraham and then to Isaac, that all nations would be blessed through his seed, who one day would attain universal pre-eminence. The "birthright," on the other hand, was evidently the right to lead the family in spiritual matters, presiding at the altars where they worshiped God together and transmitting God's Word to them, with all the primeval histories and gracious promises for the future. Sometime earlier, Esau, as a "fornicator and profane person," had "for one morsel of meat sold his birthright" to Jacob (Heb. 12:16). It seems to have been customary (though not mandatory) that this birthright should go to the eldest son, assuming he desired and deserved it. Esau apparently felt such a right was of no value to him, whereas Jacob earnestly desired this privilege, and there is no indication that the transaction he proposed was improper. Furthermore, Jacob was far better equipped to perform these functions, since "Esau despised his birthright" (Gen. 25:34).

Thus had Jacob acquired the responsibilities and privileges of the birthright. In order also to receive the paternal blessing which was rightfully his, however, he agreed to a stratagem proposed by his mother Rebekah, to persuade his blind father that he himself was Esau. When Jacob demurred at the proposed deception, Rebekah invoked her right to filial obedience on the part of Jacob and assumed all the responsibility herself (Gen. 27:13).

Rebekah paid dearly for her part in this deception, as she never saw Jacob again after that day. He was forced to flee from Esau and she died before he could return home many years later. Jacob was also guilty of lying, though he was doing so in order to obey his mother and to obtain what was rightfully his. He should have trusted God to work out the problem and to overrule his father's disobedience to God's word, rather than to resort to the method he did.

At any rate, it is very significant that, when the Lord met Jacob that night in a dream (Gen. 28:12-15), He spoke no word of rebuke to him, but only a promise to be with him and to bless him wherever he went, and his seed after him, thus confirming the very blessing pronounced by his father. It is absurd to think that God would be bound by a mere human stratagem, of course. Jacob would have received the divine blessing regardless of what Isaac or Esau may have done anyhow.

This promise received its initial fulfillment during the years spent with his uncle Laban. His faithful and capable service resulted in great prosperity for Laban (Gen. 30:27-30), even though Laban repeatedly deceived him, first in the matter of his promised wife (Gen. 29:20, 25), and then frequently in the matter of his promised wages

(Gen. 31:38-42). God blessed Jacob because of his faithfulness, by increasing his own herds (Gen. 31:5-13).

Jacob was not perfect, but it is clear that he was certainly one of the noblest and most godly men in all the Scriptures, immeasurably more so than his older brother. But if anyone still questions why God favored Jacob rather than Esau, the answer of Romans 9:13-15 to this very question should be sufficient: "As it is written, Jacob have I loved, but Esau have I hated. What shall we say then? Is there unrighteousness with God? God forbid. For he saith to Moses, "I will have mercy on whom I will have mercy, and I will have compassion on whom I will have compassion."

Thus, what God does is right—by definition! And what He says must be true—by definition. It is absurd for any man to question his Maker. "Nay but, O man, who art thou that repliest against God? Shall the thing formed say to him that formed it, Why hast thou made me thus?" (Rom. 9:20). We can always be completely certain that, whether we understand or not, God has good reason for what He says or does. Our greatest wisdom and greatest happiness is simply to trust and obey.

3. Question: "What was the role of John the Baptist in God's program?"

Answer: Coming as he did in the transition period from the Old Testament to the New Testament economy, the ministry of John the Baptist has been almost entirely neglected by modern Christians, despite its unique importance. Sermons are rarely, if ever, preached on John from most pulpits, and yet he was the greatest man who ever lived, with the exception of Christ Himself!

For example, he is the only man who ever lived of whom it was said that he was "filled with the Holy Spirit from his mother's womb" (Luke 1:15). His coming was prophesied in the Old Testament (Isa. 40:3; Mal. 3:1; 4:5, 6; Mark 1:1-3) hundreds of years before he was born. Of him it was simply said: "There was a man sent from God, whose name was John" (John 1:6).

Many people have regarded him as the last of the Old Testament prophets, but this idea was explicitly refuted by Christ when He said: "The law and the prophets were until John; since that time, the kingdom of God is preached" (Luke 16:16). Peter said: "The word which God sent unto the children of Israel, preaching peace by Jesus Christ . . . began from Galilee, after [i.e., 'with'] the baptism which John preached" (Acts 10:36, 37).

Thus, John the Baptist, rather than being the last voice of the Old Testament, is rather the first voice of the New Testament dispensation. As such, he (rather than Peter or one of the other apostles) was the first Christian witness. "The same came for a witness, to bear witness of the Light" (John 1:7). He, rather than Stephen, was the first Christian martyr, giving his life because of his testimony for Christ. Indeed, he was the first man to become a Christian and was the first one to lead others to accept Christ as their Saviour too!

As a matter of fact, it was John himself who first won these men to the Lord Jesus who were later to become the apostles. These men were John's disciples first but, when Christ came, he directed them all to follow Him (John 1:35-37). One of the criteria used to select a new apostle to replace Judas Iscariot was that he must be one who had companied with them "beginning from the baptism of John" (Acts 1:21, 22).

As the first preacher of the gospel, John preached the deity of Christ (John 1:18), the doctrine of the Trinity (John 1:33, 34), the coming kingdom (Matt. 3:2; 4:17), the necessity of the shed blood of Christ for the substitutionary atonement (John 1:29), and the forgiveness of sins (Luke 1:77). It was John who first preached that "the law was given by Moses, but grace and truth came by Jesus Christ" (John 1:17). He clearly pointed out the only way of salvation when he said: "He that believeth on the Son hath everlasting life; and he that believeth not the Son shall not see life; but the wrath of God abideth on him" (John 3:36). He preached the necessity of a godly life as evidence of regeneration (Luke 3:10-14) and "many other things" (Luke 3:18).

The powerful impact of his preaching was reinforced by the holiness of his life. He "did no miracle" (John 10:41), although he was continually filled with the Holy Spirit, and was in fact a deeply humble man (John 1:23; 3:27-30). Nevertheless he was a "holy and righteous man" (Mark 6:20), recognized as such even by the king who executed him. He was fearless even in the presence of the most powerful men in Israel (Matt. 3:7, 8) and was faithful even to death.

Though great crowds went to hear him preach, he was utterly selfless, living in the most simple and frugal manner (Mark 1:5, 6). His life was so Christ-like that many mistook him for the promised Saviour (Luke 3:15), and some even thought that Jesus was John the Baptist raised from the dead! (Matt. 14:1, 2; 16:14).

It was John also who first introduced the Christian ordinance of baptism, so that he has ever since been known as "John the Baptizer." That this was genuine Christian baptism and not some Jewish "washing" ceremony as some have thought, is evident from the fact that John baptized Jesus and all His apostles and that, when the Holy Spirit came on the day of Pentecost, and multitudes were won to Christ and baptized; none of those who had already been won and baptized by John were re-baptized.

In view of all the foregoing, it is no wonder that the Lord Jesus said: "Verily I say unto you, Among them that are born of women, there hath not risen a greater than John the Baptist" (Matt. 11:11). Of course, he was merely the forerunner of the Christ, so that Jesus added: "He that is least [that is, literally, 'lesser,' or 'later'] in the kingdom of heaven is greater than he." John himself emphasized: "He [Christ] must increase, but I must decrease" (John 3:30).

The church of the Lord Jesus Christ was "built upon the foundation of the apostles and prophets, Jesus Christ Himself being the chief corner stone" (Eph. 2:20), and it was John the Baptist who prepared that foundation!

4. Question: "Why did two members of the Jewish Sanhedrin, Joseph and Nicodemus, undertake to bury the body of Jesus after His crucifixion?"

Answer: The gospel of the Christian faith, as it has been formally defined by the Apostle Paul in I Corinthians 15:1-4, consists of three parts: (1) The death of Christ on the cross in atonement for our sins; (2) His burial; (3) His resurrection. It is through faith in the gospel that men receive salvation.

It seems a little surprising at first that the burial of Christ is thus included as an integral part of that which must be believed if one is to be saved. The reason, undoubtedly, is that it is important to believe that the death and resurrection of Christ were of the body, not the soul. It was His body that died and was buried in Joseph's tomb, and therefore His resurrection was a bodily resurrection.

As soon as it is recognized that the burial was actually a very significant event, then one immediately thinks of the role played by Joseph of Arimathea and Nicodemus, for these were the only men to have a part in burying the body of Christ. Strangely enough, these men were members of the Jewish Sanhedrin, the ruling body of the Jews, the very Council which had consistently opposed Jesus and finally condemned Him to death.

There are other mysterious aspects of the burial account. Why, for example, would Joseph own a sepulcher in such a place as Calvary, adjacent to the place of execution, where the continual sights and sounds of dying criminals would make it an almost intolerable location? He was a wealthy man, well able to purchase attractive property elsewhere, and, anyway, his home was in Arimathea, not Jerusalem! Yet the Scripture says that he himself had "hewn out in the rock . . . a new tomb" (Matt. 27:60) in this strange location, and had planted a garden there (John 19:41).

Another odd thing about the account is the surprising rapidity with which Joseph and Nicodemus accomplished the burial. As soon as Jesus was dead, Joseph appeared before Pilate requesting the body. No one else apparently had expected the death so quickly (note Mark 15:44); it is probable that various others would have requested the body if Joseph had not reached Pilate first.

It is also surprising to note the boldness of the two men. They had evidently never been open followers of Christ, but they were bold at a time when all His openly professed disciples "forsook him and fled" (Mark 14:50). Nicodemus earlier had half-heartedly defended Him in a council meeting (John 7:50-53) and at the trial itself, when Jesus was condemned to be crucified, Joseph likewise "had not consented to the counsel and deed of them" (Luke 23:51). In view of this, and the intense hatred of the Jewish leaders against Jesus and His disciples, the two friends were already on dangerous ground with their colleagues.

And yet, the Scripture says that Joseph went in "boldly" to Pilate to request the body of the Lord Jesus (Mark 15:43). There can be no doubt that this act and those which followed cost Joseph and Nicodemus very dearly. John 12:42 indicates that "many among the chief rulers" actually believed on Christ, but "because of the Pharisees they did not confess him, lest they should be put out of the synagogue." Not only would Joseph and Nicodemus have been excommunicated, but they would quite likely have lost their possessions and possibly even their lives because of this.

In John 19:38, we read that Joseph was a disciple of Jesus, "but secretly for fear of the Jews." However, the word "secretly" actually means, in the original language, "secreted," or "hiding."

Putting all the above clues together, we can hardly avoid the conclusion that Joseph and Nicodemus somehow anticipated the coming crucifixion and the role they were to play in connection with it. Joseph evidently purchased the plot of ground and prepared the garden and the tomb in anticipation of its first and only occupant. They then bought the grave clothes and the spices and hid them in the sepulcher. After the trial, they themselves went into hiding in the same place, where they could watch the awful scene on the cross without being discovered themselves.

But how did they know all this would take place, and why would they wait until the burial before identifying themselves openly with Christ?

They were diligent students of the Scriptures, of course, and the Old Testament contains many prophecies describing the first coming of Christ, including especially the circumstances connected with His sacrificial death. In particular, as they studied these passages together, they must have been struck by the statement in Isaiah 53:9: "He made his grave with the wicked, and with the rich man in his death." This passage indicated His tomb would be near where the criminals were executed and buried (therefore on the hill of Calvary) and also somehow connected with "the rich man." Joseph must have taken this prophecy as destined for fulfillment through his own ministry in preparing a temporary resting place for Jesus' body. As "the teacher of Israel" (John 3:10), Nicodemus could also have ascertained from Scripture the place and approximate time of His death.

For that matter, they could very well have spent much time themselves with Jesus, learning directly from His own lips the things which would take place. It seems unlikely that the famous night-time interview (John 3:1-21) which Nicodemus had with Jesus would be the only one he ever had, in view of what must certainly have been the intense interest awakened in him by Jesus.

On that occasion three years earlier, the Lord Jesus had told him, "As Moses lifted up the serpent in the wilderness, even so must the Son of man be lifted up; That whosoever believeth in him should not perish, but have eternal life" (John 3:14, 15). Centuries before, Moses had impaled a brazen serpent, representing sin and its penalty, on a pole in the midst of the camp of Israel, with the promise that anyone who would come and look on it, believing God's Word, would be healed of the deadly serpent poison in their bodies. In like manner, said Christ, He Himself must die on the cross, bearing our sins, so that whoever would believe on Him would be delivered from the power and penalty of sin forever.

Nicodemus evidently understood, and believed, and was "born again" (John 3:3). So did Joseph, and they prepared themselves thenceforth to render their one unique and absolutely necessary service to the Lord when His hour would come to "be lifted up" on the cross to die.

They proceeded to "go forth therefore unto him without the camp, bearing his reproach" (Heb. 13:13). After the cross, none except loving hands ever touched His bruised body, and after the burial, none except believing eyes ever saw His resurrected and glorified body. As Nicodemus and Joseph looked up at the lifeless form on the cross, they must have thought of the great prophecy of the crucifixion in Isaiah 53, especially Isaiah 53:5: "But he was wounded for our transgressions, he was bruised for our iniquities; the chastisement of our peace was upon him, and with his stripes we are healed." They are never heard from again in the Scriptures and, quite possibly, forfeited their lives for what they had done. But they knew their Lord would rise again and that, through trusting in Him, they had the confident hope of everlasting life.

5. Question: "Are the Jews still God's chosen people?"

Answer: Many churches and denominations in Christendom have believed that the Jews forfeited their claims to God's covenant promises when they refused to accept Jesus as their Messiah and when their leaders demanded that He be crucified. This belief was especially prevalent during the long centuries when they were scattered among the nations of the world, cast out of Jerusalem and the land of Israel, and with no country of their own.

However, with the almost miraculous re-establishment of the Jews in the land of Israel, as a nation among nations once again, many are re-thinking their conclusion that the Jews had permanently lost their position as the chosen people of God. Marvelous promises and prophecies were made concerning the land and the people of Israel in the Old Testament, but many Christians have tended to "spiritualize" these prophecies and to apply them to the Christian church instead of Israel. But now it appears that at least some of them are being fulfilled today in the literal nation of Israel. For example: "I will take you from among the heathen, and gather you out of all the countries, and will bring you into your own land" (Ezek. 36:24).

Many peoples, of course, resent the idea that God would have a "chosen people" at all, especially the Jews. "How odd of God, To choose the Jews" is the familiar couplet. The intense anti-Semitism of the Middle Ages, as well as in Nazi Germany more recently and Communist Russia today, is no doubt in large measure a reaction against such seeming divine favoritism.

God's choice, however, was not based on ordinary human criteria. As Moses told his people: "The Lord did not set his love upon you, nor choose you, because ye were more in number than any people; for ye were the fewest of all people" (Deut. 7:7).

Several factors were involved in God's selection:

(1) His instructions to mankind as a whole had been challenged by a united rebellion of the people against Him at Babel (Gen. 11:1-9), and He consequently had forcibly confounded their languages and divided them thereby into distinct nations (Gen. 10:32).

(2) His promise of a coming Redeemer, to reconcile a lost world to Himself, required that God Himself should become man some day, and He would thus have to be born into some one particular nation and people.

(3) Such a nation would have to be specially prepared, both by divine revelation and by national experience, to be the nation through which the Saviour would come. The choice, furthermore, would have to be made long before this purpose was accomplished, in order to allow the necessary time for these preparations.

(4) All of the nations formed as a result of the judgment at Babel were already in rebellion against God and thus unsuitable for this purpose.

(5) God therefore, in sovereign grace, chose one man, Abraham, a direct descendant of the patriarch Shem, to establish a new nation, through which "all families of the earth would be blessed" (Gen. 12:3).

Abraham's faith in God's Word was subjected to severe testing, again and again. But "he was strong in faith, giving glory to God, and being fully persuaded that, what he had promised, he was able also to perform" (Rom. 4:20, 21). Consequently, God confirmed to him an unconditional covenant. "Now to Abraham and his seed were the promises made. He saith not, And to seeds, as of many; but as of one, And to thy seed, which is Christ" (Gal. 3:16).

Furthermore, the promises to Abraham included not only the eventual coming of Christ into his family, but also the permanent possession of the Promised Land. "In the same day the Lord made a covenant with Abram, saying, Unto thy seed have I given this land, from the river of Egypt unto the great river, the river Euphrates" (Gen. 15:18). No condition whatsoever was attached to this gift, provided by God's grace in response to Abraham's obedient faith. The same promise was confirmed to his son Isaac (Gen. 26:3-5) and his grandson Jacob (Gen. 28:13-15; 35:10-12), both again unconditionally.

Consequently the promise is still in effect and will be fulfilled completely in time to come. There have been many occasions when the children of Israel had to be disciplined, because of unbelief and disobedience. This discipline, more than once, has included subjugation to other nations and even forced expulsion from their own land.

Their greatest sin, resulting in their most severe chastisement, was in the national rejection and crucifixion of the promised Redeemer when He finally came. Jesus said: "For there shall be great distress in the land, and wrath upon this people. And they shall fall by the edge of the sword, and shall be led away captive into all nations: and Jerusalem shall be trodden down of the Gentiles, until the times of the Gentiles be fulfilled" (Luke 21:23, 24).

Nevertheless, God's unconditional covenant with Abraham has not been forgotten. "I say then, Hath God cast away his people? God forbid. . . . God hath not cast away his people which he foreknew" (Rom. 11:1, 2). "Blindness in part is happened to Israel, until the fulness of the Gentiles be come in" (Rom. 11:25).

God, of course, in His wisdom, has used Israel's rejection of Christ as the very means by which He would suffer and die in atonement for the sins of men in all nations, and following which He would "visit the Gentiles, to take out of them a people for his name" (Acts 15:14). Even in this age, many individual Jews—including all the original Christians—have accepted Christ, and thus have already inherited a portion of the promises. Eventually, during the period of Christ's second coming, the Jewish nation as a whole will turn to Christ in repentance and faith. "And so all Israel shall be saved: as it is written, There shall come out of Sion the Deliverer, and shall turn away ungodliness from Jacob: For this is my covenant unto them, when I shall take away their sins" (Rom. 11:26, 27).

God keeps all His promises, including those to His people Israel. "Thus saith the Lord; If heaven above can be measured, and the foundations of the earth searched out beneath, I will also cast off all the seed of Israel for all that they have done, saith the Lord" (Jer. 31:37).

Chapter XV

CHRISTIAN HOLIDAYS

1. *Question: "Is Christmas pagan or Christian?"*

Answer: There is no doubt that many of our present-day Christmas-New Year customs have little relevance to Biblical Christianity. Such things as the commercialism, the drunkenness, the highway deaths, and the general letdown in morals that have come to be associated with the so-called "Holiday Season" obviously have no basis in New Testament Christianity. The same is true of the Christmas tree, the holly and mistletoe, the Santa Claus myth, and similar more pleasant Christmas traditions.

As a matter of fact, many of these things seem more properly associated with the festival of Saturnalia, and other similar periods of feasting and revelry which were almost universally practiced in the ancient pagan world near the end of the year than they do with Christianity. There is in fact much historical evidence that these were pagan customs which became grafted on to the modified forms of Christianity that began to be prominent in the centuries following the apostolic age.

There is no indication in the New Testament that the early Christians observed Christmas at all. Furthermore, many authorities believe now that Jesus was born, not in the winter, but more probably in the early fall. It is not surprising, therefore, that there have been various groups of Christians, both in the past and in the present, who have reacted against Christmas and New Year celebrations so vigorously as to reject them altogether and to prohibit their members from taking any part in them.

On the other hand, there is much in our Christmas observances which, even though not explicitly found in the Bible, makes it a legitimate and wholesome application of the significance of the incarnation to the world. In a society which is becoming increasingly secularized and fragmented, it is surely good to have an annual and universal remembrance of the great historical fact that "in this was manifested the love of God toward us, because that God sent his only

200

begotten Son into the world, that we might live through him" (I John 4:9). Even rank unbelievers and hardened cynics somehow seem to sense, at Christmastime, that "Christ Jesus came into the world to save sinners" (I Tim. 1:15), and this makes it a good time for evangelism.

Christmas is a time for family reunions, for communicating with old friends, and for reconciling differences that may have come between oneself and his friends and relatives. Surely this is an appropriate remembrance of Him who "hath committed unto us the word of reconciliation" (II Cor. 5:19). Except for the spirit of commercialism and covetousness that tends to intrude, the practice of exchanging gifts at Christmas is a reminder of the One who "so loved the world that he gave his only begotten Son, that whosoever believeth on him might not perish, but have everlasting life" (John 3:16). And while we are giving gifts to our loved ones, it is singularly appropriate to give a special gift to the Lord Jesus, first "our own selves," and then special gifts to those who in a special way are "ministering" in His Name (II Cor. 8:4, 5).

The emphasis on the children at Christmastime is surely wholesome, as it reminds parents again of their solemn responsibility to "bring them up in the nurture and admonition of the Lord" (Eph. 6:4). We are also confronted anew with the amazing fact that, when God became a man, He first became a babe and a child and a youth, thus experiencing and understanding the entire range of man's problems and needs.

The Christmas tree and other traditions have been adequately divested of their original pagan connotations by now so that a Christian can, in good conscience, utilize them to encourage the spirit of love and reconciliation that honors Christ. Thus, even those who are still unsaved participate in some measure in the "common grace" shed abroad on all men when Christ came into the world. As the Scripture says: "For the grace of God that bringeth salvation hath appeared unto all men" (Titus 2:11).

As far as the date of Christmas is concerned, this is unimportant in comparison with its message. Certainly the Saturnalian aspects of the Christmas and New Year celebrations ought to be avoided by Christians, as these are clearly pagan and anti-Christian in both origin and character. Apart from this, it is singularly appropriate to observe the entrance of God into man's life at the time of the winter solstice, when the sun is at its farthest retreat and the nights are longest, for "the appearing of our Saviour Jesus Christ hath abolished death and hath brought life and immortaility to light through the gospel" (II Tim. 1:10).

As noted above, it is unlikely that December 25 is the actual birth date of Christ. Perhaps the most probable date, though no one really knows, is about September 29. This was the first day of the great Jewish Feast of Tabernacles, when thousands of pilgrims from all over Israel went up to Jerusalem to dwell in small "tabernacles" or booths, commemorating their wilderness wanderings and anticipating the coming kingdom, when God Himself would "tabernacle" with them (note Rev. 21:3). This would have been a good time for the Roman census, with the weather still warm and most of the harvest in, and with people traveling anyway. Shepherds would still have their flocks in the field, whereas none of this seems at all likely in the winter time. This same date was later celebrated by Christians as Michaelmas (meaning "Michael sent"), Michael being the great archangel of God. It is at least reasonable to suppose this observance may have had its origin in the coming of the angels to announce the birth of Christ to the shepherds (Luke 2:9-14).

"The Word was made flesh and dwelt among us." In this verse, "dwelt" is literally the Greek word "tabernacled." It is altogether fitting that the God whom the Feast of Tabernacles anticipated should actually first have been seen by men on that very day. "We beheld his glory, the glory as of the only begotten of the Father, full of grace and truth."

If one counts back 280 days (the normal period of human gestation), he arrives at the previous December 25. And then he realizes that the great miracle of the incarnation was not the birth of Christ, which was a fully normal human birth in every respect, but rather the miraculous conception, when the Holy Spirit placed that "holy thing" in the womb of the Virgin Mary! (Luke 1:35).

It was on that great day that the eternal Son, the second person of the divine Trinity, left the courts of heaven and "took upon him the form of a servant and was made in the likeness of men" (Phil. 2:7), knowing that this eventually would take Him to the "death of the cross."

It is true that this world is surfeited with unrighteousness and that even Christmas in large measure has become a time of license and covetousness, but there is still much beauty and truth and love in the world, and it is not possible that God should allow Satan (and his Saturnalia) altogether to corrupt its everlasting witness to the One who came that men might have life as it really is.

2. Question: *"Who were the three wise men and what was the star that led them to the birthplace of Christ?"*

Answer: The wise men who came to Jerusalem searching for the child who was "born king of the Jews" (Matt. 2:1, 2) were of the "Magi," a class of royal scholars in Persia who were trained in astronomy and in all the wisdom of the ancient world. They were undoubtedly thoroughly familiar with the Old Testament Scriptures. Ever since at least the time of Daniel, who had been prime minister of Persia under Darius and Cyrus (6:1-3, 28), the great kings and scholars of the Persian empire must have been well acquainted with, not only the prophecies of Daniel, but also all the prophecies of the Old Testament, concerning the coming Redeemer and Saviour.

Daniel, for example, had prophesied that the Messiah would come into Jerusalem as its Prince 483 years after the Persian emperor Artaxerxes would give the decree to the Jews returning from captivity to rebuild their city and its wall (Dan. 9:25, 26; Neh. 2:7, 8). This decree had been given in about 446 B.C. They would have realized, of course, that Messiah would have to be born thirty or more years before He would be ready to come to Jerusalem in this manner.

The exact date of the birth of Jesus is not known, but we do know that He was over thirty years of age when He entered Jerusalem as its promised king (Luke 19:37-42), only to be "cut off, but not for himself," exactly as Daniel had prophesied. The Persian scholars must, therefore, have been well aware that the time of His birth was near, and were watching for other signs that might identify it.

They knew also (from Micah 5:1, 2) that He would be born in Bethlehem, the city of David, as the promised "seed of David (Isa. 9:6, 7), even though He was destined some day to reign over the whole world (Isa. 11:9, 10); Zech. 9:9, 10). They would know also, from Balaam's prophecy (Num. 24:17), that His appearance would somehow be signalled by a "star," which would "come out of Jacob."

There are numerous references in the Old Testament to the various mythological figures (Job 9:8-10; 38:31-33; Amos 5:8, etc.) associated with the stellar constellations, and there is no doubt that astrology and the worship of the "host of heaven" had a very powerful and pervasive influence on the peoples of antiquity. The Persian Magi, especially, were thoroughly schooled in both astronomy and astrology. Ancient paganism was essentially the worship of the sun, moon, planets, and stars, and was for all practical purposes the same everywhere—whether in Babylonia, India, Persia, Egypt, Greece, Rome, or elsewhere. The gods and goddesses were identified with the particular heavenly bodies whose names they bore, and their exploits were associated with the various motions of these bodies.

But it should not be thought that the ancients were so naive as actually to attribute personality, even deity, to inanimate objects such as stars—or to the graven images which they erected on earth to represent these stars and their constellations. They knew they were worshiping real persons, with real powers. In actual fact, they were worshiping the true "host of heaven," (II Kings 17:16; II Chron. 18:18), the "principalities, the powers, the rulers of the darkness of this world, the spiritual wickedness in heavenly places" (Eph. 6:12), the "devils" which were the realities behind the "idols" (I Cor. 10:19-21), the great multitude of the angelic "stars of heaven" which followed Lucifer, the "day star" (Rev. 12:3-8; Isa. 14:12-15) in his primeval rebellion against God.

Astrology, therefore, is essentially identical with paganism and pantheism, all culminating ultimately in Satanism, the "worship" of the creature rather than the Creator" (Rom. 1:25). God's people, of course, are absolutely forbidden to practice astrology, witchcraft, spiritism, or any other form of occult "science" (Isa. 8:19, 20; 47:12-15). The startling modern revival of astrology and Satan worship, even among intellectuals, is another sign of the near approach of the day when "all the world" will "worship the dragon" (Rev. 13:3, 4), who seeks to destroy the promised Saviour, the virgin-born "seed of the woman" (see Rev. 12:3-5, 17; Gen. 3:15; Isa. 7:14; 9:6, 7).

But false religion is all the more deceptive when based on a core of truth. It is very significant that the twelve signs of the Zodiac—the twelve constellations which mark the "ecliptic" of the sun's passage through the heavens during the twelve months of the year, each with three associated "decans," or lateral supporting constellations—seem to antedate all recorded history and are the same in all the nations of antiquity, whether Babylonia, Egypt, Arabia, China, Greece, or others. This is all the more remarkable in view of the fact that the constellations in most cases bear no resemblance whatever to the figures they are supposed to depict. It seems most probable that there was some primeval agreement among the early progenitors of the human race, probably before or soon after the great Flood, that the stars would permanently symbolize the events and characters in a great cosmic drama, probably nothing less than the history of the cosmos and God's promised work of redemption in the future ages.

It is remarkable that the successive constellations of the Zodiac (the Biblical "Mazzaroth"—Job 38:32) do depict in startling fashion the prophecies of the Scriptures concerning the promised Saviour of the world. Their story begins with the great sign of Virgo, the heavenly Virgin, with her infant son pictured in the accompanying decan of Coma, and terminates eleven months later with Leo, the great Lion, tearing to pieces the fleeing Serpent. In between these two signs appears in various ways the great prophecy of the promised "seed of the woman" who, though mortally bruised by the Serpent, would yet rise again finally to crush completely the old Dragon, Satan, and all his works (Gen. 3:15; Rev. 12:9; 20:10).

These primeval "signs" in the stars had been quickly corrupted by Satan, through Nimrod and his great temple tower built in the original Babylon (Gen. 11:4) into the vast system of polytheism, astrology, and idolatry, which quickly spread into the whole world and continues in various forms to this present day.

Now it is highly probable that the Magi were familiar, not only with the corrupt system of astrology, but also in some measure with the original evangelical meanings of the heavenly figures. Then, when they suddenly saw appear in the constellation Coma (the Virgin's Son) a very bright star (and there is considerable secular evidence that a "nova" occurred in this constellation at about the time of Christ's birth), they interpreted it as Balaam's prophesied Star out of Jacob, and eventually set out with a caravan on the long journey to Jerusalem.

There were probably many more than just "three" wise men in the caravan. Persia was a great nation, never subjugated by the Roman Empire, and in fact at that very time constituted a serious threat to Rome. When this great entourage suddenly appeared at Herod's palace demanding to see the newborn "king of the Jews," there was naturally great consternation and alarm in Jerusalem. This was, of course, many months after the star had first appeared, and the Persians assumed that by this time such a notable child would surely have been brought to the king's palace. Instead, however, Herod merely had to send them on to Bethlehem.

During the months (possibly even two years) that had elapsed since they first noticed it, Coma had moved away from its prominent place in the sky and they had apparently lost track of the bright new star. But now in Bethlehem they suddenly saw it again, evidently back in such a position that they were assured this was the place. There is a very ancient tradition, which may be true, that as they rested at noon by David's well in Bethlehem, they saw the reflection of the star deep

205

in the well, as it stood on the meridian, directly over the well and the adjacent house where the young child was (Matt. 2:9). This, of course, was some time after His birth, and Mary and Joseph were no longer residing in the manger where He was born. Quite possibly they were living in Joseph's ancestral home.

And there, as these great kings from the East bowed before Him, was fulfilled in miniature the ancient prophecy: "The Gentiles shall come to thy light, and kings to the brightness of thy rising" (Isa. 60:3).

3. Question: "Is there a Biblical basis for the practice of making New Year's resolutions?"

Answer: There is no indication in the New Testament that the early Christians observed the New Year in any formal way at all. However, there may be a precedent for this in the Israelite economy in the Old Testament.

The civil year of the Jews began, not in January, but in mid-September, about as our modern school year. The beginning of the year (Rosh Hashanah) was marked by the great feast of trumpets, in which the trumpets were blown and the people were gathered together for a holy convocation. This was recognized as an acknowledgment that all of God's people would one day be gathered around His throne, when the Messiah (i.e., "Christ") would come to establish His kingdom. This was a time of rejoicing and expectation that perhaps, in the new year, the Lord would come to His people.

But this time of joy and anticipation was immediately followed by ten days of repentance and confession, culminating in the solemn observance of Yom Kippur, the "Day of Atonement." This was a day of mourning and confession of sins, climaxed finally by the symbolic substitutionary sacrifice of the two goats, atoning for the sins of the people. The details of this ceremony are described in Leviticus 16.

After first offering a bullock in sacrifice for his own sins, the high priest was directed by God to select two goats, one of which was chosen to be slain and his blood offered at the mercy-seat in the holy place in the tabernacle. This blood, representing the blood of all the individual believers in the congregation, who deserved to be put to death because of their own sins against the Lord, was accepted by God in substitution and was considered by Him as an atonement (or "covering") for their sins. "For the life of the flesh is in the blood: and I have given it to you upon the altar to make an atonement for your souls: for it is the blood that maketh an atonement for the soul" (Lev. 17:11).

The second goat, the "scapegoat," was then sent away into the wilderness, after the sins of the people were first confessed over his head by the high priest. The two goats thus symbolized to the people the great truths that "the wages of sin is death" (Rom. 6:23), that "without shedding of blood is no remission" (Heb. 9:22), but also that "where remission of these is, there is no more offering for sin" and that, when sins are thus forgiven, "their sins and iniquities will I remember no more" (Heb. 10:17, 18).

As this solemn ritual was repeated every New Year, the people were impelled to remember the hideous and deadly character of sin, in the sight of a holy God. As they confessed their sins, and saw God's judgment on them inflicted on the innocent substitute, they undoubtedly, if they were sincere, made a godly resolution to try, as God enabled, to live more righteously and thankfully the coming year.

They understood, of course, that in actuality "it is not possible that the blood of bulls and of goats should take away sins" (Heb. 10:4). They simply believed God's Word, that somehow, some day, He would provide the true Saviour, One whom the innocent animals could only foreshadow.

That promise was fulfilled in the very Messiah they were expecting to inaugurate the great kingdom. Before He could reign as King, as anticipated in the feast of the trumpets, He must first die and take their sins away, as symbolized on the Day of Atonement. He must be "the Lamb of God, which taketh away the sin of the world" (John 1:29).

As the New Testament puts it: "For Christ is not entered into the holy places made with hands, which are the figures of the true; but into heaven itself, now to appear in the presence of God for us: Nor yet that he should offer himself often, as the high priest entereth into the holy place every year with blood of others; For then must he often have suffered since the foundation of the world; but now once in the end of the world hath he appeared to put away sin by the sacrifice of himself" (Heb. 9:24-26).

With this precedent and these truths before us, it is proper and fitting that men today should observe the coming of a New Year as a time of remembrance and confession of sins and of prayerful determination to serve the Lord more faithfully and effectively than they have in the past. We do not have to look forward with only shadowy understanding to a coming Saviour, as did the ancient Israelites, but can rejoice in the clear light of a perfect salvation completely accomplished in the death and resurrection of our Lord Jesus Christ.

The most important and essential decision a person can make, on

New Year's Day or any other day, is to receive Jesus Christ by faith as his personal Saviour and Lord, believing that He died for his sins and rose again for his justification. One who is already a believing Christian should continually thank Him and seek to grow in grace. Each new day, and particularly each New Year, should be a time of confession and resolution. "If we confess our sins, he is faithful and just to forgive us our sins, and to cleanse us from all unrighteousness" (I John 1:9). "If we walk in the light, as he is in the light, we have fellowship one with another, and the blood of Jesus Christ his Son cleanseth us from all sin" (I John 1:7).

4. Question: "Is the resurrection story still meaningful in this scientific age?"

Answer: The resurrection of Jesus Christ is far more than just a beautiful legend that people like to recall at Easter time every year. It is the greatest event in the history of the world and is more certainly verified and relevant today than it has ever been before. In fact our one remaining hope, now that men are beginning to realize that science and technology and human institutions cannot provide the remedy for a dying world, is a return to a living faith in a living Christ.

The continued existence of the Christian church in a world which either persecutes it or ridicules it or ignores it (depending upon the circumstances of time and place) is itself proof that Christ is alive. He had said, "Upon this rock [that is, upon that firm belief in His essential deity which the Apostle Peter had just confessed] I will build my church; and the gates of hell shall not prevail against it" (Matt. 16:18).

Then, in explanation of how He could fulfill such a seemingly impossible promise, "From that time forth began Jesus to show unto his disciples how that he must . . . be killed, and be raised again the third day" (Matt. 16:21).

After His resurrection, He sent His disciples forth to do the actual work of building His church (that is, of making new disciples, then baptizing them, and then teaching them all things) with the glorious promise, "All power is given unto me in heaven and in earth. . . . and, lo, I am with you alway, even unto the end of the world" (Matt. 28:18-20).

Today, many people believe that the church also, along with the government and the school and other institutions, has failed and is dying out. This may be true as far as most "liberal" churches are concerned. Church attendance, financial contributions, and influence have declined drastically in these churches in the past decade, in almost direct proportion as clerical involvement in social activism has increased.

But true Bible-centered churches are not dying, for the good reason that they are in vital union with the Lord Jesus Christ, the Head of the church. It is significant, for example, that a recent publication has searched out the ten largest Sunday Schools in America, and all of these were found to be associated with churches that are aggressively fundamentalist, believing and preaching the entire Scriptures as divinely inspired and infallible, looking for the imminent, personal return of Jesus Christ to establish His kingdom on earth. They are all strongly evangelistic and missionary churches and, furthermore, have a strong appeal to young people. The ratio of youth to adults in the active membership is twice what it is in liberal, or even mildly conservative, churches.

The church was established in the first century directly on the preaching and acceptance of Christ's bodily resurrection (note, for example, Acts 4:33). Its continued growth for almost two thousand years gives greater evidence of the truth of the resurrection every year. This, in addition to all the other evidences for the resurrection,[1] makes the resurrection of Jesus Christ the most certain fact of all history!

And it is certainly the most important fact of history. It is God's seal and surety that death and the grave are only temporary intruders. The ultimate reality is endless life and joy in the presence of God. But salvation from sin and death and deliverance unto eternal life are brought to fruition in Jesus Christ, "if we believe on him that raised up Jesus our Lord from the dead: Who was delivered for our offences, and was raised again for our justification" (Rom. 4:24, 25).

In the world today death is the great enemy. Man's science and philosophy, with all their technological achievements, have not answered the problem of the grave. Medical science has, of course, enabled more people to live longer, but has not yet been able to increase the maximum life span. Furthermore, science and technology have now, as people are suddenly realizing, made actual extinction of life on the entire planet an imminent possibility, either through nuclear destruction or through environmental deterioration.

In fact, as the Scripture says, "The whole creation groaneth and

[1] For a brief outline of some of these evidences, see Chapter IV, Section 4.

travaileth in pain together until now" (Rom. 8:22). This is experienced in the physical world in the Law of Increasing Entropy. That is, every system or process tends to move in the direction of increasing entropy, which is synonymous with disorder or confusion. As God told Adam when he first sinned, "Cursed is the ground for thy sake" (Gen. 3:17). That is, the very "dust of the earth," the basic elements out of which all things had been made, since they constituted man's "dominion," were brought under God's Curse because of man's sin.

In the biological world, of course, the Curse is most clearly evident, in the universal experience of aging and death. Although new individuals are born and grow for a while, they begin to die as soon as they are born. Similarly, cities and cultures and social institutions of all kinds grow for a while, but eventually die. Another illustration of this trend is that of biological mutations, which are supposed to promote evolution, but which in reality are almost always harmful, causing a decreased order and viability in the intricately organized genetic system which experiences them. This explains why modern animals and plants all seem to have relatives in the fossil world which seem larger and more "fit" to survive than their present descendants, and also may explain why many species have become extinct. Now the very environment of life itself seems about to die.

Spiritually, this tendency is painfully evident in every man's personal experience. Doing "what comes naturally" is simply to deteriorate morally and spiritually. As the Apostle Paul says, "I see another law in my members, warring against the law of my mind, and bringing me into captivity to the law of sin which is in my members" (Rom. 7:23).

But "Christ hath redeemed us from the curse of the law, being made the curse for us" (Gal. 3:13). Not only is the individual soul "born again" through faith in the resurrected Christ, but "the dead shall be raised incorruptible" (I Cor. 15:52), and he shall some day have a resurrected body like that of Christ Himself.

Finally, at the second coming of Christ, "the creation itself shall be delivered from the bondage of corruption into the glorious liberty of the children of God" (Rom. 8:21). Because of Christ's victory over sin and death, the earth itself shall then be made eternally new (Rev. 21:1-5).

5. Question: "Should Christians keep the sabbath day?"

Answer: The almost universal observance of a seven-day "week" is one of those habits so ingrained in man that most of us don't stop to realize how remarkable it is. The month and the year have an obvious basis, in astronomy, but this is not true of the week. The seven-day week was not simply adopted in the Western world because of the Christian Scriptures, as is obvious from the fact that the days of the week all have pagan names.

Although not *all* nations have observed a seven-day week, the practice existed long before the Jewish nation was formed and the Ten Commandments were given. The only really satisfactory explanation for this very ancient and almost worldwide custom is found in Genesis 2:1-3. God Himself established the sabbath as a rest day commemorating creation! "Thus, the heavens and the earth were finished, and all the host of them. And on the seventh day God ended his work which he had made, and he rested on the seventh day from all his work which he had made. And God blessed the seventh day, and sanctified it: because that in it he had rested from all his work which God created and made."

Thus God ordained in the beginning that one day out of seven should be observed as a day of rest and worship. When God established Israel as the covenant nation, and gave the Ten Commandments, the fourth of those divine laws was: "Remember the sabbath day to keep it holy. Six days shalt thou labor, and do all thy work: But the seventh day is the sabbath of the Lord thy God: . . . For in six days the Lord made heaven and earth, the sea, and all that in them is, and rested the seventh day: wherefore the Lord blessed the sabbath day, and hallowed it" (Ex. 20:8-11).

Thus, from the very beginning the seventh day was set aside by God as a day of commemorating the completed creation, and of fellowship with its Creator. If man needed such a day in the Garden of Eden, he certainly needs it much more now in his fallen condition. As Jesus said: "The sabbath was made for man, and not man for the sabbath" (Mark 2:27).

Observance of the sabbath day was especially important for the people of Israel, so important, in fact, that breaking this law was punishable by death (note Num. 15:32-35). Later, as Israel fell into deep apostasy, their desecration of the sabbath was a basic cause of God's judgment upon the nation: "If ye will not hearken unto me to hallow the sabbath day, . . . then will I kindle a fire in the gates thereof, and it shall devour the palaces of Jerusalem, and it shall not be quenched" (Jer. 17:27). "What evil thing is this that ye do, and profane the sabbath day?" Nehemiah said to those that had returned to Jerusalem from their exile: "Did not your fathers thus, and did not our God bring all this evil upon us, and upon this city? yet ye bring more wrath upon Israel by profaning the sabbath" (Neh. 13:17, 18).

Although the sabbath was a day of rest, it was not intended as a day of lethargy, but rather of worship and study of the Scriptures. A time of such spiritual refreshment is really the most satisfying and fruitful way to rest from one's daily labor.

Christians today are no different in this respect. In fact, man's nature is such that he *needs* the sabbath day. It was made for man. He must spend at least one day in seven in rest from his job and in spiritual renewal, or he will inevitably deteriorate both spiritually and physically, sooner or later.

It is significant that every one of the Ten Commandments is repeated at one place or another in the New Testament and is stressed as applicable in the Christian's life. Christ has fulfilled the Law and redeemed us from its curse (Gal. 3:13), but it is still "holy, and just, and good" (Rom. 7:12). The sabbath and its fulfillment in Christ is discussed in Hebrews 4:1-10, and it specifically says "there remaineth therefore a rest [literally 'keeping of a sabbath'] to the people of God" (Heb. 4:9). The new sabbath of which the Scripture speaks here is a more meaningful sabbath than that of the Jews, because now it commemorates not only the completion of God's work in creation but also the completion of His work of salvation!

The Christian's sabbath, therefore, is pre-eminently a time of rejoicing in the work of his Lord and Saviour Jesus Christ. It is still a rest day, but it also is the Lord's Day!

It is probably pointless to argue about whether we should observe this sabbath day on Saturday or Sunday. The Orthodox Jews today follow a calendar which was established only in about the third century A.D., and we have no real assurance that their present "seventh day" is the same as the original seventh day of Creation Week. The status of sabbatical chronology prior to the exodus of Israel from Egypt is completely uncertain, and the confusion of other ancient calendars and chronology is notorious. There was even one day in history (the long day of Joshua 10:12-14) which was two days long! It is probable that our present weekly succession dates back to the time of Christ, but it is very doubtful before that.

There are many people whose jobs require them, in fact, to work on *both* Saturday and Sunday. These people need, and should take, a real "sabbath" day on some other day of the week if necessary. The word "sabbath" basically means "cessation" or "rest," not "Saturday" or "Sunday." The point is that every "seventh" day is to be taken as a sabbath day.

Normally, this should be on our modern Sunday, since this is the day when most Christians gather in their local churches to praise the Lord and study His Word. This worship on the "first day of the week" (Acts 20:7; I Cor. 16:2) follows the practice of the early Christians, who evidently began it in commemoration of Christ's resurrection on that day (Luke 24:1; John 20:19, 26). This day is highly appropriate, since the completion of His great work of redemption was demonstrated on that day. Sunday, therefore, circumstances permitting, should normally be observed (all day long!) as a day of spiritual fellowship with God's people in the church and with one's family in the home, in praise, and in study of His Word. Anything less is dishonoring to His remembrance, and harmful to one's own soul.

Chapter XVI

THE SPIRIT WORLD

1. Question: "Is Satan a real personality and, if so, why did God create him?"

Answer: Although he has persuaded many people in our modern world that he doesn't even exist, Satan very definitely is a real, personal being, the fountainhead of all unbelief and of every kind of moral and spiritual evil in the world. He is called by various names in the Bible, including Satan (meaning "adversary"—Job 1:6; Rom. 16:20; etc.), the devil (i.e., "slanderer"—Matt. 4:1; I Peter 5:8; etc.), Lucifer (Isa. 14:12), the serpent (II Cor. 11:3; Rev. 12:9; etc), and many others.

To the Christian, the existence of Satan as a real person is proved by the fact that the Lord Jesus Christ recognized him as such. He referred to him frequently by name (e.g., Luke 10:18; Matt. 4:10; etc.) and indeed called him "the prince of this world" (John 12:31; 14:30; 16:11).

The Apostle Paul called him the "god of this world" (II Cor. 4:4) and the "prince of the power of the air" (Eph. 2:2). The Apostle John said "the whole world lieth in the wicked one" (I John 5:19) and that he is the one "which deceiveth the whole world" (Rev. 12:9).

The Scriptures teach that, before man and the world were made, God had created an "innumerable company of angels" (Heb. 12:22), a heavenly host of spiritual beings, of great strength and intelligence. The highest of these beings are the cherubim, who are attendants at the very throne of God, and the "anointed cherub that covereth" that throne was originally Satan himself (Ezek. 28:14). He was "full of wisdom and perfect in beauty."

God did not create Satan as an evil being. However, the angels, like man, were created as free spirits, not as unthinking machines. They were fully able to reject God's will if they should choose to do so.

The root of all sin, in both man and angels, is the twin sin of un-

214

belief and pride—the refusal to submit to God's will as revealed by His own Word and the accompanying assertion of self-sufficiency which enthrones the creature and his own will in the place of God. This was the original sin of Satan, rejecting God's Word and trying to become God himself. He said in his heart: "I will ascend into heaven, I will exalt my throne above the stars of God: . . . I will be like the most High" (Isa. 14:13, 14).

When God created him and set him at the head of the angelic hierarchy, He undoubtedly told Satan of His plans for the universe, including the forthcoming creation of man in His own image. In view of Satan's later malevolent preoccupation with man's destruction, it seems that this intention of God provoked a spirit of resentment in Satan's mind. He developed an intense personal pride in his own exalted position, his beauty and wisdom, and was displeased that God would create a race of beings in closer fellowship with God than the angels and, furthermore, that He would give them the marvelous ability of reproduction and multiplication, a privilege not shared by the angels.

This spirit of pride and resentment then began to generate a spirit of unbelief in God's truth and sovereign righteousness. "After all," he probably reasoned, "how do I really know that God can do all He says? How do I even know that He created me? All I have is His word for it, and He probably just told me this to keep me in my place. He is probably no better than I am, except that He arrived on the scene before I did. It seems more reasonable that He also, like the other angels and me, just arose by natural processes out of the elemental energies of the cosmos. With the advantage of His prior emergence and experience, He has been able to organize and control all the rest of us, and now, with this trick He has learned of making men who can reproduce themselves, no telling where we may end up. The time has come to organize the other angels and institute a new order in the universe. I will be God myself!"

The resulting fall of man enabled sin to enter the world and Satan to usurp the dominion thereof. God has, in His inscrutable wisdom, allowed Satan to continue for a time in his rebellion, now with the earth as his base of operations and with most of mankind as his unwitting allies. As time goes on, the conflict will become more open and intense. Even now there are millions who consciously worship Satan and many more millions who are increasingly open in their hatred of God. Ultimately the "world" will "worship the dragon" (Rev. 13:3, 4), but his success will be short-lived. For "the devil that

215

deceived them was cast into the lake of fire . . . and shall be tormented day and night for ever and ever" (Rev. 20:10).

God, of course, really is the Creator, Satan's lie to the contrary notwithstanding. And He therefore will not allow His plan and purpose in creation to be defeated. He has, for a very brief time (a few thousand years out of eternity!), allowed sin and rebellion apparently to rule the world. This has been permitted in order first to respect the reality of man's freedom before God. But even more importantly, it has enabled God to reveal His grace and love as well as His power and holiness. He is now not only our Creator but also our Redeemer and Saviour, through the wonderful gift of His Son, the Lord Jesus Christ, who died for our sins and rose again.

Salvation and eternal life both now and in the future restored perfection of heaven and earth, are offered freely to all who receive Christ by faith as their Saviour and Lord. Those who reject Him must of course share the same destiny as their preferred master. To these He must finally say: "Depart from me, ye cursed, into everlasting fire, prepared for the devil and his angels" (Matt. 25:41).

2. Question: "Does demon possession still occur today?"

Answer: During the times of Christ and the apostles, there was apparently a great deal of demonic activity. One of the miracles frequently performed by Christ was the casting out of demons who had taken possession and control of various individuals. This practice of "exorcising" evil spirits was in fact among the very credentials of the early Christians (note Mark 16:17; Acts 19:11-17; etc.).

Comparatively few modern psychiatrists or other scientists believe in true demonic possession, however. They suggest that the New Testament writers naively confused mental disturbances or lunacy with the activity of evil spirits. This suggestion is itself naive, however, for these writers made a clear distinction between "lunatics" and "demon-possessed people." Of Christ it is said, for example: "They brought unto him . . . those which were possessed with demons, and those which were lunatick, . . . and he healed them" (Matt. 4:24).

There is no doubt that the Bible teaches the real existence of evil spirits or demons in the world. These are a part of the host of angelic beings created by God before He created the physical universe. Approximately a third of these "stars of heaven" were drawn into rebellion against their Creator by the "anointed cherub," Satan (note Rev. 12:3, 4, 9; Ezek. 28:14-16), and were cast out of heaven. Their present domicile is apparently the earth's atmosphere; Satan is called the "prince of the power of the air, the spirit that now worketh in the children of disobedience" (Eph. 2:2).

God has presumably permitted Satan and his angels a temporary residence near the earth because of Satan's part in the great drama of human probationary testing and redemption taking place there. The devil and his immense host of unclean spirits are engaged in a mortal struggle against their Creator, and are using many devices to thwart His work of redeeming men from the bondage of sin into which Satan had led them. "For we wrestle not against flesh and blood, but against principalities, against powers, against the rulers of the darkness of this world, against spiritual wickedness in high places" (Eph. 6:12). "And we know that . . . the whole world lieth in the wicked one" (I John 5:19).

Normally, these evil spirits work by deception rather than confrontation. In particular, they have established a vast system of religious worship, varying in detail according to the particular culture, but essentially the same everywhere, with the following marks of identification: (a) all involve a worship of the "creature rather than the Creator" (Rom. 1:25), this being evidenced in identifying God either with some image made by human hands or else with some philosophical model of ultimate truth made by human brains; (b) all involve an ultimate salvation attainable by human works and efforts of one kind or another, "denying the Lord that bought them" (II Peter 2:1), and "turning the grace of our God into lasciviousness" (Jude 4).

The philosophical aspects of these religions have often been received by their founders and leaders by what was supposedly divine revelation, but was actually demonic revelation. The "oracle," or the "medium," or the "devotee," is "possessed" by the spirit, and his words and actions controlled by the spirit during the trance. Even the naturalistic philosopher has often admitted to receiving his own humanistic "insights" by what he attributes to hunches, or "serendipity," which is nothing but demonic suggestion in less overt form.

On the more popular level, the idols and symbols which have represented the "gods," though nothing in themselves, are nevertheless activated, as it were, by individual demons, so that those who worship them are held by them in a strong grip of both fear and trust. "Wherefore, my dearly beloved, flee from idolatry, . . . the things which the Gentiles sacrifice, they sacrifice to demons, and not to God: and I would not that ye should have fellowship with demons" (I Cor. 10:14, 20).

In certain times and places, these powers of darkness become more bold and open in their opposition to God's Word. Among animistic tribes, the worship of demonic spirits is itself the accepted religion. Missionaries working with such tribes have frequently testified of seeing—and sometimes exorcising—cases of demon possession quite similar to those described in the New Testament. The apostolic period, of course, was a critical campaign in the long warfare between God and Satan, and it is likely that this accounts for the more intense and open activity of demons in Israel and the Roman world during the first century.

In the modern, Western world, Satan has found that his most effective weapon is deception, through the philosophy of pantheistic evolutionary humanism, which is really nothing but an esoteric form of creature-worship, different in degree but not in kind from animistic idolatry.

Nevertheless, as the great climax of the cosmic battle nears, open demonic activity will again increase. "In the latter times some shall depart from the faith, giving heed to seducing spirits and doctrines of demons" (I Tim. 4:1). "For there shall arise false Christs and false prophets, and shall shew great signs and wonders" (Matt. 24:34).

The sudden revival of astrology and witchcraft in so-called Christian nations, the parallel revival of the drug religions and practices of the ancient sorcerers, the continual growth of "spiritualism" (actually demonism) and a wide assortment of occult beliefs and practices, even many features of the so-called "charismatic revival" in liberal churches, the developing interest in hypnotism and "sensitivity training"—not to mention the drastic increase in mental illness in all levels of society—all are strong evidence of a vast upsurge of demon activity in these last days before Christ returns!

But those who are trusting in the Lord Jesus for their salvation have His gracious promise of security and peace. "We know that . . . he that is begotten of God keepeth himself, and that wicked one toucheth him not" (I John 5:18).

3. Question: "How can a loving God send anyone away to eternal punishment in hell?"

Answer: The reason is that, as a God of love, He will not force people into heaven against their wills. Such people will actually be less miserable in hell than they would be in heaven.

God is not only a God of love, but also of perfect holiness and absolute righteousness. There can be no sin of any kind whatever in His presence in heaven. He created man for fellowship with Himself, but of course man (Adam first, then every other person individually since Adam) has become a sinner, separated from God's presence and fellowship. No one therefore has a right in himself to be in heaven. Every person, without exception, deserves to go to hell. Essentially, hell is the place where all aspects of the presence of God will be completely withdrawn forever. Hell is thus eternal separation from God. As the Scripture says, it is a place where men "shall be punished with everlasting destruction from the presence of the Lord and from the glory of his power" (II Thess. 1:9).

Thus, in hell there will be no love, for "God is love." There will be no light, for "God is light and in him is no darkness at all." There will be no peace, or rest, or joy, since these are all attributes of God. On the contrary, there will be eternal corruption, strife, rebellion, and hatred.

Now this is exactly what we all deserve. "But God is rich in mercy, for his great love wherewith he loved us" (Eph. 2:4). "For God so loved the world that he gave his only begotten Son, that whosoever believeth on him should not perish but have everlasting life" (John 3:16). He is "not willing that any should perish, but that all should come to repentance" (II Peter 3:9).

Jesus Christ, the only Son of God, lived a perfect human life as the representative Son of man. He died for our sins, and in so dying He was utterly separated from God the Father, thus suffering the essence of hell itself in our place. And then He arose victorious over death and hell, "alive forevermore." He paid the full price for our redemption and restoration to the presence and fellowship of God for which we were created.

The only rational response a man can possibly make to this infinite manifestation of God's love is to fall on his knees before God, confess and forsake his sin, receive the Lord Jesus Christ as personal Saviour, and commit his life and soul, for time and eternity, to the service of the One who has loved him so much and paid such an awful price for his salvation.

On the other hand, if a man either rejects or ignores the love of God in Christ, he thereby chooses to remain independent of God, to continue in his own way with his own interests and ambitions and pleasures. He is too proud to acknowledge himself as the worthless, hell-deserving sinner that he is and thus unconsciously aligns himself with those other self-righteous, religious, intelligent, unbelieving people whom God permitted to reject and crucify His Son two thousand years ago.

Such a person would be utterly miserable in heaven, with his proud and sinful nature and his desire to remain independent of God. Therefore God in mercy will send him away and permit him to exist forever the way he chose.

4. Question: "Is hell a real place? If so, where is it?"

Answer: Hell is certainly a very real and fearsome place, and those who now make light of it will find this out soon enough. Jesus Christ Himself spoke more of the reality and terrors of hell than did any other single individual in all the Bible!

There are two distinct terms in the New Testament which have both been translated by the word "hell," and it is important to recognize the difference in meaning between the two. One of these is, in the Greek, "Hades" (corresponding to "Sheol" in the Hebrew Old Testament) and is the name of the present abode of the spirits of those who died without receiving Christ as their Saviour. The other is "Gehenna," a term used for the final and eternal abode of these unsaved individuals.

So far as we can tell from Scripture, the present hell, Hades, is somewhere in the heart of the earth itself. It is also called "the pit" (Isa. 14:9, 15; Ezek. 32:18-21) and "the abyss" (Rev. 9:2). Jesus' description of Hades (Luke 16:23) indicates it to be a place of conscious suffering.

Many people today consider this simplistic view of Hades to be somewhat naive and amusing. If hell exists at all, they think, it is some kind of intangible state of existence, in another dimension. They consider Biblical references to hell to be either figurative or else just "pre-scientific."

However, the Biblical descriptions are quite matter-of-fact. The writers certainly themselves believed hell to be real and geographically "beneath" the earth's surface.

To say this is not scientific is to assume science knows much more about the earth's interior than is actually the case. The great "pit" would only need to be about 100 miles or less in diameter to contain, with much room to spare, all the forty billion or so people who have ever lived, assuming their "spiritual" bodies are the same size as their physical bodies. None of our present seismic equipment, or other means of studying the earth's core, could detect a non-homogeneity of such size deep in the interior.

The temporary spiritual bodies of these dead men and women will, of course, not be consumed in the fires of Hades, since they are not physical bodies. Nevertheless their spirits are real (in fact, a man's spirit and soul are more real than his body, and will continue to exist in this real world even after the body is dead), and will undoubtedly be subject to intense suffering. The tremendous heat and pressure at such depths will serve as a fitting environment for the oppressive pangs of conscience and regret, as well as hatred of God, which will continually torment the occupants of Hades.

By contrast, the spirits of all who die "in Christ" go immediately to His presence in heaven (Phil. 1:21-23). They are "clothed upon with our house which is from heaven" (II Cor. 5:2) and are thenceforth "present with the Lord" (II Cor. 5:8). There is some indication that, prior to His death and resurrection, even true believers in God's Word and His promised deliverance, were in Hades, though in a state of expectancy and comfort (Luke 16:25), awaiting the first coming of Christ. When He died and paid the price of redemption with His own blood (Eph. 1:7), while His body lay in the tomb, He went in His Spirit to Hades, setting free the spirits of those who had died in faith and taking them with Him to the present "Paradise" (II Cor. 12:4; Eph. 4:8-10) in heaven. When He completed His great work, gaining victory over death and hell, He could say: "Behold, I am alive forevermore, Amen; and have the keys of Hades and of death" (Rev. 1:18).

Now this present order of things is only temporary, awaiting the second coming of Christ. There will be a bodily resurrection of both the saved and the unsaved, separated in time by the thousand-year reign of Christ on earth (Rev. 20:4-6). During this millennium, Satan, who now is "the prince of the power of the air" (Eph. 2:2), will be confined in Hades (Rev. 20:1-3).

At the second resurrection, "death and Hades delivered up the dead which were in them; and they were judged every man according to their works" (Rev. 20:13). That is, the unsaved souls in Hades will be reunited with their dead bodies brought back from the grave, and both will go before God for final judgment. Since these will all be individuals who have rejected or neglected Jesus Christ and His great salvation, they must all be judged according to their works. But no works constitute the perfection which is God's standard. Therefore, "death and hades were cast into the lake of fire. . . . And whosoever was not found written in the book of life was cast into the lake of fire" (Rev. 20:14, 15).

This lake of fire is the ultimate and eternal hell, "everlasting fire prepared for the devil and his angels" (Matt. 25:41; Rev. 20:10). It will not be on this present earth, which will be renewed to its original perfection by God's creative power after the last judgment (Rev. 21:1, 5), but will be somewhere far removed "from the presence of the Lord and from the glory of his power" (II Thess. 1:9).

The flames of the fiery lake will burn without light, because it is the place of outer darkness (Matt. 22:13; Jude 13). It will be a place of unending corruption and wickedness (Mark 9:48; Rev. 22:11; James 3:6), and a place where rest is impossible (Rev. 14:11). The resurrected bodies of the unsaved, though presumably subject to pain, will not be consumed by this vast "furnace of fire" (Matt. 13:41, 42; Rev. 19:20; 20:10).

It is possible that the lake of fire will be some far-distant massive body of burning gases at the edge of the universe. Of course, many prefer to believe that these fires are only figurative, even though there is nothing impossible in a literal fulfillment. If they are figurative, however, it is only because the reality which they represent is so terrible that the only way of making it meaningful in human terms is to picture it as eternal fire and everlasting torment.

But it should be realized that the main essential of hell is eternal separation from God. Its inhabitants will be those who rejected or neglected God's gracious and free gift of forgiveness and salvation through Jesus Christ. They preferred independence from God, ignoring His Way (John 14:6) and going their own way, and thus have received only that which they desired and deserved.

Today, of course, everyone who desires to be saved and to know the Lord is invited to come to Him in faith, through Jesus Christ. "For God hath not appointed us to wrath, but to obtain salvation by our Lord Jesus Christ" (I Thess. 5:9).

5. *Question: "How will men be judged on the great judgment day?"*

Answer: Perhaps the most common misconception about the final judgment is the idea that a great balance will somehow be set up by God in heaven, and each man's deeds will be weighed in the balance. If his good deeds are found to outweigh the bad, he will enter heaven; otherwise he will be sent to hell.

But this notion, widespread though it may be, is quite contrary to Scripture. The standard against which all deeds are to be measured is not any such arbitrary human criterion, but rather the very holiness of God Himself! By this standard, every man falls far short. "For all have sinned, and come short of the glory of God" (Rom. 3:23). "Whosoever shall keep the whole law, yet offend in one point, he is guilty of all" (James 2:10).

Every man who has ever lived (except one—Jesus Christ) has broken God's law and thus is not ready to meet Him. This is true regardless of his nationality or race or religion. Everyone who has read or heard of the Ten Commandments will, if he is honest, admit he has broken one or more of them, probably many times. Those who have never heard of them will nevertheless likewise agree that they have failed to live up even to their own intuitive concepts of right and wrong. "For as many as have sinned without law shall also perish without law; and as many as have sinned in the law shall be judged by the law" (Rom. 2:12).

Therefore, if a man comes to the judgment still bearing his own sins, whether few or many, he will be condemned to eternal separation from God. "The ungodly shall not stand in the judgment" (Ps. 1:5). "The fearful, and unbelieving, and the abominable, and murderers, and whoremongers, and sorcerers, and idolators, and all liars, shall have their part in the lake which burneth with fire and brimstone: which is the second death" (Rev. 21:8).

The sad truth is that no one deserves to be saved. "They are all gone out of the way, they are together become unprofitable; there is none that doeth good, no, not one" (Rom. 3:12).

And yet, the wonderful grace of God has made it possible for men to be saved in spite of the fact that they do not deserve it! "God commendeth his love toward us, in that, while we were yet sinners, Christ died for us" (Rom. 5:8).

When the Lord Jesus Christ died on the cross, He suffered the judgment of a holy God on our sins. "Therefore, as by the offence of one, judgment came upon all men to condemnation; even so by the righteousness of one the free gift came upon all men unto justification of life" (Rom. 5:18). Each individual may now say, in effect: "Though I am a wretched sinner in the sight of the infinitely holy Creator, yet the Son of God, Jesus Christ, suffered and died in my place. He went to the judgment instead of me, and I receive Him with joy and thanksgiving, as my Lord and Saviour, trusting Him to forgive my sins and give me everlasting life."

Jesus said: "He that heareth my word, and believeth on him that sent me, hath everlasting life, and shall not come into condemnation, but is passed from death unto life" (John 5:24). The names of those

223

who believe on Christ are inscribed in the Book of Life, and they are delivered from the judgment.

"And I saw the dead, small and great, stand before God, and the books were opened; and another book was opened, which is the book of life: and the dead were judged out of those things which were written in the books, according to their works" (Rev. 20:12). It is evident that the lives of the unsaved will be evaluated from the "books" (undoubtedly, the books in which their works have been listed, as well as the Book of God, the Holy Scriptures), and then they will be judged (or, literally, "condemned") according to their works. "By the works of the law shall no flesh be justified" (Gal. 2:16).

Since no man's works are perfect, they cannot save him. "And whosoever was not found written in the book of life was cast into the lake of fire" (Rev. 20:15). There will be degrees of punishment in hell, graded in accordance with the individual's degree of guilt, as measured by both the amount of light he had received and his response to that light (note Luke 12:47, 48). But most important is the fact that everyone who dies without trusting Christ as his Saviour will, according to the Word of God, spend all eternity in a conscious existence utterly separated from God and His love. "[They] that obey not the gospel of our Lord Jesus Christ, shall be punished with everlasting destruction from the presence of the Lord, and from the glory of His power" (II Thess. 1:8, 9).

On the other hand, all who have accepted by faith the work of Christ in dying for their sins, trusting Him as their Lord and Saviour, will spend eternity with Him in heaven. And just as there are degrees of punishment in hell, so there are degrees of reward in heaven.

Believers will not be judged as to salvation on the day of the last judgment, because Christ has already borne their judgment when He died for them on the cross. However, they will be judged for possible rewards, evidently at a different judgment known as "the judgment seat of Christ" (Rom. 14:10; II Cor. 5:10).

This judgment is outlined in I Corinthians 3:13-15: "Every man's work shall be made manifest: for the day shall declare it, because it shall be revealed by fire; and the fire shall try every man's work of what sort it is. If any man's work abide which he hath built thereupon, he shall receive a reward. If any man's work shall be burned, he shall suffer loss: but he himself shall be saved; yet so as by fire."

There is only one thing in life about which each man can be absolutely certain—and that is that he must eventually come before God in judgment. Therefore the one thing in life which is more essential than anything else is that he prepare for that judgment, first by receiving the Lord Jesus as his personal Saviour, and then by seeking to obey His Word in all things.

6. Question: "Is heaven a real place?"

Answer: Actually, the Bible speaks of three "heavens." One of these is the earth's atmosphere, the "open firmament of heaven" in which "fowls fly above the earth" (Gen. 1:20). Another is the vast region of the sun and moon and stars. Of these the psalmist said: "When I consider thy heavens, the work of thy fingers, the moon and the stars, which thou hast ordained; What is man, that thou art mindful of him?" (Ps. 8:3, 4).

But there is, of course, a "third heaven" (II Cor. 12:2), sometimes also called the "heaven of heavens" (II Chron. 6:18; Neh. 9:6; Ps. 148:4; etc.). This is the heaven of God's presence, the location of the throne of God. It was to this heaven that Jesus Christ ascended after His resurrection. "So then after the Lord had spoken unto them, He was received up into heaven, and sat on the right hand of God" (Mark 16:9).

Many and marvelous have been the speculations of men about life after death and heaven. But those who have actually died and thus are in a position really to know about such things are not in any position to come back and report their observations to us! "It is appointed unto men once to die and after this the judgment" (Heb. 9:27).

With one exception! Jesus said: "No man hath ascended up to heaven, but he that came down from heaven, even the Son of man which is in heaven" (John 3:13). After His death and resurrection, He said: "I ascend unto my Father" (John 20:17).

The Lord Jesus is the one man, in all history, who died and then rose again bodily from the dead, "alive forevermore" (Rev. 1:18). If we wish to have certain knowledge concerning life after death, therefore, we must learn it only from Him and from His Word, the Holy Scriptures.

Furthermore, we must somehow get the idea out of our minds that the Bible reveals truth only in vague, symbolic language which we then try to decipher and apply in terms of our own experience. Such an approach to God's Word in effect makes it impossible for God to communicate with us at all. That is, if God's Word does not mean what it says, (allowing, of course, for figures of speech, which are always clearly self-interpretative in the Biblical context itself), then how are we to know what it does mean?

225

Thus, on the question at hand, we should realize the Bible teaches that heaven is a real place, not just some intangible, spiritual concept, some kind of fourth-dimensional, anti-matter, looking-glass sort of existence.

Jesus said: "In my Father's house are many mansions: . . . I go to prepare a place for you" (John 14:2). The fact of Christ's bodily resurrection and ascension is of basic importance. The Scriptural records are emphatic in teaching that it was not His spirit but His body that was raised from the dead. It was a glorified body, but nevertheless a physical body, in the most real sense. And it was this physical body which ascended into heaven and which will some day return from heaven. "This same Jesus, which is taken up from you into heaven, shall so come in like manner as ye have seen him go into heaven" (Acts 1:11).

Thus, right now, Jesus Christ is in heaven, in His physical body! And so, for that matter, are Enoch (Heb. 11:5) and Elijah (II Kings 2:11), both of whom were taken directly into heaven without dying. The third heaven is just as real and physical as the heaven of the clouds and the heaven of the stars.

The Bible always speaks of this heaven as somewhere "up" from the earth, so that one must "ascend" when he goes there. Since the earth continually rotates on its axis, "up" could mean any and all directions away from the earth. The third heaven thus, in some sense, is all around the starry heaven, just as the latter likewise surrounds the atmospheric heaven. It cannot be reached by telescopic observations, because the second heaven is itself too vast, and possibly also, if relativity theory is valid, curving back upon itself.

Nevertheless, it is there, and Christ is there! "He that descended is the same also that ascended far above all heavens, that he might fill all things" (Eph. 4:10).

Dwelling in heaven, with Christ, are "an innumerable company of angels" and "the spirits of just men made perfect" (Heb. 12:22, 23). When a believer dies, his spirit "departs to be with Christ" (Phil. 1:23), probably carried thence by angels (Luke 16:22). "For we know that if our earthly house of this tabernacle were dissolved, we have a building of God, an house not made with hands, eternal in the heavens" (II Cor. 5:1).

However, this is not the believer's final body, but only an intermediate spirit-body, real and distinct, but not physical. The latter awaits the great resurrection day when "the Lord himself shall descend from heaven . . . and the dead in Christ shall rise" (I Thess. 4:16).

226

At that time, He "shall change our body of humiliation that it may be fashioned like unto his body of glory" (Phil. 3:21).

At the present time, the angels, who are "ministering spirits" (Heb. 1:14) apparently can cross easily and quickly from the third heaven to the earth (note Luke 1:19; 1:26; etc.). Their bodies, though capable of materialization in the form of men as occasion requires, are essentially spirit-bodies and thus not subject to gravitational forces, mass-energy relationships, and other physical restrictions common to objects in the universe of observational science. They "excel in strength" (Ps. 103:20) and can "fly swiftly" (Dan. 9:21), not limited even to the velocity of light, although of course neither their strength nor their speed is infinite, since they also are created beings.

Ultimately, the "heavenly Jerusalem" (Heb. 12:22; Gal. 4:26) will descend from heaven to the earth (Rev. 21:10), which will have been "made new" (Rev. 21:5), to serve as the perfect home for redeemed men throughout the eternal ages to come. For the present, although we may understand very little as yet concerning the actual nature and structure of heaven, we can be confident that it does really exist. The supremely important issue confronting all men, therefore, is whether they are destined for heaven or hell. "Blessed be the God and Father of our Lord Jesus Christ, which according to his abundant mercy hath begotten us again unto a lively hope by the resurrection of Jesus Christ from the dead, To an inheritance incorruptible, and undefiled, and that fadeth not away, reserved in heaven for you, Who are kept by the power of God, through faith unto salvation ready to be revealed in the last time" (I Peter 1:3-5).

7. Question: "Will we know our loved ones in heaven?"

Answer: This is a frequent question, but it can be answered quite simply if we just realize that the future life is one of increased knowledge and awareness, not one of vague intangibles and dreamy unrealities. Heaven will be a real place and those who are saved will have real bodies—just as physical and tangible and recognizable as this present world and our present bodies. We shall certainly not know any less than we do now, and there is thus no doubt that we shall recognize one another in the glorious age to come.

Our Saviour, the Lord Jesus Christ, was raised from the grave in a physical body—one that could be seen and recognized and touched (note Luke 24:36-43). In this body, He ascended into heaven, and in this same body He will one day return to earth (Acts 1:9-11). He said, "I go to prepare a place for you" (John 14:2). He is preparing a place, not a state of mind nor some vague sphere of spirit activity!

The Bible also says: "We know that when he shall appear, we shall be like him, for we shall see him as he is" (I John 3:2). Our bodies, like His, will be physical bodies, though also resurrected and made free from the limitations of our present bodies. "He shall change our vile body, that it may be fashioned like unto his glorious body" (Phil. 3:21).

The fulfillment of these promises will take place at the time of His second coming and the resurrection of the Christian dead. "For the Lord himself shall descend from heaven with a shout, with the voice of the archangel, and with the trump of God: and the dead in Christ shall rise first. Then we which are alive and remain shall be caught up together with them in the clouds, to meet the Lord in the air; and so shall we ever be with the Lord" (I Thess. 4:16, 17).

Until Christ comes again, of course, the dead bodies of believers remain in the grave. However, their spirits are translated immediately at death into the presence of the Lord. "For we know that if our earthly house of this tabernacle were dissolved, we have a building of God, an house not made with hands, eternal in the heavens. . . . We are confident, I say, and willing rather to be absent from the body, and to be present with the Lord" (II Cor. 5:1, 8). Spirits and resurrected bodies of believers will be reunited when Christ comes again. However, the resurrection of the unsaved dead will be at the time of the last judgment (Rev. 20:5, 12-15), and these will all be consigned to eternal existence in the lake of fire.

Obviously, before we can recognize our loved ones in heaven, both we and they must actually be there! Jesus made it clear that the path that leads to life is narrow and "few there be that find it" (Matt. 7:14). It is supremely important for each of us to turn from our natural life of selfishness and unbelieving pride to trust in Jesus Christ as personal Saviour and Lord, the Son of God who "tasted death for every man" (Heb. 2:9). "He that believeth on the Son hath everlasting life; and he that believeth not the Son shall not see life; but the wrath of God abideth on him" (John 3:36).

Furthermore, each Christian should do all he can (by prayer, a godly life, and faithful witnessing) to help his family and friends also come to put their trust in the Lord Jesus for their own salvation.

Chapter XVII

THINGS TO COME

1. Question: "Is the end of the world near?"

Answer: According to Scripture, the earth as such will endure forever. For example, Psalm 104:5 says: "[He] laid the foundations of the earth, that it should not be removed for ever." However, the earth will some day be drastically changed and renovated. "The earth also and the works that are therein shall be burned up" (II Peter 3:10). Jesus said: "Heaven and earth shall pass away, but my words shall not pass away" (Matt. 24:35). "Nevertheless we, according to his promise, look for new heavens and a new earth, wherein dwelleth righteousness" (II Peter 3:13).

The earth and its atmospheric heavens will thus not be annihilated but will be completely purged by fire, cleansing it of all the age-long effects of sin, decay, and death, and enabling God to erect on its foundations a renewed earth which will exist forever in divine perfection.

The inhabitants of this new earth will likewise be cleansed of all the effects of sin and death. They will, in fact, be none other than those of the present world whose sins have been forgiven on the basis of their faith in the substitutionary death of their Saviour and Lord, when He died on the cross. They will have received glorified bodies in the great resurrection day and thus will be equipped for eternal life in the ages to come on the new earth and in the new heavens.

All of these great events, of course, are awaiting the return of the Lord Jesus Christ back to this present earth. "This same Jesus, which is taken up from you into heaven, shall so come in like manner as ye have seen him go into heaven" (Acts 1:11).

There is no way in which we can predict the definite time of His coming and of the end of this present age. He could come at any moment, and Christians should be ready for Him whenever He comes. "Watch therefore, for ye know neither the day nor the hour wherein the Son of man cometh" (Matt. 25:13).

Although we cannot determine the exact time of Christ's return, He does expect us to be aware when His coming is drawing near. "When ye shall see these things come to pass," He said, "know that it is nigh, even at the doors" (Mark 13:29). To the Christian is given the assurance: "Ye, brethren, are not in darkness, that that day should overtake you as a thief" (I Thess. 5:4).

The man who studies, believes, and loves the Word of God has a guide which not only illumines his personal path, but which also enables him to see national and world events in true perspective. Such men almost without exception today believe that trends in the political, social, religious, scientific, and physical realms are all fulfilling the prophetic descriptions of the "last days," as recorded in the Scriptures. Thus, there is real encouragement to the believer to be "looking for that blessed hope, and the glorious appearing of the great God and our Saviour Jesus Christ" (Titus 2:13).

Some of these signs and trends will be discussed in the next section. However, the day of Christ's return is certainly approaching and the reader should certainly prepare himself for that day by receiving Jesus Christ as his personal Saviour and then by living as closely as possible in obedience to His Word. "Abide in him, that when he shall appear, we may have confidence and not be ashamed before him at his coming" (I John 2:28).

2. Question: "What are the signs that the return of Christ may be soon?"

Answer: As pointed out in the previous section, it is not possible to predict the exact time of the second coming of Christ (Mark 13: 32). On the other hand, Christ actually commanded us to recognize when His coming was near! "So likewise ye, when ye shall see all these things, know that it is near, even at the doors" (Matt. 24:33).

A few of "these things" are discussed very briefly below:

(1) *A general decline in morality.*—"As it was in the days of Noah, so shall it be also in the days of the Son of man" (Luke 17:26). "God spared not the old world, bringing in the flood upon the world of the ungodly" (II Peter 2:5).

(2) *A widespread decline in religious faith.*—Jesus said: "When the Son cometh, shall he find faith on the earth?" (Luke 18:8). The Apostle Paul said: "In the last days, men shall be . . . lovers of pleasures more than lovers of God: having a form of godliness, but denying the power thereof" (II Tim. 3:1, 2, 4, 5).

(3) *Prevalence of a naturalistic evolutionary philosophy in science.* —"There shall come in the last days scoffers, saying . . . all things

continue as they were from the beginning of the creation" (II Peter 3:3, 4). This teaching, that everything always has been and always will be the same as now, that there never was a real beginning and never will be an end, is nothing but the modern scientific principle of "uniformity," which is the foundation of the theory of evolution.

(4) *Rebellious attitude of most of the younger generation.*—"This know also, that in the last days, . . . men shall be disobedient to parents, unthankful, unholy, without natural affection" (II Tim. 3:1-3).

(5) *Conflict of the prosperous and the poor.*—According to the Apostle James: "Ye rich men . . . have heaped treasure together for the last days. Behold, the hire of the laborers who have reaped down your fields, which is of you kept back by fraud, crieth . . . Be patient therefore, brethren, unto the coming of the Lord" (James 5:1-7).

(6) *Rapid rise of anti-Christian leaders and philosophers.*—This tendency has, of course, existed all during the Christian age, but will evidently increase in the last days. "As ye have heard that antichrist shall come, even now are there many antichrists; whereby we know that it is the last time" (I John 2:18).

(7) *Infiltration of false teachers and leaders into Christian churches.* —Note the tragic words of Jude: "For there are certain men crept in unawares, . . . denying the only Lord God, our Lord Jesus Christ. . . . These are murmurers, complainers, walking after their own lusts; and their mouth speaketh great swelling words. . . . But, beloved, remember ye the words which were spoken before of the apostles of our Lord Jesus Christ; How that they told you there should be mockers in the last time"(Jude 4, 16-18).

(8) *Successive world wars.*—When the disciples asked Jesus to give them a "sign" of His imminent return, He indicated that ordinary "wars and rumors of wars," that is, of local or regional concern, would be characteristic of the entire age between His first and second comings (Matt. 24:3, 6). In contrast to such limited wars, "Then said he unto them, Nation shall rise against nation, and kingdom against kingdom" (Luke 21:10). This is an idiom to express a general state of warfare affecting everyone; furthermore, the first such war was called "the beginning of travail" (literally, the "first birth-pang"), indicating others of like kind should follow.

(9) *Widespread fear and confusion regarding the world's future.* —"There shall be . . . upon the earth distress of nations, with perplexity; . . . Men's hearts failing them for fear, and for looking after those things which are coming on the earth" (Luke 21:25, 26).

(10) *Restoration of Israel as a nation, and the return of Jerusalem*

to the Jews.—"Thus saith the Lord God: Behold, I will take the children of Israel from among the heathen, whither they be gone, and will gather them on every side, and bring them into their own land; And I will make them one nation in the land upon the mountains of Israel" (Ezek 37:21, 22). Jesus said: "They [i.e., the Jews] shall be led away captive into all nations: and Jerusalem shall be trodden down of the Gentiles, until the times of the Gentiles be fulfilled" (Luke 21:24). The Apostle Paul said: "Blindness in part is happened to Israel, until the fulness of the Gentiles be come in. And so all Israel shall be saved: as it is written, "There shall come out of Sion the Deliverer, and shall turn away ungodliness from Jacob" (Rom. 11:25, 26).

(11) *Worldwide preaching of the gospel.*—Only a small part of the world's people will ever turn to Christ, but it is necessary that some from all nations at least hear the gospel. Jesus said: "This gospel of the kingdom shall be preached in all the world for a witness unto all nations; and then shall the end come" (Matt. 24:14).

The above are only a few of the signs given in the Scriptures to alert believers that "the day is approaching" (Heb. 10:25). All such signs are being fulfilled today, some more intensively today than ever in the past, the others exclusively in our present generation.

Even apart from the Scriptures, the imminent danger of nuclear extermination, the population explosion, the approaching poisoning of our water and air supplies, and the general deterioration of the entire social and physical environment indicate that the world in its present form cannot survive much longer. There is surely no hope apart from Christ. "But unto them that look for him shall he appear the second time without sin unto salvation" (Heb. 9:28).

3. Question: "What prophecies must be fulfilled before Christ returns?"

Answer: One of the most striking features of the prophetic Scriptures is the admonition to Christians to be constantly ready for the return of Christ. He is to come unexpectedly, as far as the world is concerned, but believers should be ready and watching. A few such Scriptures are the following:

Watch therefore, for ye know neither the day nor the hour wherein the son of man cometh (Matt. 25:13).

And take heed to yourselves, lest at any time your hearts be overcharged with surfeiting and drunkenness, and cares of this life, and so that day come upon you unawares. For as a snare

232

shall it come on all them that dwell on the face of the whole earth (Luke 21:34, 35).

Therefore be ye also ready: for in such an hour as ye think not the Son of man cometh (Matt. 24:44).

For yourselves know perfectly that the day of the Lord so cometh as a thief in the night. For when they shall say, Peace and safety; then sudden destruction cometh upon them, as travail upon a woman with child; and they shall not escape. But ye, brethren, are not in darkness, that that day should overtake you as a thief (I Thess. 5:2-4).

And now, little children, abide in him; that when he shall appear, we may have confidence, and not be ashamed before him at his coming (I John 2:28).

These and other similar passages make it clear that the second coming of the Lord Jesus Christ could occur at any time. The first-century Christians, and even the apostles themselves, were encouraged by the Lord to be continually ready for His coming, lest He come unexpectedly and surprise them in some activity unworthy of a Christian who truly loved his Saviour.

This can only mean that His coming is always "imminent" and, therefore, that no specific events must take place before He can return. There are no prophecies which have to be fulfilled before His coming. He might come today!

On the other hand, there also are many Scriptures which prophesy of world conditions and events in the "last days," and many of these seem to precede the Lord's coming. For example, great disturbances in the heavens. "Immediately after the tribulation of those days shall the sun be darkened, and the moon shall not give her light, and the stars shall fall from heaven, and the powers of the heavens shall be shaken: And then shall appear the sign of the Son of man in heaven: and then shall all the tribes of the earth mourn, and they shall see the Son of man coming in the clouds of heaven with power and great glory" (Matt. 24:29, 30).

Many similar "signs" are given, to be fulfilled in the last days. These include the development of an apostate world church, intensification of earthquakes and similar physical catastrophes, a world totalitarian anti-Christian government, the restoration of the Jews to Israel, turmoil in the Middle East, rapid decay of morality and religion, ascendancy of the evolutionary philosophy, and numerous others.

All of this constitutes a real paradox—an apparent contradiction in Scripture, even in the teachings of Christ. For if we must wait for great signs from heaven and the emergence of a world dictator (or even, as many believe, the development of an ideal world social order) and all of these other events before Christ can return, what is the point of the many exhortations to "watch" and "be ready" for His appearing? Once these events have taken place, then would be adequate time to be concerned about the imminence of Christ's coming!

There can be no real contradictions in the Bible, however, since it is the Word of God. Certainly the Lord Jesus Christ would not contradict Himself!

There is only one way in which His coming can be *both* imminent and yet still awaiting the fulfillment of the various "signs" of His coming. That is, His second coming will not be a single instantaneous climactic event terminating history, but will encompass a period of time and a series of events, *just as did His first coming!*

The imminent, unexpected, undated coming of the Lord will not be to the earth's surface but rather to its atmosphere. At that moment all believers will be caught up to meet Him in the air. This is quite plainly set forth in I Thessalonians 4:16, 17:

> For the Lord himself shall descend from heaven . . . and the dead in Christ shall rise first: Then we which are alive and remain shall be caught up together with them in the clouds, to meet the Lord in the air: and so shall we ever be with the Lord.

It is this great event which could take place at any time, and for which men should be ready and watching. The believer should order his affairs so as to be ready always. Perhaps today!

The "signs," on the other hand, are given primarily with respect to that phase of Christ's second coming when He will return to the very surface of the earth "in power and great glory," to judge the nations and establish His own great kingdom. This will take place several years after He has come to the earth's atmosphere to "catch up" to Himself out of the earth all those who have trusted in Him as their Lord and Saviour.

The period of time intervening between the initial and terminal phases of His coming will be occupied in two great judgments: (1) the judgment of believers at His "judgment seat" in the air, not for salvation but for rewards; (2) the judgment of the unbelieving world in the form of the "great tribulation" on earth, including an urgent call for those remaining on the earth to accept Christ before they are forever lost. Many of the special signs of His coming will be fulfilled during this period. Some of the signs, of course, even now are being fulfilled in their beginning phases, but must await the departure of the true church from the earth when Christ comes before they will be completely accomplished. In the meantime, as He said: "And when these things begin to come to pass, look up, and lift up your heads; for your redemption draweth nigh" (Luke 21:28).

4. Question: "Is communism the Antichrist?"

Answer: There is no doubt that the dogmatic Communist is anti-Christian—in fact, anti-God. The basic philosophy of communism is a militant atheism, a fact emphasized by all its leaders from Karl Marx to Mao-tse-Tung. The true Christian church has been systematically persecuted and, where possible, annihilated, in every country taken over by communism. One of the strangest developments of recent times has been the widespread promotion of communistic causes and teachings by so-called "liberal" religious leaders, in spite of the acknowledged antipathy of communism to Christianity.

The real nature of communism can be understood only by recognizing it as a powerful religious system. Its god is evolution, which has supposedly originated and developed all things into their present forms. Its heaven is the future utopian state of perfect communism at the end of history. Its prophets are Marx, Lenin, Mao, and others of like kind, and its sacred Scriptures are their writings. Its devil is Christian civilization, destined for final destruction in the fires of global revolution. Its local church is the commune, or in non-converted cultures, the underground cell.

One should not think of international communism as being centered in Russia, of course. It did not originate in Russia, and even the Russian takeover in 1917 was financed and directed from outside. Neither is communism a single, monolithic system, but rather a vast and heterogeneous conglomerate of semi-competitive systems and philosophies, linked together primarily by a mutual hatred of Biblical Christianty and the climate of individual liberty and responsibility in which it thrives.

The Russian branch of communism, in fact, is due for imminent destruction! In Ezekiel 38 and 39 is found a remarkable prophecy of a latter-day confederation of communistic and Arabic nations. These include Persia, Ethiopia, Libya, Gomer (probably East Germany), Togarmah (probably Armenia and/or Turkey), and many others (note Ezek. 38:5, 6). These countries are listed in clockwise order, surrounding the nation of Israel, but they are under the command of the prince of Rosh (that is, "Russia"), Meshech (that is, the

235

original form of "Muscovy" or "Moscow"), and Tubal (the ancient form of "Tobolsk," the chief town of Russia's traditional eastern regions).

It is prophesied that in the "latter days" (Ezek. 38:16), the leader of this horde, Gog (probably a variant of the Russian "Georgi"), will decide on a sudden invasion of the land of Israel (Ezek. 38:8) and will "ascend and come like a storm" in order to "take a great spoil" (Ezek. 38:9, 13).

As has often happened in the past, however, God will once again intervene to protect Israel against what seem impossible odds, this time in the form of a tremendous convulsion of nature. "Surely in that day there shall be a great shaking in the land of Israel; . . . and the mountains shall be thrown down, and the steep places shall fall, . . . and I will rain upon him, and upon his bands, and upon the many people that are with him, an overflowing rain, and great hailstones, fire, and brimstone. . . . Yea, all the people of the land shall bury them; and it shall be to them a renown the day that I shall be glorified, saith the Lord God" (Ezek. 38:19, 20, 22; 39:13).

Although the military pre-eminence of Russia and her allies will be destroyed, another international totalitarian regime will probably emerge very quickly, in which the basic philosophy and methodology of communism will be perpetuated, and even strengthened. This will be the world system of the final Anti-Christ, also known in Scripture as "the Beast" (Rev. 13:2), and the "man of sin" (II Thess. 2:3).

Just as communism, this system also will seek to exercise international control. "Power was given him over all kindreds, and tongues, and nations" (Rev. 13:7). Similarly, it is atheistic and man-deifying. "He shall magnify himself above every god, and shall speak marvelous things against the God of gods. . . . But in his estate shall he honor the God of forces" (Dan. 11:36, 38). In fact, the system will quickly become an enforced ecumenical humanistic religion, with worship of the representative Man at its head. "As many as would not worship the image of the beast should be killed" (Rev. 13:15).

The government of Anti-Christ will exercise absolute economic controls. "No man might buy or sell, save he that had the mark, or the name of the beast, or the number of his name" (Rev. 13:17). At the same time, the great "merchants of the earth are waxed rich" (Rev. 18:3) through their financial interests in the monstrous system. Even today, socialistic and communistic systems are not really movements for the benefit of workers and peasants, as they purport to be, but rather are designed to concentrate political and financial power in the hands of an elite group of conspirators.

As far as the "masses" are concerned, they will have degenerated into not only a servile acquiescence in the anti-Christian dictatorship, but also into a morass of godless immorality. "And the rest of the men repented not of the works of their hands . . . of their murders, nor of their sorceries [literally, in the Greek, their 'religious rites using drugs'], nor of their fornication, nor of their thefts" (Rev. 9: 20, 21).

The world is now being rapidly prepared for this last attempt to destroy God and His truth from the face of the earth. "Then shall that Wicked One be revealed, . . . whose coming is after the working of Satan with all power and signs and lying wonders, . . . because they received not the love of the truth, that they might be saved. And for this cause God shall send them strong delusion, that they should believe the lie: That they might all be damned who believed not the truth, but had pleasure in unrighteousness" (II Thess. 2:8-12).

5. Question: "Will the world eventually be destroyed in a nuclear holocaust?"

Answer: The over-thirty generation still remembers the unbelievable headlines of August, 1945, describing the awful destruction in Hiroshima, when the first atomic bomb was unveiled and the world entered the nuclear age. Bible-believing Christians recall how they thought immediately of the great prophecy in II Peter 3:10: "The day of the Lord will come as a thief in the night; in the which the heavens shall pass away with a great noise, and the elements shall melt with fervent heat, the earth also and the works that are therein shall be burned up."

Yes, the earth will eventually undergo a cataclysmic destruction, which may well consist of actual atomic disintegration. The Greek word translated "elements" in the above passage actually means the basic subdivisions of matter, corresponding quite closely to the modern scientific concept of the chemical elements. The word translated "melt" means "break apart." The phrase "pass away" does not mean "be annihilated" but, rather, "pass out of sight." The "heavens" are not the stars, but the "sky" or "air." Finally, "great noise" and "fervent heat" are intrinsically associated with atomic explosions.

Peter's prophecy may well describe, therefore, a final cataclysm when the earth itself, with its atmosphere, will experience a vast nuclear chain reaction and perish in a tremendous atomic holocaust.

Although it is conceivable that man's activities may lead to this final conflagration, it seems more likely that God Himself will bring it about.

The very existence of such a remarkable prophecy in the Bible is evidence of divine inspiration. The scientific discovery that matter can be converted into energy is one of the greatest triumphs of twentieth-century science, and yet this plain forecast of atomic disintegration into "fervent heat" has been in the Bible for 1,900 years.

There are, in fact, numerous other references in the Bible indicating the fundamental equivalence of matter and energy, and also the even more remarkable fact that the structural integrity of "matter" is maintained by something which is non-material, the mysterious "binding energy" of the atom.

Peter, for example, says that "the heavens and the earth which are now, are kept in store [that is, 'preserved' or 'conserved'] by the same Word" (II Peter 3:7)—by the same omnipotent Word which first created them. Similarly, in Hebrews 1:3, the Scriptures say that the Creator, the Lord Jesus Christ, is now "upholding all things by the Word of his power." Note—"things" are held together by "power," or energy. Likewise, Paul says "in Christ all things consist" (literally, "cohere") (Col. 1:17).

Finally the Bible tells us that "the worlds" (that is, the "space-time cosmos") were framed by the Word of God, so that things which are seen were not made of things which do appear." (Heb. 11:3). These are only a few of the scores of examples of the scientific insights of the Bible, not, of course, couched in the technical jargon of modern textbooks, but expressing clearly the basic truths behind the jargon.

Furthermore, not only is the basic fact of the essential non-mechanical nature of matter stated in the cited references, but also the actual identity and source of the nuclear forces and binding energies which hold the atomic nucleus together. That source of power is nothing less than Christ Himself! He is the omnipotent Creator and Sustainer of the universe!

No wonder that Paul says: "For in him we live and move and have our being, so that he is not far from every one of us" (Acts 17:27, 28). The very atoms of our bodies are preserved from instant disintegration by the Lord Jesus Christ. The very brain cells which men employ to devise their vain speculations about their origin and destiny, denying the Word which created them, are held together by the One whom they continually blaspheme by their unbelief. If He were to withdraw His gracious sustaining power for only an instant, the whole world would collapse into chaos.

And, in fact, that is exactly what is going to happen some day! From the face of His wrath and His outraged grace and mercy, "the earth and the heaven fled away; and there was found no place for them" (Rev. 20:11). In the fires of atomic dissolution, all the age-long effects of the Curse that have filled the earth with the scars of physical convulsions, disorders, decay, and death will be purged out forever. And that which brought on the Curse—rebellion and sin, in the persons of the devil and his angels and of all those men who have rejected or neglected God's Word and His great salvation in Jesus Christ—will be separated forever from the presence of God and the redeemed (Rev. 20:10-15; II Thess. 1:9).

But then the earth, with its heavens, will be made new again! "We, according to his promise, look for new heavens and a new earth, wherein dwelleth righteousness" (II Peter 3:13). "Behold," says the Lord Jesus, "I make all things new" (Rev. 21:5). The primeval creative power of the divine Word will be exercised once more and the "times of restitution of all things" (Acts 3:21) will come. God will answer the prayers of the faithful through the ages, when they pray: "Thy kingdom come; thy will be done, in earth, as it is in heaven" (Matt. 6:10).

How utterly, fantastically foolish it is today for anyone to dare to question God's Word and to neglect His gracious gift of forgiveness and salvation. "Heaven and earth shall pass away," said Jesus, "but my words shall not pass away" (Matt. 24:35). "The world passeth away, and the lust thereof, but he that doeth the will of God abideth forever" (I John 2:17).

6. Question: "How will we spend eternity?"

Answer: Although this question is difficult to answer—indeed, impossible to answer completely—it is nevertheless of incomparable importance. The sad pre-occupation of nearly all men with "this present evil world" (Gal. 1:4), with no concern for the eternal "ages to come" (Eph. 2:7), is certainly the strangest paradox of modern times.

After all, man was created for eternity, and everyone who is ever born (indeed, in all probability, everyone who is ever conceived[1] in the womb) will continue to exist forever. Nothing can possibly be

[1] See Question XIII - 5.

more important, therefore, than a proper understanding of eternity and adequate preparation therefor.

Although science as such cannot deal with the distant future, a strong implication of eternal existence is found in the most basic law of all the sciences. This law is that of conservation of energy—nothing is created or destroyed, but all is conserved. And if the natural phenomena which are studied and comprehended by human consciousness are eternally conserved, then surely that consciousness which studies them is conserved also.

The nature of this perpetual conservation of each human personality, however, is revealed only in Scripture. Obviously it is closely correlated with God's primeval purpose in creation. As discussed under Question II - 5, the earth was created primarily for man, and man was created for personal fellowship with God. The interruption of an age of sin and rebellion has temporarily delayed the accomplishment of this purpose. Nevertheless, the incarnation of the Son of God in the person of the Lord Jesus Christ, His substitutionary death on the cross for our sins, and His triumphant resurrection for our justification have all together purchased the salvation and restoration of all who receive Him by faith as personal Lord and Saviour.

Jesus Christ is thus not only the Redeemer but also the great Divider—between those who desire to be restored to God's eternal fellowship on the one hand, and those who prefer to remain separated from Him on the other hand. "He that believeth on him is not condemned: but he that believeth not is condemned already, because he hath not believed in the name of the only begotten Son of God. And this is the condemnation, that light is come into the world, and men loved darkness rather than light, because their deeds were evil. . . . He that believeth on the Son hath everlasting life: and he that believeth not the Son shall not see life; but the wrath of God abideth on him" (John 3:18, 19, 36).

There are therefore two distinct categories of inhabitants of eternity, the saved and the unsaved, those who have received everlasting life and those upon whom God's wrath must abide forever. It is sobering to realize that most people are in the second category. "Few there be — that find — the way that leadeth unto life" (Matt. 7:14). "Ye will not come to me, that ye might have life" (John 5:40).

Those who reject or "neglect" the Lord Jesus Christ and His "great salvation" (Heb. 2:3) will spend eternity in everlasting separation "from the presence of the Lord, and from the glory of his power" (II Thess. 1:9). Since they have shown that they do not want

His presence and authority in their lives, they will actually be less miserable this way than if they were forced to go to heaven. However, such a total absence of God will, of course, mean the perpetual presence of darkness and evil and suffering. Their existence is described as one of "wandering stars, to whom is reserved the blackness of darkness for ever," like "raging waves of the sea, foaming out their own shame" (Jude 13). Jesus said they would be "where their worm dieth not, and the fire is not quenched" (Mark 9:44).

The anguish of regret and hatred will be with them forever. "The smoke of their torment ascendeth up for ever and ever: and they have no rest day nor night" (Rev. 14:11). Jesus also said: "He which is filthy, let him be filthy still" (Rev. 22:11). This is only a glimpse of what hell will be. It is "everlasting fire, prepared for the devil and his angels" (Matt. 25:41). It will be an actual physical existence in a real portion of this created universe, but it will be infinitely removed in space from God's presence. The location is called "the lake of fire" (Rev. 20:15); possibly a vast dark nebula of burning gases in some remote and inaccessible corner of the universe.

In glorious contrast, those who are saved "shall ever be with the Lord" (I Thess. 4:17), in unending joy. "For, behold, I create new heavens and a new earth: and the former shall not be remembered, nor come into mind. But be ye glad and rejoice for ever in that which I create" (Isa. 65:17, 18).

The earth and "all things" will be "made new" (Rev. 21:5), purged of all the age-long effects of sin. "And there shall be no more curse" (Rev. 22:3). The heavenly city, New Jerusalem, will "descend out of heaven from God" (Rev. 21:10) and will then be established forever on the new earth.

There it is that "God shall wipe away all tears from their eyes, and there shall be no more death, neither sorrow, nor crying, neither shall there be any more pain: for the former things are passed away" (Rev. 21:4). He will "bring in everlasting righteousness" (Dan. 9:24) and "they that turn many to righteousness shall shine as the stars for ever and ever" (Dan. 12:3). They "will dwell in the house of the Lord forever" (Ps. 23:6).

It will not, of course, be a place of eternal idleness. "His servants shall serve him" (Rev. 22:3). Just as man when first created was given responsibility over the earth, so will redeemed men be given the privilege of serving God in the new creation. And lest anyone doubt that there are enough tasks to occupy eternal time, he might remember that there are numberless worlds to explore throughout infinite space and that he can never exhaust the intricacies and potentialities of a universe created by the omnipotent and omniscient God! Even the study of the inexhaustible Word of God itself may well occupy many ages.

There will also be the joy of reunion with loved ones and friends of other years, with ample time then for fellowship and sharing of testimonies. And of meeting and getting to know Adam and Noah and David and John the Baptist and Paul, as well as Bunyan and Spurgeon and all the other disciples of the Lord, small and great, from all the ages!

But the most glorious prospect of all is that of seeing the Lord Jesus Himself! "They shall see his face; and his name shall be in their foreheads" (Rev. 22:4). Then shall Jesus' prayer be answered: "Father, I will that they also, whom thou hast given me, be with me where I am; that they may behold my glory, which thou hast given me" (John 17:24).

Thus we shall spend eternity with Christ, and will never cease to praise Him for "His great love wherewith he loved us" (Eph. 2:4). Therefore we "reckon that the sufferings of this present time are not worthy to be compared with the glory which shall be revealed in us" (Rom. 8:18). "Unto him be glory in the church by Christ Jesus throughout all ages, world without end. Amen." (Eph. 3:21).

SUBJECT INDEX

Abortion, 183-184
Abraham and Isaac, 187-189
Adam, 68-69, 88
Age of the earth, 22, 90, 93, 96
Aging, biological, 101-102, 210
Amorites, 72
Angels, 25, 70, 78, 204, 214, 217,
    226-227
Animals on Noah's Ark, 106-107
Antichrist, 235-237
Ape-men, 88-89
Apostasy, 124-126, 230-231
Archaeology, 2, 71-72
Ark, of Noah, 103, 105-107
Astrology, 70, 78, 203-205, 218
Atmosphere, circulation of, 2, 73
Atomic disintegration, 237-239

Babel, Tower of, 70-71, 112, 198, 205
Baptism, 53, 140-143, 193-194
Behaviorism, 122
Bethlehem, 30, 203, 205
Bible
    Archaeological confirmation of, 2,
        71-72
    Facts of science in, 2-3, 63-64, 73,
        237, 238
    Inspiration of, 1-6, 58, 67, 133-134,
        139, 153, 179
    Structure of, 3
    Study of, 10, 146, 153, 170
    Translations of, 11-13
    Used in judgment, 159, 224
Birth control, 185
Blood, life of flesh in, 2
Blum, Harold F., 86, 87

Cain's wife, 98-100
Calling, divine, 146-149
Campbell, Alexander, 140
Carbon-14 dating, 146-149
Cataclysm, supposed pre-Adamic,
    90-92
Cause, First, 14-16
Cayce, Edgar, 2
Christ
    Attitude toward Old Testament, 4-6,
        58, 65, 74, 81-82, 104
    Burial, 194-197
    Death, 41-46

Deity, 17-18, 27-28, 32, 41-43, 119,
    135
Doctrine, 118-121, 135
Humanity, 34-35, 119, 135
Lordship, 57-59, 121, 159, 161, 164
Messiah, 28-30, 203
Name, 58
Physical appearance, 31-33, 39-40
Resurrection, 42, 46-49, 74-76, 127,
    208-210, 221, 225
Second coming, 49-50, 185-186,
    226, 229-235
Sinlessness, 33-35, 127
Social teachings, 39-41
Virgin birth, 8, 31, 33, 35-38, 120,
    202
Work, 120, 135
Christianity, uniqueness of, 126-128
Christmas, 200-202, 203-206
Chronology, human, 88-89, 97
Church, in general, 117, 131-132
Church, local, 53, 131-133, 136-138,
    147, 168, 209, 213
Classification, biological, 83-84
Communism, 39, 69, 80, 235-237
Conception, 182-184, 239
Conscience, 157-159
Conservation of energy, 2, 15, 63-65,
    80, 83, 240
Creation
    Allegorical theory, 81
    Date, 96-98
    Genesis record, 68, 81-82, 90-95
    Miracles of, 65
    Purpose, 23-26, 34, 95, 116, 215,
        240-242
    Universe, 21-23, 77-78, 211, 215
Creation Research Society, 105
Cults, 133-136, 153
Curse, Adamic, 46, 63, 95, 175-176,
    178, 209-210, 239, 214

Daniel, 1, 5
Darwin, Charles, 80, 104, 111
Dating, geologic, 96-98, 108-110
Day of Atonement, 206-207
Day-age theory, 92-94
Death, origin of, 92, 95, 101-102, 110,
    209-210
Deeper life, 151-153

SCRIPTURE TEXT INDEX

249

251

252

254